Technical
Analysis
Explained

OTHER BOOKS BY MARTIN J. PRING

HOW TO FORECAST INTEREST RATES:
A Guide to Profits for Consumers, Managers and Investors (1981)

INTERNATIONAL INVESTING MADE EASY:
Proven Money-Making Strategies with as Little as $5000 (1981)

THE McGRAW-HILL HANDBOOK OF COMMODITIES AND FUTURES (1985)

Technical Analysis Explained

The Successful Investor's Guide to Spotting Investment Trends and Turning Points

Second Edition

Martin J. Pring

McGraw-Hill Book Company

New York St. Louis San Francisco Auckland Bogotá Hamburg
Johannesburg London Madrid Mexico Montreal New Delhi
Panama Paris São Paulo Singapore Sydney Tokyo Toronto

Library of Congress Cataloging in Publication Data
Pring, Martin J.

  Technical analysis explained.

  Bibliography: p.
  Includes index.
  1. Investment analysis. I. Title.
HG4529.P75 1985   332.63'22   84-21861
ISBN 0-07-050885-2

ISBN 0-07-050885-2

The editors for this book were William A. Sabin and Georgia
Kornbluth, the designer was Mary Ann Felice, and the production
supervisor was Teresa F. Leaden. It was set in Optima by Achorn
Graphics.

Printed and bound by R. R. Donnelley & Sons, Company.

THIS BOOK IS DEDICATED TO MY WIFE, DANNY.

Contents

Preface

There is no reason why anyone cannot make a substantial amount of money in the stock market, but there are many reasons why most people will not. As with most endeavors in life, the key to success in the stock market is knowledge and action. This book has been written in an attempt to throw some light on the internal workings of the market and therefore help expand the "knowledge" aspect, leaving the "action" to the patience, discipline, and objectivity of the individual investor.

Over the years many excellent books have been written on the technical approach to investing in the stock market. Since the goal of most investors and speculators is to make money, most of these books have concentrated on short-term trading techniques and stock selection. As a result there is a dearth of material explaining the technical position of "the market" itself. The majority of stocks move in sympathy with the overall trend of the market, so an analysis of the macro picture is a good starting point for any serious investment strategy.

In order to answer the question "What do I need to know to obtain a good working knowledge of the market?" an attempt has been made to combine the more useful facets of technical analysis in one volume, with the historical perspective presented in the appendix. Since changes in interest rates have a pronounced influence on the stock market, several chapters have been devoted to this subject, although strictly speaking it is not "technical analysis" in the sense understood in this book.

Since the publication of the first edition in 1980 there have been many institutional changes and innovations in financial markets. Technical analysis has also grown in popularity, and for this reason additional chapters have been included in this edition to cover gold, commodities, and currencies. The volatility of the early 1980s, associated with powerful inflationary and deflationary cross currents, have emphasized the always important concept of group rotation and the diverging performance of individual stocks which are also covered in separate chapters. Besides expanding the coverage of several other chapters such as that on sentiment, this edition also includes discussions of flags, pennants, and wedges, and point and figure charting. With the addition of these areas, the coverage of technical analysis is now complete.

Much of the technical work published today tends to develop indicators geared to giving exact timing signals. The reputation of such indicators is often based on a relatively short, 5- to 10-year statistical history. When researched back over a considerably longer period, the consistent success of such indicators invariably proves to be misleading over the many different market conditions such as inflation, deflation, war, and peace. This is because no "perfect" indicator has ever been developed and one probably never will be.

To be successful, technical analysis should be regarded as an art, not a science. While many of the mechanistic techniques described in subsequent pages offer reliable indications of changing market conditions, all suffer from the common characteristic that they do sometimes fail to operate satisfactorily. This characteristic presents no problem to the consciously disciplined investor, since a good working knowledge of the principles underlying major movements in the market, and a balanced view of its overall technical position, offer a much superior framework within which to operate.

There is, after all, no substitute for independent thought. The action of the technical indicators portrays the underlying characteristics of the market, and it is up to the analyst to put the pieces of the jigsaw puzzle together and come up with a working hypothesis.

The task is by no means easy, as initial success can lead to overconfidence and arrogance. Charles H. Dow, the father of technical analysis, once wrote that "pride of opinion caused the downfall of more men on Wall Street than all the other opinions put together. . . ."

This is because the market is essentially a reflection of people in action. Normally such activity develops on a reasonably predictable path. Since people can—and do—change their minds, price trends in the market can deviate unexpectedly from their anticipated course. If serious trouble is to be avoided, investors must adjust their attitudes as changes in the technical position emerge.

In addition to pecuniary rewards, a study of the market can also reveal much about human nature, both from observation of other people in action and from the aspect of self-development. As investors react to the constant struggle through which the market will undoubtedly put them, they will also learn a little about their own makeup. Washington Irving might well have been referring to this challenge of the stock market when he wrote: "Little minds are taxed and subdued by misfortune but great minds rise above it."

MARTIN J. PRING

Acknowledgments

The material for this book has been gathered from a substantial number of sources, and I am greatly indebted to the many organizations that have given their permission to reproduce charts and diagrams. Special thanks go to my associates at *The Bank Credit Analyst* (Montreal), in particular to Tony Boeckh for his encouragement in the development of many of the charts and techniques illustrated in the book and for permission to reproduce them. Thanks also to Linda LaRoche and Cindy Jones for their help, patience, and encouragement in the development of many of the charts, and to Kiril Sokoloff (editor and publisher of *Street Smart Investing*) for his constant encouragement.

Acknowledgment is also due to Bill DiIanni for his useful suggestions and updates on Chapter 2, "Dow Theory"; and to David Weis and ContiCommodity Services, Inc., for their help in reproducing some of the breadth data on the commodity markets. Thanks also to Ian Notley, North America's leading cycles analyst, for his comments on Chapter 14, "Time: Longer-Term Cycles," and for his help in reproducing several of the commodity price charts from the trend and cycle department at Dominion Pitfield.

Above all, this book would not have been possible without the help and encouragement of my wife, Danny, who not only typed the manuscript but also translated it into readable English.

Technical
Analysis
Explained

Introduction

To investors willing to buy and hold common stocks for the long term, the stock market has offered excellent rewards over the years in terms of both dividend growth and capital appreciation. The market is even more challenging, fulfilling, and rewarding to resourceful investors willing to learn the art of cyclical timing through a study of technical analysis.

The advantages of cyclical investing over the "buy-and-hold" approach were particularly marked between 1966 and 1982.

The market made no headway at all—as measured by the Dow Jones Industrial Average (DJIA)—in the 16 years between 1966 and 1982. Yet there were some substantial price fluctuations.

The potential rewards of cyclical investing are better appreciated when it is realized that even though the DJIA was unable to record a net advance between 1966 and 1982, the period did encompass five cyclical advances totaling over 1500 Dow points.

Had a cyclically oriented investor been fortunate enough both to sell at the five tops in 1966, 1968, 1973, 1979, and 1981 and to reinvest the money at the troughs of 1966, 1970, 1974, 1980, and 1982, the total investment (excluding transactions costs and capital gains tax) could have grown from a theoretical $1000 (that is, $1 for every Dow point) in 1966 to over $10,000 by October 1983. In contrast, the investor following a buy-and-hold approach would have realized a mere $250 gain over the same period. Even during the spectacular rise which began in August 1982, the investor would have found technical analysis useful, since that period witnessed a considerable divergence of performance between various market sectors.

In practice, of course, it is impossible to consistently buy and sell at exact cyclical market turning points, but the enormous potential of this approach still leaves substantial room for error even when commission costs and taxes are taken into consideration. For example, using the rather conservative assumption that the cyclically oriented investor would have required a 15 percent price movement from the primary peak or trough before the indicators on which his or her judgment was based signaled a change in investment posture, the results would still show a substantial gain over the buy-and-hold strategy.

Consequently, the rewards can be substantial for those who can identify major market junctures and take the appropriate action.

If it is to be successful, the approach involves taking a contrary position to the majority or consensus view of the outlook for the market. This requires patience, objectivity, and discipline, since it means acquiring stocks at a time of depression and gloom and liquidating them in an environment of euphoria and excessive optimism. The aim of this book is to explain the technical characteristics which may be expected at major market turning points so that they may be assessed as objectively as possible. The book has therefore been designed to give a better understanding of market action, thus enabling the investor to minimize future mistakes and capitalize on major swings.

TECHNICAL ANALYSIS DEFINED

The technical approach to investment is essentially a reflection of the idea that the stock market moves in trends which are determined by the changing attitudes of investors to a variety of economic, monetary, political, and psychological forces. The art of technical analysis, for it is an art, is to identify changes in such trends at an early stage and to maintain an investment posture until a reversal of that trend is indicated.

Human nature remains more or less constant and tends to react to similar situations in consistent ways. By studying the nature of previous market turning points, it is possible to develop some characteristics which can help identify major market tops and bottoms. Technical analysis is therefore based on the assumption that people will continue to make the same mistakes that they have made in the past. Human relationships are extremely complex and are never repeated in identical combinations. The stock market, which is a reflection of people in action, never repeats a performance exactly, but the recurrence of similar characteristics is sufficient to permit the technician to identify major juncture points.

Since no single indicator has signaled or indeed could signal every cyclical market juncture, technical analysts have developed an arsenal of tools to help identify these points.

THREE BRANCHES OF TECHNICAL ANALYSIS

Technical analysis can be broken down into three essential areas: sentiment indicators, flow-of-funds indicators, and market structure indicators.

From the point of view of the analysis of the U.S. stock market, with which this book is primarily concerned, it is possible to obtain data and indicators on all three. For other financial markets the available statistics are more or less confined to the market structure indicators.

Sentiment Indicators

Sentiment or *expectational indicators* monitor the actions of many market participants—for example, the so-called "odd lotter," mutual funds, and floor specialists. Just as the pendulum of a clock is continually moving from one extreme to another, so the sentiment indexes (which monitor the emotions of those various investors) move from one extreme at a bear market bottom to another at a bull market top. The logic behind the use of such indicators is that different groups of investors are consistent in their actions at major market turning points. For example, insiders (i.e., key employees or major stockholders of a company) and New York Stock Exchange (NYSE) members as a group have a tendency to be correct at market turning points; in aggregate, their transactions are on the buy side toward market bottoms and on the sell side toward tops.

Conversely, mutual funds and advisory services as a group are wrong at market turning points, since they consistently become bullish at market tops and bearish at market troughs. Indexes derived from such data are able to show that certain readings have historically corresponded with market tops and others with market bottoms. Since the consensus or majority opinion is normally wrong at market turning points, these indicators of market psychology are a useful basis on which to form a contrary opinion.

Flow-of-Funds Indicators

The second area of technical analysis involves what are loosely termed *flow-of-funds indicators*. This approach analyzes the financial position of various investor groups in an attempt to measure their potential capacity for buying or selling stocks. Since there has to be a purchase for each sale, the "ex post" or actual dollar balance between supply and demand for stock must always be equal. The price at which a stock transaction takes place has to be the same for the buyer and the seller, so naturally the amount of money flowing out of the market must equal that which is being put in. The flow-of-funds approach is therefore concerned with the before-the-fact balance between supply and demand, known as the "ex ante" relationship. If at a given price there is a preponderance of buyers over sellers on an ex ante basis, it follows that the actual (ex post) price will have to rise to bring buyers and sellers into balance.

The *short interest ratio* is perhaps the most widely used indicator of this type. It is calculated by taking the monthly NYSE short interest position (i.e., the number of NYSE shares that have been sold short) and dividing it by the average daily volume for the month in question. Since every share sold short must eventually be repurchased, a high short interest of 1.8 to 2.0 or more is considered to be bullish, since it represents 1.8 to 2.0 days of potential buying power. (The short interest ratio is also a measure of sentiment, since high readings represent an extremely bearish feeling among investors.)

Flow-of-funds analysis is also concerned with trends in mutual fund cash positions and other major institutions such as pension funds, insurance companies, foreign investors, bank trust accounts, and customers' free balances, which are normally a source of cash on the buy side; and new equity offerings, secondary offerings, and margin debt on the supply side.

This money flow analysis also suffers from disadvantages. While the data measure the availability of money for the stock market, e.g., mutual fund cash position or pension fund cash flow, they give no indication of the inclination of these market participants to use this money for the purchase of stocks, nor of the elasticity or willingness to sell at a given price on the sell side. The data for the major institutions and foreign investors are not sufficiently detailed to be of much use, and in addition they are reported well after the fact. In spite of these drawbacks, flow-of-funds statistics may be used as background material.

A superior approach to flow-of-funds analysis is derived from an examination of liquidity trends in the banking system, which measures financial pressure not only on the stock market but on the economy as well.

Market Structure Indicators

The final area of technical analysis is the one with which this book is mainly concerned, embracing *market structure* or the *character of the market indicators*. These indications monitor the trend of various price indexes, market breadth, cycles, stock market volume, etc., in order to evaluate the health of bull and bear markets.

In a general sense, "the market" refers to the 30 stocks that make up the DJIA or to some other index such as the Standard and Poor's 500; these account for a substantial amount of the outstanding capitalization on the NYSE. Most of the time the majority of the other market averages and indicators of internal structure rise and fall with the DJIA, but toward the end of major market movements the paths of many of these indexes diverge from the senior average. Such divergences offer signs of technical deterioration during advances, and technical strength following declines. Through judicious observation of these signs of latent strength and weakness, the technically oriented investor is alerted to the possibility of a reversal in the trend of the market itself.

Since the technical approach is based on the theory that the stock market is a reflection of mass psychology ("the crowd") in action, it attempts to forecast future price movements on the assumption that crowd psychology moves between panic, fear, and pessimism on one hand and confidence, excessive optimism, and greed on the other. As discussed here, the art of technical analysis is concerned with identifying such changes at an early phase, since these swings in emotion take several years to accomplish. Studying these market trends enables the technically oriented investor to buy or sell stocks with a degree of confidence, on the principle that once a trend is set in motion it will perpetuate itself.

Price movements in the market may be classed as minor, intermediate, and major. Minor movements, which last less than 3 or 4 weeks, tend to be random in nature and are not discussed in this book.

Intermediate movements usually develop over a period of 3 weeks to as many months, sometimes longer. While not of prime importance, they are nevertheless useful to identify. It is clearly important to distinguish between an intermediate reaction in a bull market and the first downleg of a bear market, for example.

Major movements (sometimes called primary or cyclical) typically work themselves out in a period of 1 to 5 years.

DISCOUNTING MECHANISM OF THE MARKET

All price movements have one thing in common: they are a reflection of the trend in the hopes, fears, knowledge, optimism, and greed of the investing public.

The sum total of these emotions is expressed in the price level, which is, as Garfield Drew[1] noted, ". . . never what they [stocks] are worth but what people think they are worth. . . ."

This process of market evaluation was well expressed by an editorial in *The Wall Street Journal*[2]:

> The stock market consists of everyone who is "in the market" buying or selling shares at a given moment, plus everyone who is not "in the market" but might be if conditions were right. In this sense, the stock market is potentially everyone with any personal savings.

---

[1] Garfield Drew, *New Methods for Profit in the Stock Market,* Metcalfe Press, Boston, 1968, p. 18.
[2] *The Wall Street Journal,* Oct. 20, 1977. Reprinted by permission of *The Wall Street Journal.* Copyright Dow Jones and Co. Inc. 1977. All rights reserved.

It is this broad base of participation and potential participation that gives the market its strength as an economic indicator and as an allocator of scarce capital. Movements in and out of a stock, or in and out of the market, are made on the margin as each investor digests new information. This allows the market to incorporate all available information in a way that no one person could hope to. Since its judgments are the consensus of nearly everyone, it tends to outperform any single person or group. . . . [The market] measures the after-tax profits of all the companies whose shares are listed in the market, and it measures these cumulative profits so far into the future one might as well say the horizon is infinite. This cumulative mass of after-tax profits is then, as the economists will say, "discounted back to present value" by the market. A man does the same thing when he pays more for one razor blade than another, figuring he'll get more or easier shaves in the future with the higher-priced one, and figuring its present value on that basis.

This future flow of earnings will ultimately be affected by business conditions everywhere on earth. Little bits of information are constantly flowing into the market from around the world as well as throughout the United States, and the market is much more efficient in reflecting these bits of news than are government statisticians. The market relates this information to how much American business can earn in the future. Roughly speaking, the general level of the market is the present value of the capital stock of the U.S.

This implies that investors are looking ahead 6 months or more, and buying their stocks now so that they can liquidate at a higher price when the anticipated news or development actually takes place. If expectations concerning the development are better or worse than originally thought, then through the market mechanism investors sell either sooner or later, depending on the particular circumstances. Thus the familiar maxim "sell on good news" applies only when the "good" news is right on or below the market's (i.e., the investor's) expectations. If the news is good but not as favorable as expected, a quick reassessment will take place, and the market (other things being equal) will fall. If the news is better than anticipated, the possibilities are obviously more favorable. The reverse will, of course, be true of a declining market. This process explains the paradox of markets peaking out when economic conditions are strong and forming a bottom when the outlook is most gloomy.

The reaction of the market to news events can be most instructive, for if the market, as reflected in the averages, ignores supposedly bullish news about the economy or a large corporation and sells off, it is certain that the event was well discounted, i.e., already built into the price mechanism. Such a reaction should therefore be viewed bearishly. If the market reacts more favorably to bad news than might be expected, this in turn should be interpreted as a positive sign. There is a good deal of wisdom in the saying "A bear argument known is a bear argument understood."

THE STOCK MARKET AND THE BUSINESS CYCLE

The major movements in stock prices are caused by major trends in the emotions of the investing public. These emotions are themselves a reflection of the anticipated level and growth rate of future corporate profits, and the attitude of investors toward those profits.

There is a definite link between primary movements in the stock market and cyclical movements in the economy, since on most occasions trends in corporate profitability are an integral part of the business cycle. If the stock market were influenced by basic economic forces only, the task of determining the changes in the primary movements of the market would be relatively simple. In practice it is not, and this is due to several factors.

First, changes in the direction of the economy can take some time to develop. During the period of development, other psychological considerations—for example, political developments or purely internal factors such as a speculative buying wave or selling pressure from margin calls—can affect the equity market and result in misleading rallies and reactions of 5 to 10 percent or more.

Second, while changes in the market usually precede changes in the economy by 6 to 9 months, the lead time can sometimes be far shorter or longer. In 1921 and 1929, the economy turned before the market.

Third, even when an economic recovery is in the middle of its cycle, doubts about its durability can quite often arise. When these are accompanied by political or other adverse developments, rather sharp and confusing corrections can be set off.

Fourth, even though profits may increase, investors' attitudes toward those profits may change. For example, in the spring of 1946 the Dow Jones Industrial Average stood at 22 times the price/earnings ratio. By 1948, the comparable ratio was 9.5 when measured against 1947 earnings. In this period profits had almost doubled and price/earnings ratios had fallen, but stock prices were lower.

TECHNICAL ANALYSIS—TREND DETERMINATION

Because technical analysis involves a study of the action of the market, it is not concerned with the extremely difficult and subjective tasks of forecasting trends in corporate profitability or of assessing the attitudes of investors toward those profits. Technical analysis is concerned only with the identification of major turning points in the *market*'s assessment of these factors. Since "the market" is a reflection of changes in the balance of opinion between buyers and sellers as expressed in the price mechanism, the essence of technical analysis is to identify important changes in the trends of these prices.

The approach taken here differs from that found in standard presentations of technical analysis. The various techniques used to determine trends and identify their reversals will be examined in Part 1, "Trend-Determining Techniques," which deals with moving averages, rates of change, trend-lines, price patterns, etc. Following this is a more detailed explanation of the various indicators and indexes themselves and of how they can be combined to build a picture from which the quality of the internal structure of the market can be determined. A study of the market character is a cornerstone of technical analysis, since reversals of price trends in the major averages are almost always preceded by latent strength or weakness in the market structure. Just as a careful driver does not judge the performance of a car from the speedometer alone, so technical analysis looks further than the price trends of the popular averages.

The character or health of the market will therefore be analyzed in Part 2, "Market Structure." Since trends of investor confidence are responsible for price movements, this emotional aspect is examined from four viewpoints, namely:

Price

Time

Volume

Breadth

Changes in stock prices reflect changes in investor attitude, and *price* indicates the level of that change.

Time, the second dimension, measures both the recurring cycles in investor psychology and their lengths. Changes in confidence go through distinct cycles, some long and some short, as investors swing from excesses of optimism toward deep pessimism. The degree of price movement in the market is usually a function of the time element. The longer it takes for investors to move from a bullish to a bearish extreme, the greater the ensuing price change is likely to be.

Volume reflects the intensity of changes in investor attitudes. For example, if stock prices advance on low volume, the enthusiasm implied from the price rise is not nearly as strong as that present when a price rise is accompanied by very high volume.

The fourth dimension, *breadth,* measures the extent of the emotion. This is important, for as long as stocks are advancing on a broad front, the trend in favorable emotion is dispersed among most stocks and industries, thereby indicating a broad economic recovery in general and a widely favorable attitude toward stocks in particular. On the other hand, when interest has narrowed to a few blue-chip stocks, the quality of the trend has deteriorated, and a continuation of the bull market is highly suspect.

Technical analysis measures these psychological dimensions in a number of ways. Most indicators monitor two or more aspects simultaneously; for instance, a simple price chart measures both price (on the vertical axis) and time (on the horizontal axis). Similarly, an advance/decline line measures breadth and time.

Part 3, "Interest Rates and the Stock Market," and Part 4, "Other Aspects of Market Behavior," deal with the important subjects of interest rates and their relation to movements of equity prices, speculation, and other aspects of market sentiment.

Finally, Part 5, "Specific Financial Markets," considers the application of technical analysis to other financial markets including gold, currencies, and commodities.

A small glossary at the end of the book explains some terms used but not defined in the text.

CONCLUSION

Financial markets move in trends caused by the changing attitudes and expectations of investors with regard to the business cycle. Since investors continually make the same type of mistake from cycle to cycle, an understanding of the historical behavior and relationships of certain price averages and stock market indicators can be used to identify major market turning points. Since no one indicator can ever be expected to signal all such trend reversals, it is essential to use a number of them together so that an overall picture can be built up.

This approach is by no means infallible, but a careful, patient, and objective use of the principles of technical analysis will put the odds of success very much in favor of the investor who incorporates it into an overall investment strategy.

Trend-
Determining
Techniques

1

Financial Markets and the Business Cycle

INTRODUCTION

Although our basic concern here is with the technical trends of the U.S. stock market, it is important to understand that there are two other important markets—the debt market and commodities—both of which compete with the equity market for the investment dollar. Since these other two markets have a tendency to peak and trough at different junctures than the stock market but in a consistent, chronological manner, an understanding of the interrelationship of debt, equity, and commodity markets will provide a useful framework for identifying major reversals in the stock market. The following discussion will use the U.S. dollar price of gold bullion as a proxy for the commodity markets. Although the price performance of gold bullion has differed from general commodity price trends from time to time, it has nevertheless been a useful measure of inflationary expectations.

THE DISCOUNTING MECHANISM OF FINANCIAL MARKETS

The introduction briefly discussed the discounting mechanism as it applied to the stock market. However, the trend of all financial markets is essentially determined by investors' expectations of movements in the economy, the effect those changes are likely to have on the price of the asset in which a specific financial market is dealing, and the psychological attitude of investors to these fundamental factors.

Market participants typically anticipate future economic and financial developments and take action by buying or selling the appropriate asset, so that normally a market will reach a major turning point well ahead of the occurrence of an actual development.

An expanding level of economic activity is normally favorable for stock prices, a weak economy is bullish for bond prices, and an inflationary economy is favorable for gold and gold-related assets. These three markets are often moving in different directions at the same time, since they are essentially trying to discount different things.

An economy is rarely stable but is either expanding or contracting. As a result, financial markets are also in a continual state of flux. A hypothetical economy, as shown in Figure 1.1, revolves around a point of balance known as *equilibrium*. Roughly speaking, equilibrium can be thought of as a period of zero growth in which the economy is neither expanding nor contracting. In practice, this state of affairs is rarely if ever attained, since an economy as a whole possesses tremendous momentum, in either the expansionary or the contractionary phase, so that the turnaround rarely occurs at an equilibrium level. In any event the "economy" consists of a host of individual sectors, many of which are operating in different directions at the same time. Thus, at the beginning of the business cycle, leading economic indicators such as housing starts might be rising, while lagging indicators such as capital spending or employment levels could be falling. Investors in financial markets are not concerned with periods of extended stability or equilibrium, for such periods do not produce volatile price swings and opportunities to make quick profits.

Since the financial markets lead the economy, it follows that greatest profits can be made just before the point of maximum economic distortion, or disequilibrium. Once investors realize that an economy is changing direction and returning toward the equilibrium level, they discount this development by buying or selling the appropriate asset. Obviously, the more dislocated and volatile an economy becomes, the greater is the potential, not only for a return toward the equilibrium level but for a strong swing well beyond it to the other extreme. Under such conditions the possibilities for

Business cycle peak

Equilibrium

Expansion
Recession

Business cycle trough

FIGURE 1.1 Hypothetical business cycle. (SOURCE: *Martin J. Pring*, International Investing Made Easy, *McGraw-Hill, New York, 1981, p. 16.*)

making money in financial markets are greater because they too will normally become subject to wider price fluctuations.

MARKET MOVEMENTS AND THE BUSINESS CYCLE

The major movements of interest rates, equities, and gold prices are related to movements in the level of business activity. Figure 1.2 represents a business cycle which typically has a life of between 3 and 5 years. As in Figure 1.1, the horizontal line reflects a level of zero growth, above which are periods of expansion and below which are periods of contraction. Thus, after the peak has been experienced, the economy continues to grow but at a declining rate until the line crosses below the equilibrium level and an actual contraction in business activity takes place. The idealized peaks and troughs of the financial markets as they relate to the business cycle are shown on Figure 1.2 by the arrows.

Periods of expansion generally last longer than those of contraction; for this reason, bull markets in equities and gold, and bear markets in bond prices, generally last longer than bear markets in equities and gold, and bull markets in bonds.

Figure 1.3 also shows how the three markets of interest rates, gold, and equities relate to the typical business cycle. In the example, interest rates have been plotted inversely to correspond with bond prices. Consequently, a bull market for bonds is represented by a rising line, and a bear market by a descending one. The bond market is the first financial market to begin a bull phase. This usually occurs after the growth rate in the economy has slowed down considerably from its peak rate and is quite often delayed until the initial stages of the recesssion. Generally speaking, the sharper the economic contraction, the greater will be the potential for a rise in bond prices

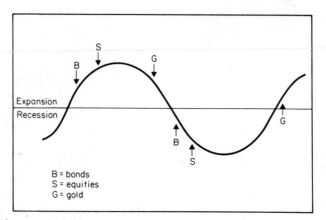

FIGURE 1.2 Hypothetical business cycle showing peaks and troughs. (SOURCE: *Martin J. Pring, International Investing Made Easy, McGraw-Hill, New York, 1981, p. 20.*)

(i.e., a fall in interest rates). Alternatively, the stronger the period of expansion, the smaller the amount of economic and financial slack, and the greater the potential for a decline in bond prices (and a rise in interest rates).

Following the bear market low in bond prices, economic activity begins to contract more sharply. At this point participants in the equity market are able to "look through" the valley in corporate profits, which are now declining sharply because of the recession, and begin accumulating stocks. After the recovery has been under way for some time, investors start to feel uncomfortable about the outlook for inflation; therefore a bottom occurs in the gold asset markets if it has not done so already. At this point all three financial markets are in a rising trend.

Gradually the economic and financial slack which developed as a result of the recession is substantially absorbed, putting upward pressure on the price of credit, i.e., interest rates. Since rising interest rates mean falling

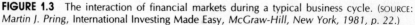

FIGURE 1.3 The interaction of financial markets during a typical business cycle. (SOURCE: *Martin J. Pring, International Investing Made Easy, McGraw-Hill, New York, 1981, p. 22.*)

bond prices, the bond market peaks out and begins its bear phase. Some excess plant and labor capacity still exists, and so rising business activity results in improved productivity and a continued positive outlook. Because the stock market discounts trends in corporate profits, it remains in an uptrend until participants sense that the economy is becoming overheated and the potential for an improvement in profits is very little. At this point there is less reason to hold equities and they in turn enter into a bear phase.

The price of gold is determined basically by the interaction of two types of market participants. The first group deals in gold as an industrial commodity affected by fundamental demand-supply relationships; the second invests in gold as a hedge against inflation. Essentially, the level of business activity has a more or less identical effect on both types of market participants, since the trend of industrial demand and the growth rate of price inflation are both normally rising during a business cycle expansion, and falling during a contraction. The price of gold and gold-related assets therefore discounts trends in business activity, but lags behind equity prices. This occurs because both forms of market demand for gold—i.e., commodity and investment demand—are oriented to lagging indicators of an economic cycle. For example, since gold is considered to be a good store of value, its investment demand depends substantially on the rate of price inflation. Since the peak rate of price inflation is typically experienced around the beginning of the recessionary stage of the business cycle, the cyclical high in the price of gold should theoretically be achieved several months ahead of the point where the rate of price inflation turns down.

Once this juncture has been reached, all three financial markets are falling and will continue to do so until the debt markets bottom out. This final stage, which develops around the same time as the beginning stages of the recession, is usually associated with a free fall in prices in at least one of the financial markets. If a panic is to develop, this is one of the most likely points for it to take place.

MARKET EXPERIENCE, 1964–1983

Figure 1.4 shows how the peaks and troughs developed for the various markets between 1964 and 1983. The horizontal line corresponds with the periods when the economy moved from a stage of expansion to contraction in a similar manner to that used in Figure 1.1. The jagged lines represent a rough approximation of the peaks and troughs of economic growth throughout the period. B, S, and G relate to the prices of short-term (i.e., money market) debt instruments: the NYSE Advance/Decline Line[1] as published in

---

[1] This indicator is discussed at length in Chapter 17.

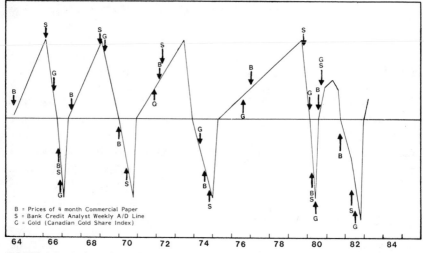

FIGURE 1.4   Peaks and troughs in U.S. Financial Markets, 1964–1983. (SOURCE: Pring Market Review.)

the *Pring Market Review* and the Toronto Stock Exchange Gold Share Index. The share index has been used in place of the actual gold price since it has a longer trading history.

It can be seen from Figure 1.4 that the peaks and troughs of the various markets have turned out in practice very much as might be expected. While the chronological sequence has been perfect, the leads and lags in each cycle have varied considerably, because special circumstances can affect a particular market and cause it to reverse at an earlier or later point than might be expected from a study of the business cycle. For example, in the 1970–1974 cycle most commodities peaked during the spring of 1974, but the U.S. dollar price of gold bullion made its cyclical high later in the year because the legalization of gold purchases for American residents in December 1974 had the effect of delaying the bearish phase of the cycle. (The share index, however, peaked in March 1974.)

On the other hand, the Toronto Stock Exchange Gold Share Index peaked almost simultaneously with the stock market in 1980, etc. Figure 1.4 therefore shows that while the chronological sequence of peaks and troughs worked well during the 1964–1983 period, the difficulty lies in the constant variability of the leads and lags. In forecasting, this approach is most useful as a framework or road map. For example, if the technical position of the debt markets suggests that they have made a peak, yet gold and stock markets are still acting well, the framework would suggest that the next major top was going to be that of equities and so forth. Similarly, if it is evident that the gold price has peaked, the technical position of the debt markets should be assessed in anticipation of a bear market low, and so forth.

SUMMARY

1. A typical business cycle embraces three individual cycles for interest rates, equities, and gold, all of which are influenced by the same economic and financial forces but each of which responds in different ways.

2. The leads and lags vary in each cycle and have little forecasting value.

3. The chronological sequence in the peaks and troughs of the various financial markets can be used as a framework for identifying the position of a specific market within its bull or bear market cycle.

2

Dow Theory

The Dow theory is the oldest and by far the most publicized method of identifying major trends in the stock market. An extensive account will not be necessary here, as there are many excellent books on this subject. Nevertheless, a brief explanation of the theory is in order since the basic principles incorporated in the Dow theory are used in other branches of technical analysis.

The object of the theory is to determine changes in the primary or major movement of the market. Once a trend is established, it is assumed to exist until a reversal is proved. The theory is concerned with the *direction* of a trend and has no forecasting value as to its ultimate duration or size.

If an investor, starting in 1897, had purchased the stocks in the Dow Jones Industrial Average following each Dow theory buy signal, and had liquidated the position on sell signals and reinvested the money on the next buy signal, the original investment of $44 in 1897 would have risen to about $18,000 by July 1981.[1] If instead the investor had held onto the original $44 investment throughout the 80 years, the investment would also have grown, but only to $960. In reality the substantial profit earned by following the Dow theory would have been trimmed by transaction costs and capital gains taxes. Even if a wide margin for error is allowed, the investment performance using this approach would still have been far superior to the results of a buy-and-hold strategy.

It should be recognized that the theory does not always keep pace with events; it occasionally leaves the investor in doubt, and it is by no means infallible, since small losses are sometimes incurred. These points empha-

---

[1] This assumes the averages were available in 1897. Actually, Dow theory was first published in 1900.

size that, while mechanical devices can be useful for forecasting the stock market, there is no substitute for additional supportive analysis on which to base sound, balanced judgment.

Dow theory evolved from the work of Charles H. Dow, which was published in a series of *Wall Street Journal* editorials between 1900 and 1902. Dow used the behavior of the stock market as a barometer of business conditions rather than as a basis for forecasting stock prices themselves. His successor William Peter Hamilton developed Dow's principles and organized them into something approaching the theory as we know it today. These principles were outlined rather loosely in his book *The Stock Market Barometer,* published in 1921. It was not until Robert Rhea wrote *Dow Theory* in 1932 that a more complete and formalized account of the principles was finally published.

The theory assumes that the majority of stocks follow the underlying trend of the market most of the time. In order to measure "the market," Dow constructed two indexes: the (Dow Jones) Industrial Average, a combination of 12 (now 30) blue-chip stocks, and the (Dow Jones) Rail Average, comprising 12 railroad stocks. Since the Rail Average was intended as a proxy for transportation stocks, the evolution of aviation and other forms of transportation has necessitated modifying the old "Rail" Average in order to incorporate other forms of this industry. Consequently, the name of this index has been changed to "Transportation Average."

INTERPRETING THE THEORY

In order to interpret the theory correctly, it is necessary to have a record of the daily closing[2] prices of the two averages and the total of daily transactions on the New York Stock Exchange (NYSE). The six basic tenets of the theory are as follows:

1. The Averages Discount Everything

Changes in the daily closing prices reflect the aggregate judgment and emotions of all stock market participants, both current and potential. It is therefore assumed that this process discounts everything known and predictable that can affect the demand-supply relationships of stocks. Although acts of God are obviously unpredictable, their occurrence is quickly appraised and their implications discounted.

---

[2] It is important to use closing prices, since intraday fluctuations are more subject to manipulation.

FIGURE 2.1

2. The Market Has Three Movements

There are simultaneously three movements in the stock market.

Primary Movement: The most important is the primary or major trend, more generally known as a bull (rising) or bear (falling) market. These movements last from less than 1 year to several years.

A *primary bear market* is a long decline interrupted by important rallies. It begins as the hopes on which the stocks were first purchased are abandoned. Its second phase evolves as the level of business activity and of profits declines. The bear market reaches a climax when stocks are liquidated regardless of their underlying value (because of the depressed state of the news or because of forced liquidation caused, for example, by margin calls). This represents the third stage of the bear market.

A *primary bull market* is a broad upward movement, averaging at least 2 years, which is interrupted by secondary reactions. The bull market begins when the averages have discounted the worst possible news and confidence begins to revive about the future. The second stage of the bull market is a response of equities to known improvements in business conditions, while the third and final phase evolves from overconfidence and speculation when stocks are advanced on projections that usually prove to be unfounded.

Secondary Reactions: A secondary or intermediate reaction is defined as ". . . an important decline in a bull market or advance in a bear market, usually lasting from three weeks to as many months during which interval the movement generally retraces from 33 to 66 percent of the primary price change since the termination of the last preceding secondary reaction."[3] This relationship is shown in Figure 2.1.

[3] Robert Rhea, *Dow Theory*, Barron's, New York, 1932.

Occasionally a secondary reaction can retrace the whole of the previous primary movement, but normally the move falls in the ½ to ⅔ area, often at the 50 percent mark. As discussed in greater detail below, the correct differentiation between the first leg of a new primary trend and a secondary movement within the existing trend provides Dow theorists with their most difficult problem.

Minor Movements: The third movement lasts from a matter of hours up to as long as 3 weeks. It is important only in that it forms part of the primary or secondary moves; it has no forecasting value for longer-term investors. This is especially important since short-term movements can be manipulated to some extent, unlike the secondary or primary trends.

3. Lines Indicate Movement

Rhea defined a line as ". . . a price movement two to three weeks or longer, during which period the price variation of both averages moves within a range of approximately 5 percent (of their mean average). Such a movement indicates either accumulation [*stock moving into strong and knowledgeable hands and therefore bullish*] or distribution [*stock moving into weak hands and therefore bearish*]."[4] (Words in italics added by the present author.)

An advance above the limits of the "line" indicates accumulation and predicts higher prices, and vice versa. When a line occurs in the middle of a primary advance, it is really forming a horizontal secondary movement and should be treated as such.

4. Price/Volume Relationships Provide Background

The normal relationship is for volume to expand on rallies and contract on declines. If volume becomes dull on a price advance and expands on a decline, a warning is given that the prevailing trend may soon be reversed. This principle should be used as background information only, since the conclusive evidence of trend reversals can be given only by the price of the respective averages.

5. Price Action Determines the Trend

Bullish indications are given when successive rallies penetrate peaks while the trough of an intervening decline is above the preceding trough. Conversely, bearish indications arise from a series of declining peaks and troughs.

[4] Ibid.

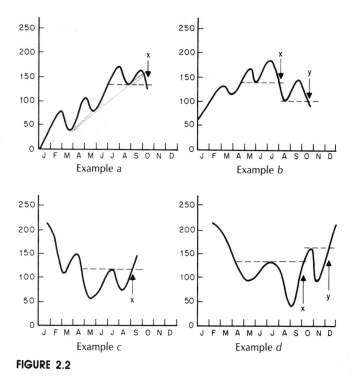

Example a

Example b

Example c

Example d

FIGURE 2.2

Figure 2.2 shows a theoretical bull trend interrupted by a secondary reaction. In example a the index makes a series of three peaks and troughs, each higher than its respective predecessor. Then, following the third decline, the index rallies but is unable to surpass its third peak. The ensuing decline takes the average below its low point, confirming a bear market as it does so at point X. Similarly, in example b, following the third peak in the bull market, a bear market is indicated as the average falls below the previous secondary trough. In this instance the preceding secondary was part of a bull market, not the first trough in a bear market, as shown in example a. Many Dow theorists do not consider penetration at point X in example b to be a sufficient indication of a bear market. They prefer to take a more conservative stance by awaiting a rally and subsequent penetration of that previous trough marked as point Y in example b.

In such cases, it is wise to approach the interpretation with additional caution. If a bearish indication is given from the volume patterns and if a clearly identifiable speculative stage for the bull market has already materialized, it is probably safe to assume that the bearish indication is valid. In the absence of such characteristics it is wiser to give the bull market the benefit of the doubt and adopt a more conservative position.

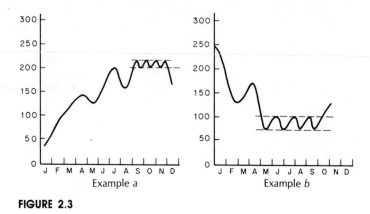

Example a   Example b

FIGURE 2.3

Examples c and d represent similar instances at the bottom of a bear market.

The examples in Figure 2.3 show how the primary reversal would appear if the average had formed a "line" at its peak or trough.

The importance of being able to distinguish between a valid secondary movement and the first leg of a new primary trend is now evident. This is perhaps the most difficult part of the theory to interpret, and unquestionably the most critical.

It is first essential to establish that the secondary reaction has retraced at least one-third of the ground of the preceding primary movement as measured from the termination of the preceding secondary. The secondary should also extend for at least 3 to 4 weeks.

Vital clues can also be obtained from volume characteristics and from an assessment of the maturity of the prevailing primary trend. The odds of a major reversal are much greater if the market has undergone its third phase, characterized by speculation and false hopes during a primary upswing, or a bout of persistent liquidation and widespread pessimism during a major decline. While a change in the primary trend can occur without a clearly identifiable third phase, generally such reversals prove to be relatively short-lived. On the other hand, the largest primary swings usually develop when the characteristics of a third phase are especially marked during the preceding primary movement. Hence, the excessive bouts of speculation in 1919 and 1929 were followed by particularly sharp setbacks. Intermediate-term movements are discussed more extensively in Chapter 3.

6. The Averages Must Confirm

One of the most important principles of Dow theory is that the movement of the Industrial Average and the Transportation Average should always be considered together, i.e., the two averages must confirm each other.

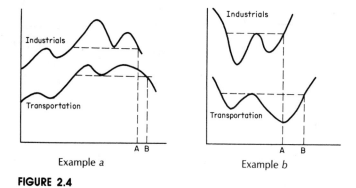

Example *a*   Example *b*

FIGURE 2.4

The need for confirming action by both averages would seem fundamentally logical, for if the market is truly a barometer for future business conditions, in an expanding economy investors should be bidding up the prices both of companies that produce goods and of companies that transport them. It is not possible to have a healthy economy where goods are being manufactured but not sold (i.e., shipped to market). This principle of confirmation is shown in Figure 2.4.

In example *a*, the Industrial Average is the first to signal a bear trend (point *A*), but the actual bear market is not indicated until the Transportation Average confirms at point *B*. Example *b* shows the beginning of a new bull market. Following a sharp decline, the industrials make a new low. A rally then develops, but the ensuing reaction holds above the previous low. When prices push above the preceding rally, a bull signal is given by the industrials at point *A*. In the meantime the Transportation Average makes a series of two succeeding lows. The question that arises is which average is correctly representing the prevailing trend. Since it is always assumed that a trend is in existence until a reversal is proved, the conclusion should be drawn at this point that the Transportation Average is portraying the correct outcome.

It is only when this average exceeds the peak of the preceding secondary at point *B* that a new bull market is confirmed by both averages, thereby resulting in a Dow theory buy signal.

The movement of one average unsupported by the other can often lead to a false and misleading conclusion—which is well illustrated in Figure 2.5 by the following example, which occurred in 1930.

The 1929–1932 bear market had begun in September 1929 and was confirmed by both averages in late October. In June 1930 both averages made a new low, then rallied and reacted in August. Following this correction the industrials surpassed their previous peak. Many believed that this signaled the end of a particularly sharp bear market and that it was only a matter of time before the rails would follow suit. As it turned out, the action

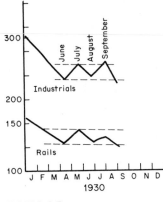

FIGURE 2.5

of the industrials was totally misleading; the bear market still had another 2 years to run.

Dow theory does not specify a time period beyond which a confirmation of one average by the other becomes invalid. Generally, the closer the confirmation, the stronger the ensuing move is likely to be. For example, confirmation of the 1929–1932 bear market was given by the Rail Average just one day after the Industrial Average. The sharp 1962 break was confirmed on the same day.

One of the major criticisms of Dow theory is that many of its signals have proved to be late, often 20 to 25 percent after a peak or trough in the averages has occurred. One rule of thumb that has enabled Dow theorists to anticipate probable reversal at an earlier date is to observe the dividend yield on the industrials. When the yield on the Industrial Average has fallen to 3 percent or below, this has historically been a good indication of the maturity of the bull market and therefore representative of the so-called third stage. Similarly a yield of 6 percent has been a reliable indicator at market bottoms.

The Dow theorist would not necessarily use these levels as actual buying or selling points, but would probably consider altering the percentage of his equity exposure if a significant nonconfirmation were to develop between the Industrial Average and the Transportation Average when the yield on the Dow reached these extremes. Such a strategy would help improve the investment return of the Dow theory but would not always result in a superior performance. At the 1976 peak, for example, the yield on the Dow never reached the magic 3 percent level, and prices fell 20 percent before a mechanical signal was confirmed by both averages. Moreover, in the postwar period long-term interest rates have reached higher and higher peaks in each succeeding cycle, so that if inflationary pressures continue and this

TABLE 2.1   85-Year Record of the Dow Theory

Buy signals			Sell signals		
Date of signal	Price of Dow	% gain from sell signal when short	Date of signal	Price of Dow	% gain from buy signal
Jul. 1897	44		Dec. 1899	63	43
Oct. 1900	59	6	Jun. 1903	59	0
Jul. 1904	51	14	Apr. 1906	92	80
Apr. 1908	70	24	May 1910	85	21
Oct. 1910	82	4	Jan. 1913	85	3
Apr. 1915	65	24	Aug. 1917	86	32
May 1918	82	5	Feb. 1920	99	22
Feb. 1922	84	16	Jun. 1923	91	8
Dec. 1923	94	loss 3	Oct. 1929	306	226
May 1933	84	73	Sep. 1937	164	95
Jun. 1938	127	23	Mar. 1939	136	7
Jul. 1939	143	5	May 1940	138	loss 7
Feb. 1943	126	8	Aug. 1946	191	52
Apr. 1948	184	4	Nov. 1948	173	loss 6
Oct. 1950	229	loss 32	Apr. 1953	280	22
Jan. 1954	288	loss 3	Oct. 1956	468	63
Apr. 1958	450	4	Mar. 1960	612	36
Nov. 1960	602	2	Apr. 1962	683	13
Nov. 1962	625	8	May 1966	900	43
Jan. 1967	823	9	Jun. 1969	900	9
Dec. 1970	823	9	Apr. 1973	921	12
Jan. 1975	680	26	Oct. 1977	801	18
Apr. 1978	780	3	Jul. 1981	960	23
Aug. 1982	840	13			
Average of all cycles, 11%			Average of all cycles, 35%		

secular trend of higher rates is extended, it may not be unreasonable to expect future bear markets to end with yields well in excess of 6 percent on the DJIA.

Over the years many criticisms have been leveled at the theory on the basis that from time to time (as in periods of war) the rails have been over-regulated, or that the new Transportation Average no longer reflects investors' expectations about the future movement of goods. The theory has stood the test of time, however, as Table 2.1 indicates. Indeed, the existence of criticism is perfectly healthy, for were the theory to gain widespread acceptance and were its signals purely mechanistic instead of requiring experienced judgment, they would be instantly discounted, rendering Dow theory useless for profitable investment.

SUMMARY

Dow theory is concerned with determining the direction of the primary trend of the market, not the ultimate duration or size of the trend. Once confirmed by both averages, the new trend is assumed to be in existence until an offsetting confirmation by both averages has taken place.

Major bull and bear markets each have three distinct phases. The identification of these phases and the appearance of any divergence in the normal volume/price relationship both offer useful indications that a reversal in the major trend is about to take place. Such supplementary evidence is particularly useful when the action of the price averages themselves is inconclusive.

Typical Parameters for Intermediate-Term Trends

SOME BASIC OBSERVATIONS

In the two previous chapters the discussion centered around the main or primary trend of the stock market, i.e., the price movement that corresponded with changes in economic activity over the course of a typical 3- to 4-year business cycle. Though it is clearly important to have an idea of the direction and maturity of the primary trend, it is also helpful to obtain some kind of understanding of the typical character and duration of the intermediate trend, not only for the purpose of improving success rates in trading but also to help assess when the primary movement may have run its course.

Successful analysis of intermediate trends offers the following advantages:

1. Changes in intermediate trends aid in the identification of turning points in the primary trend.
2. Intermediate-term trading involves fewer transactions than trading minor price movements and therefore results in lower commission costs.

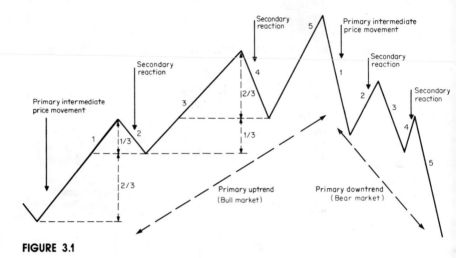

FIGURE 3.1

3. Intermediate-trend reversal points occur several times a year and can, if properly interpreted, allow a relatively high and quick return on capital.

INTERMEDIATE CYCLES DEFINED

Typically a primary trend consists of five intermediate trends, three of which form part of the prevailing trend whereas the remaining two run counter to that trend. In a bull market the intermediate counter trends are represented by price declines; in a bear market they form rallies which separate the three intermediate downwaves as shown in Figure 3.1.

It is apparent from the previous discussion that there are essentially two types of intermediate price movements. The first, which goes in the direction of the primary trend, may be called a primary intermediate price movement. The second is an important price movement that lasts from 3 weeks to 3 months (occasionally longer) and normally retraces between one-third and two-thirds of the preceding primary intermediate movement. This price movement, which runs counter to the main trend, is called a secondary movement or reaction. Since a primary intermediate price movement operates in the same direction as the primary or main market trend, it almost always lasts longer than its secondary counterpart. Its price magnitude is normally greater as well.

Since these countertrends or reactions against the main trend are notoriously difficult to forecast in terms of character, magnitude, and duration, they should generally be avoided from a trading point of view as they will almost invariably be subject to confusing whipsaws. By their very nature

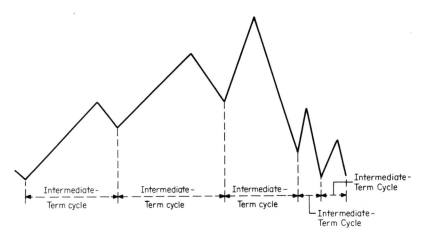

FIGURE 3.2

they tend to fool the majority and can therefore prove extremely treacherous. In this respect, although it is possible to design successful mechanized systems based on intermediate price movements, almost invariably poor or losing signals come from secondary market movements which occur against the main trend. Intermediate-term trends that move in the same direction as the primary trend are generally easier to profit from. Traders who do not have the patience to invest for the longer term will therefore find that successful analysis of intermediate movements offers superior results, especially because the day-to-day or minor swings are to a large degree random in nature and therefore even more difficult to capitalize on.

A secondary reaction need not always be a bull market correction or a bear market rally since it can take the form of a sideways movement or consolidation under the same idea as Charles Dow's line formation (see the discussion in Chapter 2).

Since intermediate movements can go either with or against the main trend, it is possible to recognize that there is also an intermediate cycle, just as there is a primary trend cycle which occurs between two bear market lows.

An intermediate cycle consists of a primary intermediate price movement and a secondary reaction. It extends from the low of one intermediate trend to the low of the other, as shown in Figure 3.2.

In a bull market the up phase of the cycle should be longer in time and greater in magnitude. The low on the secondary reaction should be higher than its predecessor. In a bear market the reverse conditions hold true, i.e., declines are longer and greater, and rallies are short and sharp but of less magnitude. Accordingly the technician is first alerted to the possibility of a basic reversal in the primary trend when: first, a third intermediate cycle is

TABLE 3.1 Primary Intermediate Upmoves, 1898–1933 (Percentage)

Proportion of intermediate moves	Price magnitude
25	7–14
50	15–28
25	28–117
100	
Median 20	

nearing completion; second, the overall technical structure looks weak (strong in a bear market) as the previous intermediate low (high) is approached; and third, that level is finally and decisively broken on the downside (upside).

It should not be assumed from the above discussion that primary movements can never encompass more or fewer than three primary intermediate price movements, for often they do. Readers are therefore cautioned to expect three as a normal event, but not to be caught off guard if there are fewer or more.

AMPLITUDE AND DURATION OF PRIMARY INTERMEDIATE UPMOVES

Between 1897 and 1933 Robert Rhea, the author of *Dow Theory*, classified 53 intermediate trend advances within a primary bull market which ranged in magnitude from 7 to 117 percent, as shown in Table 3.1.

I have classified 35 intermediate-term moves between 1933 and 1982, the median of which averaged 22 percent from low to high. The results are shown in Table 3.2.

The median average primary intermediate advance since 1897 appears therefore to be around 20 to 22 percent.

The median primary intermediate upmove does not appear to be much different in the 1933–1982 period from that classified by Rhea. However,

TABLE 3.2 Primary Intermediate Upmoves, 1933–1982

	Swings from low to high, percent	Duration, weeks
Mean average	30	22
Median	22	24
Range	10–105	3–137

TABLE 3.3 Primary Intermediate Downmoves, 1898–1932
(Percentage)

Proportion of intermediate moves	Price magnitude
25	3–12
50	13–27
25	28–54
Median 18	

the median duration appears to have increased considerably, from 13 weeks in the 1898–1933 period to 24 weeks in the 1933–1982 period.

AMPLITUDE AND DURATION OF PRIMARY INTERMEDIATE DOWNMOVES

Using Rhea's classification, 39 cases of a primary intermediate decline developed between 1900 and 1932, as summarized in Table 3.3.

My research shows that between 1932 and 1982 there were 35 primary intermediate declines with a median of 16 percent, the decline being measured as a percentage from the high. The results are summarized in Table 3.4.

The results in the 1932–1982 period did not differ appreciably from those classified by Rhea. His median average swing was 18 percent compared to a more recent 16 percent, whereas the median duration in the earlier period was 13 weeks compared to 14 weeks in the 1932–1982 period.

AMPLITUDE, DURATION, AND RETRACEMENT OF BULL MARKET INTERMEDIATE CORRECTIONS

Bull Market Secondary Reactions

Between 1898 and 1933 Rhea classified 43 cases of bull market secondaries. In terms of retracement of the previous primary intermediate upmove, they ranged from 12.4 to 180 percent with a median of 56 percent. This

TABLE 3.4 Primary Intermediate Downmoves, 1932–1982

	Swings from high	Duration (weeks)
Mean average	18	17
Median	16	14
Range	7–40	3–43

compared with a range in the 1933–1982 period from 25 to 148 percent, with a median of 51 percent. The duration of the median in the earlier period was 5 weeks compared to 8 weeks between 1933 and 1982. The median percentage loss from the previous primary intermediate peak was 12 percent (the mean average was 13 percent) between 1933 and 1982.

Bear Market Rallies

Rhea estimated that the median bear market rally retraced 52 percent of the previous decline, which compares to my own median estimate of 61 percent in the 1932–1982 period. The two ranges were 30 and 116 percent and 26 and 99 percent, respectively. Median durations were 6 weeks in 1898–1933 and 7 weeks in 1932–1982. Rallies off the low averaged 12 and 10 percent for mean and median, respectively, for the 1933–1982 period.

CAUSES OF SECONDARY REACTIONS

Since the primary trend of stock prices is determined by the *attitudes* of investors to the future flow of profits, which are in turn determined to a large degree by the course of the business cycle, it would at first seem illogical to expect these longer-term movements to be interrupted by what can often prove to be very uncomfortable reactions (or in the case of a bear market, very deceptive rallies).

History shows that secondary reactions occur not only because of technical distortions which arise in the market as a result of overoptimism (or overpessimism), but also because new factors emerge which suggest that business conditions are not going to be as extreme as had originally been anticipated, or even that they are going to materialize in the opposite direction. For example, after the first intermediate-term rally in a bull market, the ensuing reaction may develop because investors who had been discounting a strong recovery now see some chinks appearing and might even be forecasting an actual decline in business conditions. Another possibility might be fear of rising interest rates which could choke off the recovery. Since prices had discounted a strong recovery, this change in perception causes investors to pull back and prices to fall accordingly. At the same time many investors get carried away during the rally phase and leverage themselves up. As prices begin to fall, this causes their equity to shrink, forcing them to liquidate. This process adds further fuel to the price decline.

A bear market rally generally takes place because of a better outlook for business conditions than had previously been anticipated. The catalyst to the rally is the rush by traders and investors to cover their short positions (for a definition and explanation of short selling, see the Glossary). It should be added that the *apparent* motivating force for the correction need not necessarily be directly linked to the outlook for business or interest rates. It could be the anticipated resolution or worsening of a political or military problem, for example. Essentially the change in anticipated conditions combined with the unwinding of the technical distortions of the previous primary intermediate trend and its associated sharp price movement are sufficient to fool the majority. Only when business conditions are correctly anticipated to change from recovery to recession (or vice versa) is the primary trend likely to reverse.

In his excellent book, *Profits in the Stock Market*, H. M. Gartley[1] pointed out that in the 40 years ending in 1935 two-thirds of all bull market corrections developed in two waves of liquidation separated by a minor rally which retraced between one-third and two-thirds of the first decline. Observation of such corrections since 1935 also bears out the finding that most intermediate corrections consist of two rather than one or three phases of liquidation. Unfortunately, intermediate corrections within a bear market cannot be so easily categorized since some are one-move affairs, some rally out of a small base, while still others unfold as a very volatile sideways movement.

RELATIONSHIP BETWEEN PRIMARY INTERMEDIATE MOVES AND SUBSEQUENT REACTIONS

In *Profits in the Stock Market* Gartley published a series of diagrams using the classification of intermediate trends established by Robert Rhea. Gartley's conclusion was that the smaller the primary intermediate-term movement was in magnitude, the larger tended to be the retracement, and vice versa. He noted that this was just as valid for bull market reactions as for bear market rallies. For the period since 1933 there seems to be little statistical evidence to refute this hypothesis. For example, the rally off the 1962 low was only 18 percent compared to the mean average of 30 percent between 1933 and 1982. This represented part of a double bottom formation and therefore the first primary intermediate rally. This relatively small advance was followed by a somewhat large 71 percent retracement. However, the ensuing rally from late 1962 until mid-1963 was 32 percent and was followed by a small 25 percent retracement of the gain. The curious reader may wish to be satisfied that what goes up does not necessarily come down, and vice versa, by studying some of the charts in Appendix B, not only of the DJIA but also other averages and indicators, to see that this is *normally* the case.

---

[1] Lambert Gann Publishing, Pomeroy, Wash.

FIGURE 3.3

USING INTERMEDIATE CYCLES TO IDENTIFY PRIMARY REVERSALS

Number of Intermediate Cycles

A primary movement may normally be expected to encompass 2½ intermediate cycles (see Figure 3.3). Unfortunately, not all primary movements correspond to the norm; an occasional primary movement may consist of 1, 2, 3, or even 4 intermediate cycles. Furthermore, these intermediate cycles may be of very unequal length or magnitude, making their classification and identification possible only after the event. It is still possible, however, to use intermediate-cycle analysis as a basis for identifying the maturity of the primary trend in the majority of cases, in which the intermediate cycles are clearly identifiable.

Whenever prices are well advanced on a primary intermediate trend following the complication of two intermediate cycles, the technician should be alerted to the fact that a reversal of the primary trend itself may be about to take place. Similarly if only one intermediate cycle has been completed the chances of prices reaching higher levels (lower levels in a bear market) are clearly quite high.

Characteristics of Final Intermediate
Cycle in a Primary Trend

In addition to actually counting the number of intermediate cycles, it is also possible to relate the characteristics of a particular cycle to those of a typical pivotal or reversal cycle of a primary trend. These characteristics are discussed below.

Reversal from Bull to Bear Market: Since volume leads price, the failure of volume to increase above the levels of the previous intermediate-cycle up phase is a bearish sign. Alternatively, if volume, over a period of 3 to 4 weeks, expands on the intermediate rally close to the previous peak in volume but fails to move prices significantly, this represents churning and should also be treated bearishly. Accompaniment of either of these characteristics by a downward crossover of a 40-week moving average (see Chapter 7) or a divergence in an intermediate-term momentum index (see Chapter 8) is an additional reason for caution.

There are essentially two broad characteristics which suggest that the downward phase of an intermediate cycle could be the first downleg of a bear market. The first is a substantial increase in volume during the price decline. The second is a cancellation or retracement of 80 percent or more of the up phase of that same intermediate cycle. The greater the retracement, the greater the probability that the basic trend has reversed, especially as a retracement in excess of 100 percent means that any series of rising troughs has been broken, thereby placing the probabilities in favor of a change in the primary trend.

Reversal of Bear to Bull Market: The first intermediate up phase of a bull market is usually accompanied by a substantial expansion in volume which is significantly greater than that of previous intermediate up phases. In other words, the first upleg in a bull market attracts noticeably more volume than any of the intermediate rallies in the previous bear market. Another sign of a basic reversal occurs when prices retrace at least 80 percent of the previous decline. Again the greater the proportion of retracement, the greater are the odds of a reversal in the basic trend. If the retracement is greater than 100 percent, then the odds clearly indicate that a reversal in the downward trend has taken place, since this will have broken the series of declining troughs.

Since volume normally expands substantially as the intermediate down phase during a bear market reaches its low, a shrinkage in volume during an intermediate decline could well be a warning that the bear market has run its course. This is especially true if the price does not reach a new low during this intermediate decline, since the suggestion would be that the series of declining intermediate cyclical lows, characteristic of a bear market, may no longer be intact. An example of this can be seen in Chart 4.7a (page

58), where the overall peak in volume was seen in the June 1962 decline rather than the August–October sell-off. In Chart 4.7b there was no perceptible slackening of volume at the lows, but the volume expansion during the January rally, combined with the bettering of the October–November high, i.e., 100 percent retracement, offered a valuable clue that the bear market was over. The final decline in October represented the down phase of the third intermediate cycle in the bear market, which should have been a warning of its probable maturity.

SUMMARY

1. The typical primary trend can be divided into 2½ primary intermediate cycles, each consisting of an upmove and a downmove. In a bull market each successive upwave should reach a new cyclical high, and in a bear market each successive downwave of the intermediate cycle should reach a new low. The breaking of such a pattern of rising lows and falling peaks is an important but *not* unequivocal warning of a reversal in the primary trend. For more conclusive proof, technicians should resort to a similar conclusion from a *consensus* of indicators.

2. A secondary movement or reaction is that part of an intermediate cycle which runs counter to the main trend—a downward reaction in a bull market or a rally in a bear market. Secondary intermediate movements typically last from 3 weeks to 3 months and retrace between one-third and two-thirds of the previous primary intermediate price movement. Secondary price movements may also take the form of a line or horizontal trading pattern.

3. The character of intermediate cycles can be used to help identify primary trend reversals.

4

Price
Patterns

The techniques discussed in this chapter and in Chapters 5 to 10 are concerned with the analysis of either a market average or an indicator of the market's internal structure, but these basic principles can just as validly be applied to individual stocks.

The concept of price patterns is demonstrated in Figures 4.1 and 4.2. Figure 4.1 represents a typical stock market cycle in which there are three trends—two basic and one minor. The two basic trends are the primary bull or rising trend (A to B) and the bear market or declining phase (C to D). The minor trend is essentially a horizontal or transitional one which separates the two major market movements. Sometimes a highly emotional market can change without warning, as in Figure 4.2, but this rarely happens. Consider a fast-moving train, which takes a long time to slow down and then go into reverse; the same is normally true of the stock market.

To the market technician, the transitional phase takes on great significance since it marks the turning point between a rising and a falling market. If prices have been advancing, the enthusiasm of the buyers has outweighed the pessimism of sellers up to this point, and prices have risen accordingly. During the transition phase, the balance becomes more or less even until finally, for one reason or another, it is tipped in a new direction as the relative weight of selling pushes the trend (of prices) down. At the termination of the bear market the reverse process occurs.

From a technical viewpoint these transition phases are almost invariably signaled by clearly definable price patterns and formations whose successful completion alerts the technician to the fact that a major reversal in trend has taken place.

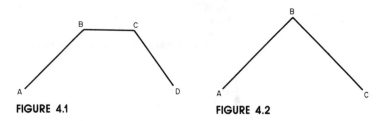

FIGURE 4.1   **FIGURE 4.2**

   This phenomenon is illustrated in Figure 4.3, which represents the price action at the end of a long rising trend. As soon as the index rises above line *BB* it is in the transitional area, although this is only apparent some time after the picture has unfolded.

   Once into the area the index rises to line *AA*, which is technically termed a *resistance area*. The word "resistance" is used because at this point the index shows a resistance to a further price rise. This arises because as the supply-demand relationship comes into balance at *AA*, the market quickly turns in favor of the sellers because prices react. This temporary reversal may occur because buyers refuse to pay up for stock, or because the higher price attracts more sellers, or for a combination of both reasons. The important fact is that the relationship between the two groups is temporarily reversed at this point.

   Following the unsuccessful assault on *AA*, prices turn down until line *BB*, known as a *support level*, is reached. Just as the price level at *AA* reversed the balance in favor of the sellers, so the support level *BB* alters the balance yet again. This time the trend moves in an upward direction, for at *BB* prices again become relatively attractive for buyers who "missed the boat" on the way up, while sellers who feel that the price will again reach *AA* hold off. For a while there is a standoff between buyers and sellers within the confines of the area bounded by lines *AA* and *BB*. Finally the price falls below *BB*, and a new major (downward) trend is signaled.

   In order to help explain this concept, the "battle" between buyers and sellers can be thought of as one fought by two armies engaged in trench warfare. In Figure 4.4, example *a*, two armies A and B are facing off. Line *AA* represents army A's defense, and *BB* is army B's line of defense. The arrows indicate the forays between the two lines as both armies fight their way to the opposing trench but are unable to penetrate the line of defense.

FIGURE 4.3

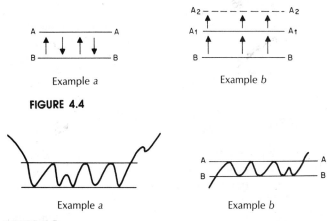

Example a   Example b

FIGURE 4.4

Example a   Example b

FIGURE 4.5

In the second example army B finally pushes through A's trench. Army A is then forced to retreat and make a stand at the second line of defense (line AA_2). In the stock market, line AA represents selling resistance which, once overcome, signifies a change in the balance between buyers and sellers in favor of the buyers, so that prices will advance quickly until new resistance is met. The second line of defense, line AA_2, represents resistance to a further advance.

On the other hand, army B might quite easily break through AA_2, but the farther it advances without time to consolidate its gains the more likely it is to become overextended, and the greater is the probability of its suffering a serious setback. At some point, therefore, it makes more sense for this successful force to wait and consolidate its gains.

If stock market prices extend too far without time to digest their gains, they too are more likely to face a sharp and seemingly unexpected reversal.

The transitional or horizontal phase separating rising and falling price trends is a pattern known as a *rectangle*. This formation corresponds to the "line" formation developed from Dow theory. The rectangle in Figure 4.3 marking the turning point between the bull and bear phases is termed a *reversal* pattern. Reversal patterns at market tops are known as *distribution* areas or patterns, and those at market bottoms are called *accumulation* patterns (see Figure 4.5a). Had the rectangle been completed with a victory for the buyers as the price pushed through line AA (see Figure 4.5b), no reversal of the rising trend would have occurred. The "breakout" above AA would therefore have reaffirmed the underlying trend. In this case the corrective phase associated with the formation of the rectangle would have temporarily interrupted the bull market and become a *consolidation* pattern. Such formations are also referred to as *continuation* patterns.

During the period of formation, there is no way of knowing in advance which way the price will ultimately break; therefore it should always be assumed that *the prevailing trend is in existence until it is proved to have been reversed.*

There are certain characteristics that apply to all types of price patterns.

SIZE AND DEPTH

The significance of a price formation or pattern is a direct function of its size and depth. In other words, the longer a pattern takes to complete and the greater the price fluctuations within the pattern, the more substantial the ensuing move is likely to be. It is as important to build a strong base from which stock prices can rise as it is to build a large, strong, deep foundation for the construction of a skyscraper. In the case of stocks, the foundation is an accumulation pattern which represents an area of indecisive combat between buyers and sellers. The term "accumulation" is used because market bottoms always occur when business news is bad. Such an environment stimulates the sale of stock by uninformed investors who were not expecting developments to deteriorate. During an accumulation phase more sophisticated investors and professionals would be positioning or accumulating stock in anticipation of improved conditions 6 to 9 months ahead. During this period stock is moving from weak, uninformed investors into strong and knowledgeable hands. At market tops the process is reversed as those who accumulated stocks at or near the bottom sell to the less sophisticated market participants, who become more and more attracted to the stock market as prices rise, business conditions improve, and forecasts for the economy are revised upward. Thus the longer the period of accumulation, the greater the amount of stock that moves from weak into strong hands, and the greater is the base from which prices can rise. The reverse is true at market tops, where a substantial amount of distribution inevitably results in a protracted period of price erosion or base building.

The longer the formation of a rectangle pattern takes (see Figure 4.6) and the more often it fails to break through its outer boundaries, the greater is the significance of the ultimate penetration.

The time taken to complete a formation is important because of the amount of stock changing hands, and also because a movement in price

FIGURE 4.6

FIGURE 4.7

beyond the boundaries of a pattern means that the balance between buyers and sellers has altered. When the price action has been in a stalemate for a long time and investors have become used to buying at one price and selling at the other, a move beyond either limit is a fundamental change which has great psychological significance.

MEASURING IMPLICATIONS

Most of the results obtained with technical analysis procedures do not indicate the eventual duration of a trend. Price patterns are the exception, since their construction offers some limited forecasting possibilities.

There are two alternative methods of charting, and the choice of scale determines the significance of the measuring implications. The two types of graph used in technical analysis are (1) arithmetic and (2) ratio or logarithmic.

Arithmetic Scale

Arithmetic charts consist of an arithmetic scale on the vertical or y axis, with time being shown on the horizontal or x axis, as illustrated in Figure 4.7. All units of measure are plotted using the same vertical distance, so that the difference in space between 2 and 4 is the same as that between 20 and 22. This scale is not particularly satisfactory for stock price measurement, since a rise from 2 to 4 represents a doubling of the price, while one from 20 to 22 represents only a 10 percent increase. On an arithmetic scale both moves are represented by the same vertical distance. A relatively large move of 10 points or more was not uncommon from 1966 to 1978, when the DJIA ranged between 600 and 1000. A 10-point move in 1932, though, when the average was as low as 40 to 50, represented a 20 to 25 percent change. For this reason, long-term movements are commonly plotted on a ratio or logarithmic scale.

FIGURE 4.8

FIGURE 4.9

Ratio Scale

Indexes or stock prices plotted on this scale show identical distances for identical percentage moves.

In Figure 4.8 the vertical distance between 1 and 2 (a 2:1 ratio) is ½ inch. Similarly, the 2:1 distance between 4 and 2 is also represented on the chart as ½ inch. A specific vertical distance on the chart will represent the same percentage change in the index being measured whatever the price level. For example, if the scale in Figure 4.8 were extended, ½ inch would always represent a doubling, whether from 1 to 2, 16 to 32, 50 to 100, and so on, just as ¼ inch would indicate a rise of 50 percent, or 1 inch a quadrupling of prices. Graph paper using ratio or logarithmic scale is easily obtained from any large office supplier.

An alternative method of portraying a ratio scale chart is to use arithmetic paper but plot the logarithm of an index instead of the actual index number itself. Hence, the DJIA at 1004 would be plotted at 3.001, which is the base 10 logarithm for 1000, and 758 would be plotted at 2.880, etc.

Figure 4.9 shows a rectangle which has formed and completed a (distribution) top. The measuring implication of this formation is the vertical distance between its outer boundaries, i.e., the distance between lines *AA* and *BB* projected downward from line *BB*. If *AA* represents 100 and *BB* 50, then the downside objective will be 50 percent, using a ratio scale. When projected downward from line *BB*, 50 percent gives a measuring implication of 25. While this measuring formula offers a rough guide, this is usually a *minimum* expectation, and prices often go much farther than their implied objective. In a very high proportion of cases the objective level derived from the measuring formula becomes an area of support or resistance where the price trend is temporarily halted. Should a rectangle appear as a bottom reversal pattern or as a consolidation pattern, the measuring rules remain consistent with the example given for the distribution formation. This is shown in the series in Figure 4.10.

If the minimal objective proves to be the ultimate extension of the new trend, a substantial amount of accumulation or distribution, whichever is

| Example a | Example b | Example c |

FIGURE 4.10

appropriate, will have to occur before prices can move in their original direction. Thus, if a 2-year rectangle is completed and the downward price objective is reached, even though further price erosion does not take place it is still usually necessary for a base (accumulation) to be formed of approximately the same size as the previous distribution (in this case 2 years) before a valid uptrend can take place.

CONFIRMATION OF A VALID BREAKOUT

Price

So far it has been assumed that any move out of the price pattern (however small) constitutes a valid signal of a trend reversal (or resumption if the pattern is one of consolidation). Quite often misleading moves known as "whipsaws" occur, so that it is helpful to set up certain criteria to minimize the possibility of such a misinterpretation. In terms of price it has been found useful to await a 3 percent penetration of the boundaries before concluding that the breakout is valid. This filters out a substantial number of misleading moves, even though the resulting signals are less timely.

Volume

A further confirmation of the validity of a breakout can be derived from an examination of the volume characteristics that accompany it. Volume usually goes with the trend, i.e., volume advances with a rising trend of prices and falls with a declining one. This is a normal relationship, and anything which diverges from this characteristic should be considered a warning sign that the prevailing price trend may be in the process of reversing. Figure 4.11 shows a typical volume/price relationship.

The volume, that is, the number of shares changing hands, is shown by the vertical lines at the bottom of the chart. Volume expands marginally as the index approaches its low, but as the accumulation pattern is formed, activity recedes noticeably. Volume is always measured on a relative basis,

FIGURE 4.11

so that heavy volume is "heavy" only in relation to a recent period. As the pattern nears completion, disinterest prevails and volume almost dries up. Then, as if by magic, activity picks up noticeably as the index moves above its level of resistance (bounded by the upper line in the rectangle). It is sometimes possible to draw a trendline joining the lower volume peaks, as shown in Figure 4.11. It is this upward surge in trading activity that confirms the validity of the breakout. A similar move on low volume would have been suspect, as it would have resulted in a failure of volume to move with the trend.

Following the sharp price rise from the rectangle, enthusiasm dies down as prices correct in a sideways movement and volume contracts. This is a perfectly normal relationship, since volume is correcting (declining) with price. Eventually volume and price expand together, and the primary upward trend is once again confirmed. Finally the buyers become exhausted, and the index forms yet another rectangle—characterized as before by falling volume, but this time destined to become a reversal pattern.

It is worth noting that while the volume from the breakout in rectangle *B* is high, it is relatively lower than that which accompanied the move from rectangle *A*. In relation to the overall cycle this is a bearish factor, since volume usually leads price. In this case volume makes its peak just before entering rectangle *B*, while the peak in prices is not reached until rectangle *C*. Chart 4.1 shows how this occurs in the marketplace.

Volume contracts throughout the formation of rectangle *C* and expands as prices break out on the downside. This expanded level of activity associated with the violation of the support at the lower boundary of the rectangle emphasizes the bearish nature of the breakout, although expanding volume is not a prerequisite for a valid signal with downside breakouts as it is for an upside move. More often than not, following the downside breakout prices will reverse and put on a small recovery or retracement rally. This advance is invariably accompanied by declining volume, which itself reinforces the bearish indications. It is halted at the lower end of the rectangle, which now becomes an area of resistance.

Some of the more common reversal formations will now be discussed.

CHART 4.1 Dow Jones Rail Average, 1946. This chart shows a classic rectangle formation as traced out by the Rail Average at the peak of the 1942–1946 bull market. Note the declining trend of volume, as indicated by the dashed line, during the formation of the rectangle. Worth special mention is the saucerlike formation of the volume during the late July–early August rally. The expansion of activity accompanying the downside breakout in late August completed the bearish implication of the successful completion of this pattern.

FIGURE 4.12

HEAD AND SHOULDERS

The head and shoulders (H&S) is probably the most reliable of all the chart patterns. These formations occur at both market tops and market bottoms. Figure 4.12 shows a typical head-and-shoulders distribution pattern. (See also Chart 4.3.)

The pattern consists of a final rally (the head) separating two smaller though not necessarily identical rallies (the shoulders). The first shoulder is the penultimate advance in the bull market, and the second is in effect the first bear market rally.

The volume characteristics are of critical importance in assessing the validity of these patterns. Activity is normally heaviest during the formation of the left shoulder and also tends to be quite heavy as prices approach the peak. The real tip-off that a head-and-shoulders pattern is being formed comes with the formation of the right shoulder, which is invariably accompanied by distinctly lower volume. The line joining the bottoms of the two shoulders is called the "neckline."

The measuring formula for this price formation is the distance between the head and the neckline projected downward from the neckline, as shown in Figure 4.12. It follows that the deeper the pattern, the greater its bearish significance once it has been completed. It is essential to await a 3 percent decline below the neckline.

Head-and-shoulders patterns can be formed in a period as short as 3 to 4 weeks or can take as long as several years to develop. Generally speaking, the longer the period, the greater the amount of distribution that has taken place, and therefore the longer the ensuing bear trend is likely to be. The larger head-and-shoulders formations are often very complex and comprise several smaller ones, as shown in Figure 4.13.

The H&S patterns illustrated in Figures 4.12 and 4.13 have a horizontal neckline, but there are many other varieties (as Figure 4.14 shows), all of which possess the same bearish implications as the horizontal variety once they have been completed.

CHART 4.2 *The New York Times* average, 1928–1930. During January and May of 1929 it appeared as if *The New York Times* average, shown here, was forming a broadening top. Three ascending peaks, *O, Q,* and *S,* were separated by two declining troughs *P* and *R,* but since the third bottom (*T*) remained above *R,* no negative signal was given. The break above the line joining *O, Q,* and *S* indicated that the "top" would not be completed. A sharp upward move followed as prices ran up to the ultimate peak of the 1921–1929 bull market. Even though this formation was never completed, the very fact that prices moved in such a volatile manner was a strong warning of the underlying weakness. A small right-angled broadening formation seemed to develop in July and August, but this would eventually prove to be the left shoulder of a 2½-month H&S pattern, the completion of which terminated the long bull market.

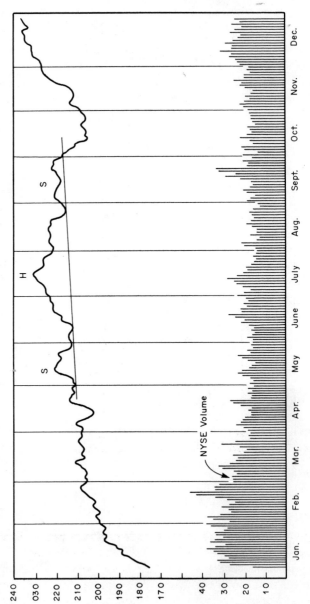

CHART 4.3 Dow Jones Transportation Average, 1976. Between mid-April and September 1976, the Dow Jones Transportation Average formed and completed a head-and-shoulders distribution pattern. The breakout in September proved to be a "bear trap," since the average resumed its advance and reached a major peak at 246 in May 1977. Nevertheless, the 1976 head-and-shoulders pattern did indicate the presence of distribution, and as a result the progress of the average was halted for a considerable time.

FIGURE 4.13

Example *a*

Example *b*

Example *c*

FIGURE 4.14

FIGURE 4.15

Figure 4.15 shows a head-and-shoulders pattern at a market bottom; this variety is usually called an "inverse head and shoulders."

Volume is usually relatively high at the bottom of the left shoulder and during the formation of the head. The major factor to watch for is activity on the right shoulder, which should contract during the decline to the trough and expand substantially on the breakout (see Chart 4.5). Like the H&S distribution patterns, the inverse (accumulation) H&S can have a number of variations in trendline slope, number of shoulders, etc. Some of these are shown in Figure 4.16.

CHART 4.4 *The New York Times* average, 1928. This chart of *The New York Times* average of 50 railroad and industrial stocks shows the formation of an upward-sloping H&S during March, April, and May 1928. The minimum downside objective of about 182 was achieved fairly quickly, but a 3-month period of base building commensurate with the head-and-shoulders pattern was still necessary before the effect of the distribution was canceled out and prices were able to resume their primary advance. Note the heavy volume on the left shoulder and head and the relatively low volume on the right shoulder. Also, activity declined substantially during the formation of the triangle but began to expand during the breakout in September.

CHART 4.5 Dow Jones Industrial Average, 1898. This downward-sloping inverse head and shoulders developed in the spring of 1898. Note how the April rally developed on very low volume. The subsequent reaction successfully tested the March low, and the ensuing breakout rally was accompanied by a bullish expansion of volume. By August the DJIA had reached 60.97, and by April 1899 it rose to 77.28.

Head-and-shoulders patterns are extremely reliable formations, and their successful completion usually offers an excellent indication of a trend reversal.

H&S FAILURES

Sometimes the price action exhibits all the characteristics of a H&S distribution pattern but either refuses to penetrate the neckline or penetrates it

Example *a*   Example *b*   Example *c*

FIGURE 4.16

CHART 4.6 Dow Jones Industrial Average, 1936–1937. Following a substantial advance from 1932, the first post-Depression bull market ended in 1937. This chart shows a classic double top. Note how the volume during the July–August rally was substantially below that of the January–March peak.

temporarily and then starts to rally. This represents a H&S failure and is usually followed by an explosive rally.

Chart 4.7*b*, which shows the daily close for the DJIA in 1975, illustrates this phenomenon very clearly as the "failure" of a head-and-shoulders pattern results in a fairly worthwhile rally. Nevertheless a H&S that does not "work" indicates that while there is still some life left in the situation, the end may not be far off. In the example cited above, the rally ended rather abruptly in July.

Unfortunately, the pattern itself gives no indication that it is going to fail. Sometimes such evidence can be gleaned from other technical factors. Such failures tend to be fairly rare but do point out the necessity of waiting for a decisive breakout on the downside. If any action is contemplated, it should be taken when the price breaks above the right shoulder on heavy volume. Usually such signals offer substantial profits in a very short period of time and are well worth acting on. Inverse H&S patterns can also fail. Again, the failure is usually followed by an extremely sharp selloff, as participants who bought in anticipation of an *upward* breakout are flushed out and the new bearish fundamentals become more widely known.

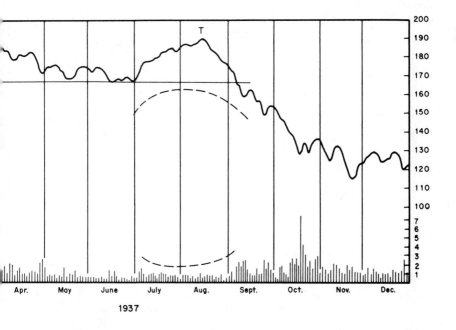

DOUBLE TOPS AND BOTTOMS

A double top consists of two peaks separated by a reaction or valley in prices. The main characteristic of a double top is that the second top is formed with distinctly less volume than the first (see Chart 4.6).

Minimum downside measuring implications, as shown in Figure 4.17, are similar to the H&S patterns. A double bottom is shown in Figure 4.18.

The pattern is typically accompanied by high volume on the first bottom, very light volume on the second, and very heavy volume on the breakout. Usually the second bottom is formed above the first, but these formations are equally valid whether or not the second reaction reaches (or even slightly exceeds) the level of its predecessor.

Some "double" patterns extend to form triple tops or bottoms, sometimes even quadruple or other complex formations. Some of the variations are shown in Figure 4.19.

The measuring implications of all such patterns are derived by measuring the distance between the peak (trough) and lower (upper) end of the pattern and projecting this distance from the neckline (see Chart 4.7).

CHART 4.7 Dow Jones Industrial Average, 1962. Chart 4.7 depicts two classic double bottoms in the DJIA formed during 1962 and 1974. Note how the second of each pair was accompanied by lower volume than the first. While volume expanded during the 1962 break-out, the increase in activity was not particularly spectacular. The rise in activity during January 1975 left little doubt that a new bull market had begun.

FIGURE 4.17

FIGURE 4.18

Example a   Example b   Example c

FIGURE 4.19

BROADENING FORMATIONS

Broadening formations occur where a series of three or more price fluctuations widen out in size so that peaks and troughs can be connected with two diverging trendlines. The easiest types of broadening formations to detect are those with a "flattened" bottom or top, as shown in examples a and b, Figure 4.20.

The pattern in example a is sometimes referred to as a right-angled broadening formation. Since the whole concept of widening price swings suggests highly emotional activity, volume patterns are difficult to characterize, though at market tops volume is usually heavy during the rally phases. The patterns, both at bottoms and tops, are similar to the H&S

Example a   Example b

FIGURE 4.20

Example a   Example b

FIGURE 4.21

FIGURE 4.22

variety, except that the "head" in the broadening formation is always the last to be formed. Bearish significance is obtained from a downside breakout confirmed by a 3 percent penetration of the neckline. Volume can be heavy or light, but additional bearish emphasis arises if activity expands at this point.

Since a broadening formation with a flattened top is an accumulation pattern, it is an important requirement that volume expand on the breakout, as shown in example b, Figure 4.20.

These two types of broadening formation can also develop as consolidation patterns, as represented in Figure 4.21.

Unfortunately, there does not appear to be a reliable point beyond which it is safe to say that the pattern has become one of continuation rather than reversal. The best defense in such cases is to extend the diverging trendlines, i.e., the dashed lines in Figure 4.21, and await a 3 percent penetration by the index as confirmation.

When completed, right-angled broadening formations of the reversal and continuation type result in a particularly dynamic move. It is almost as if they are aborted head-and-shoulders formations in which the move is so powerful that there is not time to complete the right shoulder.

The final type of broadening formation, known as an "orthodox broadening top," is shown in Figure 4.22.

This pattern comprises three rallies, with each succeeding peak higher than its predecessor, and each peak separated by two bottoms with the second bottom lower than the first. Orthodox broadening formations are associated with market peaks rather than troughs.

CHART 4.8 Dow Jones Industrial Average, 1954–1978. This chart shows the DJIA from 1954 to 1977. Between 1966 and 1977 the progress of this average was halted at the 1000 level. The reactions of 1966, 1970, and 1974 took the DJIA to succeeding new lows, resulting in what would appear to be a broadening formation with a flat top. Should the DJIA rise above the 1000 level (indicated by the dashed line) accompanied by high volume, this would represent an immensely bullish indication that the secular rise of the U.S. stock market had resumed.

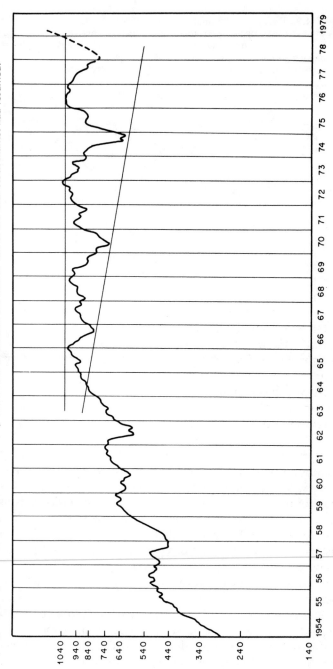

CHART 4.9   Dow Jones Industrial Average, 1919–1920. This daily chart of the DJIA during 1919 shows a classic right-angled broadening formation. This period marked the peak of a huge run-up in commodity prices and preceded the 1920–1921 Depression. The extreme volatility of financial markets at this time is clearly reflected not only in the action of the Dow but also in the volume of stocks traded.

These patterns are extremely difficult to detect until sometime after the final top has been formed, since there is no clearly definable level of support whose violation could serve as a benchmark. The violent and emotional nature of both price and volume swings further compounds the confusion and increases the complexity of defining these situations. Obviously under such conditions a breakout is difficult to pinpoint, but if the formation is reasonably symmetrical, a 3 percent move below the descending trendline joining the two bottoms—or even a 3 percent decline below the second bottom—usually serves as a timely warning that an even greater decline is in store.

Measuring implications are similarly difficult to ascertain, but normally the volatile character of a broadening top formation implies the completion of a substantial amount of distribution. Consequently, price declines of considerable proportion usually follow the successful completion of such patterns.

Mar.   Apr.   May   June   July   Aug.   Sept.   Oct.   Nov.   Dec.

1920

TRIANGLES

Triangles are the most common of all the price patterns discussed in this chapter but unfortunately the least reliable. Triangles may be consolidation or reversal formations, and they fall into two categories, symmetrical and right-angled.

Symmetrical Triangles

A symmetrical triangle is composed of a series of two or more rallies and reactions in which each succeeding peak is lower than its predecessor and the bottom from each succeeding reaction is higher than its predecessor (see Figure 4.23). A triangle is therefore the opposite of a broadening formation, since the trendlines joining peaks and troughs *converge,* unlike the (orthodox) broadening formation, where they *diverge.*

FIGURE 4.23

FIGURE 4.24

Example *a*   Example *b*

FIGURE 4.25

Example *a*   Example *b*

FIGURE 4.26

These patterns are also known as "coils," for the fluctuation in price and volume diminishes as the pattern is completed. Finally, both price and (usually) volume react sharply, as if a coil spring had been wound tighter and tighter and then snapped free as prices broke out of the triangle. Generally speaking, triangles seem to "work" best when the breakout occurs somewhere between half and three-fourths of the distance between the widest peak and rally and the apex (as in Figure 4.24).

The volume and 3 percent confirmation rules used for other patterns are also appropriate for triangles.

Right-Angled Triangles: Right-angled triangles are really a special form of the symmetrical type in that one of the two boundaries is formed at an angle of 90 degrees, i.e., horizontal to the vertical axis. (These triangle variations are illustrated in Figure 4.25 and Chart 4.10.) Whereas the symmetrical triangle gives no indication of which way it is ultimately likely to break, the right-angled triangle, with its implied level of support or resistance and contracting price fluctuations, does give an indication. Because one difficulty of interpreting these formations is that many rectangles begin as right-angled triangles, considerable caution should be used when interpreting these elusive patterns. Such a situation is shown in Figure 4.26 where a

CHART 4.10 Dow Jones Industrial Average, 1938. This excellent example of a right-angled triangle occurred at the bottoms of the 1937–1938 bear market. Note the substantial increase in volume that accompanied the upside breakout. Following the breakout, the average traced out a right-angled broadening formation with a flat top. Usually breakouts from these consolidation patterns are followed by a dramatic rise. In this case, however, the 158 level in November was destined to become the high for the 1938–1939 bull market.

Example *a*

Example *c*

Example *b*

Example *d*

FIGURE 4.27

potential downward sloping right-angled triangle in example *a* develops into a rectangle in example *b*.

Measuring objectives for triangles are obtained by drawing a line parallel to the base of the triangle through the peak of the first rally. This line (*BB* in Figure 4.27) represents the price objective which prices may be expected to reach or exceed.

The reverse procedure at market tops is shown in examples *c* and *d*. The same technique is used to project prices when triangles are of the consolidation variety.

SUMMARY

1. Stock prices move in trends, and once a trend has been established, the assumption is that it will perpetuate itself until a reversal has been proved. Reversals in these price trends take some time to bring about, and they are characterized by a temporary period in which the enthusiasm of buyers and sellers is roughly in balance. Such transitional periods between bull and bear phases can be identified by clearly definable price patterns which, when accompanied by the appropriate trends in volume, offer good and reliable indications that a reversal in trend has taken place.

2. Until a pattern has been formed and completed, the assumption should be that the prevailing trend is still operative, i.e., that the pattern is one of consolidation or continuation. This principle takes on added importance when the major trend has been in existence for only a relatively short period, because the more mature the trend, the greater is the probability of an important reversal.

3. Price patterns can be formed over periods ranging from 2 to 3 weeks to as many years. Their significance is derived from both their length and their depth. The longer the time required to form a pattern and the greater the price fluctuations within a pattern, the more substantial the ensuing price movement is likely to be.

4. While measuring formulas can be derived for many of the patterns, these are generally minimum objectives, since price trends usually extend much farther than indicated.

5

Flags,
Pennants,
Wedges,
and Gaps

The price patterns described in Chapter 4 develop as either reversal or continuation formations. The price patterns discussed in this chapter are almost invariably of the continuation variety.

FLAGS

A *flag*, as the name implies, looks like a flag on the chart. It represents a quiet pause accompanied by a trend of declining volume which interrupts a sharp, almost vertical rise or decline. As the flag is completed, prices break out in the same direction that they were moving in before its formation. Flags for both an up and a down market are shown in Figure 5.1. Essentially, the flag formation is a parallelogram in which the rally peaks and reaction lows can be connected by two lines that run parallel to each other. In the case of a rising market the flag is usually formed with a slight downtrend, whereas in a falling market it has a slight upward bias. Flags may also be horizontal.

In a rising market this type of pattern usually separates two halves of an

Example a   Example b

FIGURE 5.1   [SOURCE: *Martin J. Pring (ed.),* The McGraw-Hill Handbook of Commodities and Futures, *McGraw-Hill, New York, 1985, p. 42-2.*]

almost vertical rise. Volume is normally extremely heavy just before the flag formation begins. As the pattern develops, volume gradually dries to almost nothing, only to explode as the price works its way out of the complete formation. Flags can take as little as 5 days to as much as 3 to 5 weeks to form. Essentially they represent a period of controlled profit taking in a rising market.

In a falling market the formation of the flag is also accompanied by declining volume. Since this type of flag represents a formation with an upward bias in price, the volume implication (i.e., rising price with declining volume) is essentially bearish in nature. When the price breaks down from the flag, the almost vertical slide which preceded the formation of the flag resumes. Although volume tends to pick up at this point, it does not have to be explosive, unlike the breakout from a flag formed during an upmove, which should be.

It is most important to make sure that the price and volume characteristics agree. If, following a sharp rise for example, the price consolidates in what appears to be a flag formation but volume fails to contract appreciably, great care should be taken before coming to a bullish conclusion since prices may well react on the downside. A flag which takes more than 4 weeks to develop should also be treated with caution. This is because these formations are by definition temporary interruptions of a sharp uptrend. A period of longer than 4 weeks therefore represents an unduly long time for profit taking.

Flag formations are usually reliable patterns from a forecasting point of view, for not only is the direction of ultimate breakout indicated but also the ensuing move is usually well worthwhile from a trading point of view. Flags seem to form at the halfway point of a move. Once the breakout has taken place, a useful method for setting a price objective is to estimate the size of the price move in the period immediately before the flag formation began and then to project this move in the direction of the breakout. Since flags

FIGURE 5.2   [SOURCE: *Martin J. Pring (ed.),* The McGraw-Hill Handbook of Commodities and Futures, *McGraw-Hill, New York, 1985, p. 42-3.*]

take a relatively short period to develop, they do not show up on weekly or monthly charts.

PENNANTS

A pennant develops under exactly the same circumstances and has the same characteristics as a flag. The only difference is that this type of consolidation formation is constructed by joining a series of converging rallies and peaks as shown in Figure 5.2. In a sense the flag corresponds to a rectangle and the pennant to a triangle. If anything, volume tends to contract even more during the formation of a pennant than while a flag is forming. In every other way, however—measuring implications, time taken to develop, volume characteristics, etc.—pennants are identical to flags.

WEDGES

A wedge is very similar to a triangle in that two converging lines can be constructed from a series of peaks and troughs as shown in Figure 5.3, but whereas a triangle consists of one rising and one falling line, or one horizontal line, the converging lines in a wedge both move in the *same* direction. A falling wedge represents a temporary interruption of a rising trend, a rising wedge a temporary interruption of a falling trend. It is normal for volume to contract during the formation of both types of wedges.

Since wedges can take anywhere from 2 to 8 weeks to complete, they sometimes occur on weekly charts but are too brief to appear on monthly charts.

Rising wedges are fairly common as bear market rallies. Following their completion, prices usually break very sharply, especially if volume picks up noticeably on the downside.

FIGURE 5.3   [SOURCE: *Martin J. Pring (ed.), The McGraw-Hill Handbook of Commodities and Futures, McGraw-Hill, New York, 1985, p. 42-4.*]

SAUCERS AND ROUNDING TOPS

Examples *a* and *b* in Figure 5.4 show the formation of a saucer and a rounding top. A saucer pattern occurs at market bottoms while a rounding top develops at market peaks. A saucer is constructed by drawing a circular line under the lows which roughly approximates an elongated or saucer-shaped letter U. As the price drifts toward the low point of the saucer and investors lose interest, downward momentum dissipates. This lack of interest is also characterized by the volume level, which almost dries up at the time the price is reaching its low point. Gradually both price and volume pick up until eventually each explodes into an almost exponential pattern.

The price action of the rounded top is almost the exact opposite to that of the saucer pattern. On the other hand, volume characteristics are almost the same. As a result, if volume is plotted below the price it is almost possible to draw a complete circle, as shown in example *b* of Figure 5.4. The tip-off to

Example *a*   Example *b*

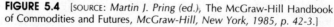

FIGURE 5.4   [SOURCE: *Martin J. Pring (ed.), The McGraw-Hill Handbook of Commodities and Futures, McGraw-Hill, New York, 1985, p. 42-3.*]

the bearish implication of the rounded top is that volume shrinks as prices reach their highest levels and then expands as they fall. As discussed in greater detail in Chapter 16, both these characteristics are bearish.

Rounding tops and bottoms are fine examples of a gradual changeover in the supply-demand balance that slowly picks up momentum in the opposite direction to the previous trend. Quite clearly, it is difficult to obtain breakout levels for such patterns since they develop slowly and do not offer any clear support or resistance levels on which to establish a valid signal. Even so, trying to identify such formations is worthwhile since they are usually followed by substantial moves.

These patterns can also be observed as consolidation as well as reversal phenomena; they take from as little as 3 weeks to as long as several years to complete.

KEY REVERSAL DAYS

A key reversal day occurs after a long move, either up or down, has taken place. The key reversal day is the pivotal point between an upmove and a downmove, or between a downmove and an upmove.

At the beginning of the day in question the price continues to move sharply in the direction of the previous trend. Since this usually occurs following a long exponential-type move, it appears that the price may never reverse its trend. However, by the end of the day the price has "key-reversed" so that it closes in the opposite direction to that which was indicated at the opening. In an up market the price closes down on the day; in a down market the price closes up on the day. Key reversal days are associated with an explosion of volume well above levels of the recent past and represent an exhaustion of buying power at peaks and selling power or liquidation at troughs (see Figure 5.5a and b).

Example a   Example b

FIGURE 5.5 [SOURCE: *Martin J. Pring (ed.), The McGraw-Hill Handbook of Commodities and Futures, McGraw-Hill, New York, 1985, p. 42-5.*]

A key reversal is in a sense a 1-day price pattern, and thus it implies a short-term trend reversal. However, since such a reversal develops after a long and sustained move, it is often followed by an important change in trend.

The price range on key reversal days usually dwarfs anything that has gone before. Often the price moves as much in the first 2 to 4 hours as it would in 2 to 5 normal trading days, usually opening well above or below the previous day's close. If the price does not make a significant new high or low, the day does not qualify as a key reversal day. Price action which occurs within a price pattern does not qualify as a key reversal, even though it possesses the appropriate volume characteristics. Although such a "pattern-contained" reversal does have some short-term significance, it cannot be treated with anywhere near the reverence accorded a key reversal that takes place after an extended move.

GAPS

General

A gap occurs when the lowest price of a specific trading period is above the highest level of the previous trading period (Figure 5.6, example a), or when the highest price for a specific trading period is below the lowest price of the previous trading period (example b in Figure 5.6). On a daily bar chart the trading period would be regarded as a day; on a weekly chart, a week; etc.

By definition, gaps can occur only on bar charts on which intraday, weekly, or monthly prices are plotted. A gap is represented on the chart by an empty vertical space between one period of trading and another. Daily gaps are far more common than weekly ones since a gap on a weekly chart can fall only between Friday's price range and Monday's price range, i.e., a 1 to 5 chance relative to a daily chart. Monthly gaps are even more rare

Example a   Example b

FIGURE 5.6 [SOURCE: Martin J. Pring (ed.), The McGraw-Hill Handbook of Commodities and Futures, McGraw-Hill, New York, 1985, p. 42-5.]

since such "holes" on the chart can only develop between monthly price ranges. A gap is closed or "filled" when the price comes back and retraces the whole range of the gap. This process sometimes takes a few days, at other times it takes a few months or weeks, and more rarely, it never occurs. There is an old principle that the market abhors a vacuum and that all gaps are eventually filled. It is certainly true that almost all gaps are eventually filled, but since this is not *always* the case, and because it could take months or even years to fill a gap, trading strategies should not be implemented solely on the assumption that the gap will be filled in the immediate future. In almost all cases, however, some kind of attempt is made to fill the gap; but quite often a partial filling on a subsequent test is all that is necessary before the price again reverts to the direction of the prevailing trend. Indeed, within a day's trading many gaps are made between ticks, but these do not show up on intraday charts. Consequently, though gaps should be treated with respect, their importance should not be overemphasized. Gaps which occur during the formation of a price pattern are usually closed fairly quickly and do not have much significance. Such occurrences are termed common or area gaps. Another type of gap which has little significance occurs when a stock goes ex dividend.

There are three other types which are worthy of consideration: breakaway, runaway, and exhaustion gaps.

Breakaway Gaps

As the name implies, a breakaway gap is created when a price breaks out of a price pattern (as in Figure 5.6a and b). Generally speaking, the presence of the gap emphasizes the bullishness or bearishness of the breakout, depending on which direction it takes. Even when a gap is present, it is important for an upside breakout to be accompanied by a relatively high level of volume. In other words, it is necessary for a change to bullish sentiment not only to develop in terms of price but to be backed up with money on the buying side, i.e., volume. It should not be concluded that every gap breakout that takes place is a valid one, because there is no such thing as a "sure thing" in technical analysis. However, a breakout which does develop with a gap is more likely to be valid than one that does not. Gap breakouts which occur on the downside are not required to be accompanied by heavy volume.

Continuation or Runaway Gaps

These gaps occur during a straight-line advance or decline when price quotations are moving rapidly and emotions are running very high. Either such gaps are closed very quickly, e.g., within a day or so, or they tend to

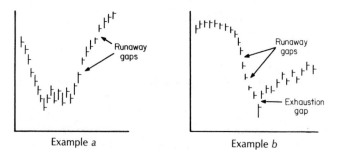

Example a   Example b

FIGURE 5.7 [SOURCE: *Martin J. Pring (ed.),* The McGraw-Hill Handbook of Commodities and Futures, *McGraw-Hill, New York, 1985, p. 42-6.*]

remain open for much longer periods and are not generally closed until the market makes a major or intermediate swing in the opposite direction to the price movement which was responsible for the gap. This type of gap often occurs halfway between a previous breakout and the ultimate duration of the move. For this reason, runaway gaps are sometimes called measuring gaps (see Figure 5.7a).

Exhaustion Gaps

A price move sometimes contains more than one runaway gap. While this indicates that a very powerful trend is in force, the presence of a second or third gap should also alert the technician that the move is soon likely to run out of steam. Hence there is a possibility that a second or third runaway gap represents an exhaustion gap which is associated with the terminal phase of a rapid advance or decline and is the last in a series of runaway gaps. At the time, of course, it is not easy to ascertain whether the gap in question is another runaway gap or an exhaustion gap.

One clue that may be given on the day that the gap is created is unusually heavy volume in relation to the price change of that day. In such cases volume usually works up to a crescendo well above previous levels. Sometimes the price will close near the vacuum (or gap) but well away from its extreme reading of the day. Creation of an "island" by the next day's trading, which completely isolates the "gap" day by a vacuum from the previous day's trading, is usually an excellent sign that the "gap" day was in fact a key reversal day. Although such a sign of exhaustion is only a signal of temporary reversal, it is sufficient to indicate to highly leveraged traders that they should liquidate or cover their positions.

If the gap is the first one during a move, it is more likely to be a runaway than a breakaway gap, especially if the price objective called for by a price pattern has not yet been achieved. An exhaustion gap should not normally

FIGURE 5.8

be regarded as a sign of a major reversal but merely as a signal that some form of consolidation should be expected.

ISLAND REVERSALS

An island reversal is a compact trading range created at the end of a sustained move and isolated from previous price behavior by an exhaustion gap and a breakaway gap. A typical island reversal is shown in Figure 5.8.

The island itself is not usually a pattern denoting a major reversal. However, islands often appear at the end of an intermediate or even a major move and form part of an overall price pattern, such as the top (or bottom) of a head-and-shoulders pattern (or an inverse head-and-shoulders pattern).

SUMMARY

1. Flags, pennants, and wedges are short-term price patterns which usually develop halfway along a sharp price movement. Their development is normally complete within 3 weeks and represents a period of dramatically reduced price volatility and contracting volume. They are almost always continuation patterns.

2. Saucer formations and rounding tops are usually reversal formations and are typically followed by a substantial price movement. In both formations volume contracts toward the center and is at its greatest at either extremity.

3. A key reversal day indicates that a price movement has exhausted itself at least temporarily. A key reversal has three characteristics: First, it should occur after prices have made a sustained move to a new high or low. Second, it must be accompanied by heavy volume. Third, the price must close in the opposite direction to the previous move—e.g., higher following a downmove.

4. A gap is essentially a vacuum or hole in a bar chart. Ex dividend and area gaps have little significance. Breakaway gaps develop at the beginning of a move, runaway gaps in the middle of a move, and exhaustion gaps at the end of a move.

5. Island reversals are small price patterns or congestion areas isolated from the main price trend by two gaps. They often signal the termination of an intermediate move.

Trendlines

A review of any stock chart will quickly reveal that prices move in trends and that quite often a series of ascending bottoms in a rising market can be joined together by a straight line, just as can the tops of a descending series of rally peaks. These lines, known as "trendlines," are a simple but invaluable addition to the technical arsenal (see Figure 6.1).

Since some trends can be sideways, it naturally follows that trendlines can also be drawn horizontally. The neckline of a head-and-shoulders pattern or the upper or lower boundary of a rectangle is really a trendline, and just as the penetration of those lines warns of a change in trend, so does the penetration of rising or falling trendlines likewise represent points of support (rising trendline) and resistance (declining trendline).

It may be recalled that the completion of a rectangle pattern can signify either (1) a reversal in the previous trend, in which case it becomes known as a reversal pattern, or (2) a resumption of the previous trend, when it is defined as a consolidation or continuation pattern. Similarly, the penetration of a trendline by an index will result in either a reversal of that trend or its continuation. Figure 6.2 illustrates this point from the aspect of a rising price trend.

In example a the trendline joining the series of troughs is eventually penetrated on the downside. Since the fourth peak represented the highest point in the bull market, the downward violation of the trendline signaled that a bear market was under way.

In example b the upward price trend and trendline penetration are identical to example a, but the action following this warning signal is entirely different, since the trendline violation merely signaled that the advance would continue, but at a greatly reduced pace.

Unfortunately, there is no way of telling at the time of the violation which possibility will prove to be the eventual outcome. Nevertheless, valuable

Example *a*

Example *b*

FIGURE 6.1

Example *a*

Example *b*

FIGURE 6.2

clues can be obtained from the application of other techniques described in subsequent chapters and from an appraisal of the state of health of the market's overall technical structure, which is examined in Parts 2 through 4. Using the techniques discussed in Chapter 2 can also help. For example, in a rising market, a trendline penetration may occur at the time of or just before the successful completion of a reversal pattern. Some possibilities are shown in Figure 6.3.

In example *a* the rising trendline joins a series of bottoms, but the last two troughs represent reactions from a right shoulder and head which are part of an ascending head-and-shoulders pattern. Examples *b* and *c* represent a similar situation for a rectangle and broadening top.

Figure 6.4 illustrates the same phenomenon from the point of view of a reversal of a bear market. If the violation occurs simultaneously with or just after the completion of a reversal pattern, the two breaks have the effect of reinforcing each other; but sometimes, as in Figure 6.5, the trendline violation occurs *before* the completion of the pattern. In such cases, since a trend is assumed to continue until a reversal is proved, the violation should be regarded as a sign of interruption of the prevailing movement rather than one of reversal. In an advance, it is necessary to await a decline in the indicator below the previous trough before confirmatory evidence of an actual trend reversal is given.

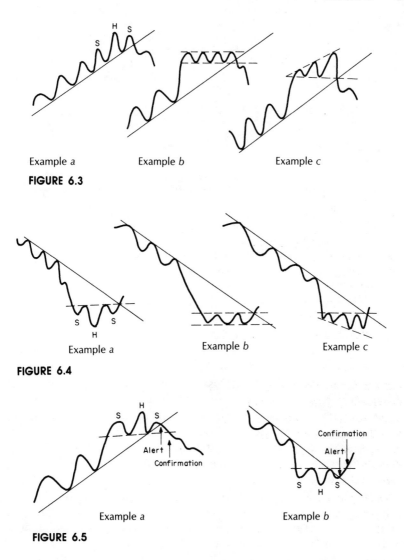

Example a   Example b   Example c

FIGURE 6.3

Example a   Example b   Example c

FIGURE 6.4

Example a   Example b

FIGURE 6.5

The opposite will occur in the case of a declining market (see Figure 6.5). In these instances the trendline penetration is treated as an alert. Additional evidence of the likely significance of a trendline violation can be derived from the level of volume by utilizing the principles outlined in Chapter 2. For example, if a series of ascending peaks and troughs is accompanied by successively less volume, it is a sign that the advance is running out of steam (since volume is no longer going with the trend). Under such circumstances a trendline violation is likely to be of greater significance than if volume

Example *a*   Example *b*

FIGURE 6.6

continues to expand with each successive rally. Although it is not necessary for a downside penetration to be accompanied by high volume, expansion of activity at such a point is clearly more bearish since it emphasizes the switch in the supply/demand balance in favor of the sellers.

Just as a return move often occurs following a breakout from a price pattern, so a similar move known as a "throwback" sometimes develops following a trendline penetration.

Example *a* in Figure 6.6 shows a trendline reversing its previous role as support while the "throwback" move turns it into an area of resistance. Example *b* shows the same situation for a declining market.

The importance of plotting charts on logarithmic as opposed to arithmetic paper was discussed in Chapter 4. The choice of ratio scale is even more critical for a timely and accurate use of trendline analysis, because at the end of a major movement prices tend to accelerate in the direction of the prevailing trend, i.e., they rise faster at the end of a rising trend and decline more sharply at the termination of a bear market. In a bull market (Chart 6.1) prices rise slowly after an initial burst, then advance at a steeper and steeper angle as they approach the ultimate peak, looking rather like the left-hand cross section of a mountain.

As Figure 6.7 shows, this exponential movement takes the price well away from the trendline if the index concerned is being plotted on an arithmetic scale. Consequently, the price has to fall that much farther before a penetration of the trendline can take place.

SIGNIFICANCE OF TRENDLINES

It has been established that a break in trend caused by a penetration of a trendline results in either an actual trend reversal or a slowing down in the pace of the trend. Although it is not always possible to assess which of these alternatives will develop, it is still important to understand the significance of a trendline penetration; the following guidelines should help in assessing the situation.

CHART 6.1 Dow Jones Transportation Average, 1965–1970. This chart shows the 1966–1968 bull market for the Transportation Average. The downward penetration of the trendline joining the 1966 and early 1968 bottoms signaled the end of the bull market. Note how the index breaks down from what might have been a right-angled triangle consolidation pattern, had it been able to surpass its 1966 and 1967 peaks.

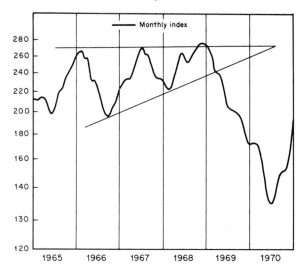

Number of Times the Trendline Has Been Touched

A trendline obtains its authority from the number of times it has been touched, i.e., the larger the number, the greater the significance. This is because a trendline represents an area of support or resistance, so that each successive "test" of the line contributes to the significance of this support or resistance and therefore the authority of the line itself.

Example *a* (arithmetic scale)   Example *b* (ratio scale)

FIGURE 6.7

FIGURE 6.8

FIGURE 6.9

Length of the Line

The size or length of a trend is an important factor, as with price patterns. If a series of ascending bottoms occurs over a 3- to 4-week span, the resulting trendline is of only minor importance. Should the trend extend over a period of 1 to 3 years, however, its violation marks a significant juncture point. The construction of trendlines is often a matter of judgment established through trial and error. For example, in Figure 6.8 two bottoms are formed at marginally different levels, so that the resulting trendline AA becomes relatively flat; consequently, its penetration is of no use from the point of view of signaling a breakdown or reversal of the major trend. Although trendline BB is shorter than AA in this case, it more closely resembles the trend, and its violation is that much more significant, for by the time prices violate AA the bear market is almost over.

A very sharp trend (as in Figure 6.9) is difficult to maintain and is liable to be broken rather easily, even by a short sideways movement.

All trends are eventually violated, but the steeper ones are more likely to be broken more quickly. Consequently, the violation of a particularly steep trend is not as significant as that of a slower, more sustainable one. Penetration of a steep line will usually result in a short corrective movement, following which the trend resumes, but at a greatly reduced and more sustainable pace.

MEASURING IMPLICATION

Trendlines have measuring implications when broken, just as price patterns do. For a rising trendline, the vertical distance between the peak in the index and the trendline is measured (A_1 in Figure 6.10). This distance is then projected down from the point at which the violation occurs (A_2).

The term "price objective" is perhaps a misleading one, for although such objectives are usually reached when a trendline is the reversal type,

FIGURE 6.10   **FIGURE 6.11**

they are more often exceeded, so that (as with price patterns) the objective becomes more of a minimum expectation. When prices fall significantly below the objective, as in Figure 6.11, this area often becomes one of resistance to the next major rally or support for a subsequent reaction (Chart 6.3).

In the case of a falling trendline these principles are reversed (see Figure 6.12 and Chart 6.2).

Time and again these price objective areas prove to be important support or resistance points, but unfortunately there is no way of determining which is likely to prove the actual juncture point for any rally or reaction. This really emphasizes the point made earlier that there is no way of determining the duration of a move in prices. It is only possible to speculate on the probability that a certain area will prove to be an important juncture point. Consequently, when many other technical indicators are pointing out that a reversal in trend is about to take place, these trendline basing points can be used as a strong confirmation.

CHART 6.2 Dow Jones Transportation Average, 1944–1952. The 1946–1949 bear market trendline was broken on the upside in early 1950. The measuring objective for this monthly index was achieved in late 1950, after which the average paused for some months before resuming its cyclical advance.

CHART 6.3   Dow Jones Transportation Average, 1974–1978. The bull market trendline (*AB*) joining the 1974 bottoms was violated in 1975. The ensuing rally took this average above its previous high, but the substantial resistance marked by this extended trendline eventually proved too great, so the average was forced to temporarily turn down. A secondary trendline *CD* was also violated. Even though the average was able to advance to a new cyclical high, an extension of *CD* also proved to be a formidable resistance barrier.

CORRECTIVE FAN PRINCIPLE

At the beginning of a new primary bull market the initial intermediate rally is likely to be relatively steep and the ensuing rate of advance unsustainable. This is because the rally is often a technical reaction to the previous overextended decline, as speculators who were caught short rush to cover their positions. Therefore, the steep trendline constructed from the first minor reaction is quickly violated.

This is represented as line *AA* in Figure 6.13. A new trendline is then constructed, using the bottom of this first intermediate decline (*AB*). This new line rises at a less rapid rate than the initial one. Finally the process is repeated, resulting in the construction of a third line, *AC*. These lines are

FIGURE 6.12   **FIGURE 6.13**

known as "fan" lines. The principle has been established that once the third trendline has been violated, the end of the bull market is confirmed. In some respects these three rally points and trendlines can be compared to the three stages of a bull or bear market, as outlined in Chapter 2. The fan principle is just as valid for downtrends as it is for uptrends and can also be used for determining intermediate as well as cyclical movements.

TREND CHANNELS

So far only the possibilities of drawing trendlines joining bottoms in rising markets and tops in declining ones have been examined, but it is also useful to draw lines that are parallel to those "basic" trendlines, as shown in Figure 6.14.

In a rising market the parallel line, known as a "return" trendline, joins the tops of rallies (AA, example a), and during declines the return line joins the series of bottoms (BB, example b). The area between these trend extremities is known as a "trend channel."

The return line is useful from two points of view. First, it represents an area of support or resistance, depending on the direction of the trend. Second, and perhaps more important, penetration of the return trendline often signifies reversal of at least a temporary proportion in the basic trend (see Figure 6.15).

In example a prices have been rising for some time; then, as is characteristic of the terminal phase of a trend, they accelerate sharply with such force that the return line is penetrated on the upside. This is normally a bearish sign since it indicates exhaustion of a move, especially if such action is accompanied by high volume.

Consider the situation where a man is sawing a thick piece of wood. At first his sawing strokes are slow but deliberate; gradually he realizes his task

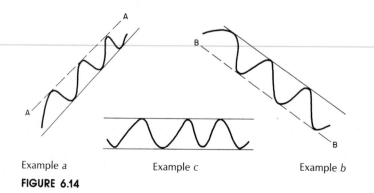

Example a   Example c   Example b

FIGURE 6.14

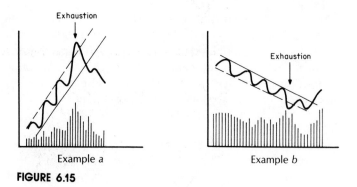

FIGURE 6.15

is going to take some time, becomes frustrated, and slowly increases the speed of his strokes. Finally he bursts into a frantic effort and is forced to give up his task for at least a temporary period because of complete exhaustion. Example *b* in Figure 6.15 shows an exhaustion move in a declining market. In this case the expanding volume at the low represents a selling climax.

SUMMARY

1. Trendlines are perhaps the easiest technical tool to understand, but considerable experimentation and practice are required before the art of their interpretation can be successfully mastered.

2. Generally speaking (given the guidelines described in this chapter), the more obvious the construction of a trendline, the greater the significance of its violation is likely to be.

7

Moving Averages

It is now evident that trends in stock prices can be very volatile, almost taking on a haphazard characteristic at times. One technique for overcoming this phenomenon is the *moving average* (MA).

A moving average attempts to tone down the fluctuations of stock prices into a smoothed trend, so that distortions are reduced to a minimum. Three basic types of moving averages are used in the technical analysis of stock trends: simple, weighted, and exponential. Since the construction and use of these averages is different, the discussion of this subject will deal with each type in turn.

SIMPLE MOVING AVERAGE

A simple moving average is by far the most widely used, but not necessarily the best. It is constructed by totaling a set of data and dividing that total by the number of observations. The resulting number is known as the *average* or *mean average*. In order to get the average to "move," a new item of data is added and the first item on the list subtracted. The new total is then divided by the number of observations and the process repeated ad infinitum.

For example, if the calculation of a 10-week MA were required, the method would be as shown in Table 7.1.

On March 9 the total of the 10 weeks ending on that date was 966, and 966 divided by 10 results in an average of 96.6. On March 16 the number

TABLE 7.1

Date		Index	10-week total	Moving average
Jan.	8	101		
	15	100		
	22	103		
	29	99		
Feb.	5	96		
	12	99		
	19	95		
	26	91		
Mar.	5	93		
	12	89	966	96.6
	19	90	955	95.5
	26	95	950	95.0
Apr.	2	103	950	95.0

90 is added, and the observation of 101 on January 8 is deleted. The new total of 955 is then divided by 10. If a 13-week moving average had been required, it would have been necessary to total 13 weeks of data (as of April 2, the thirteenth week of observation) and divide by 13. A 13-week moving average is shown in Figure 7.1, example a, by the dashed line. It can be observed that a rising moving average indicates market strength and a declining one denotes weakness.

Reference to the price index and its 13-week moving average shows that the moving average changes direction well after the peak or trough in stock prices and is therefore "late" in changing direction. This is because the moving average is plotted on the thirteenth week, whereas the average price

Example a   Example b

FIGURE 7.1

of 13 weeks' observations actually occurs halfway through the observation period, which in this instance is the seventh week. Consequently, if it is to correctly reflect the trend that it is attempting to measure, the plot of the moving average should be centered, i.e., plotted on the seventh week, as shown in Figure 7.1, example *b*.

If the centering technique had been used, it would have been necessary in our example to wait 6 weeks before ascertaining whether the average had changed direction.

A time delay, while an irritant, is not particularly critical when analyzing other time series such as economic data; but given the relatively rapid movement of stock prices and consequent loss of profit potential, a delay here is totally unacceptable. It has thus been found that for the purposes of stock market analysis the best results are achieved by plotting the moving average on the final week.

Changes in the trend of the index or stock being measured are identified not by a change in direction of the moving average, but by a crossover of the moving average by the index itself. A change from a rising to a declining market is signaled when the index moves below its moving average. The reverse set of conditions will confirm the termination of a declining trend. Since the use of moving averages gives clear-cut buy and sell signals, it helps to eliminate some of the subjectivity associated with the construction and interpretation of trendlines.

More often than not it pays to take action based on moving-average crossovers, since this technique is one of the most reliable tools in the technical arsenal. However, the degree of accuracy depends substantially on the choice of moving average. This is discussed later, but some of the characteristics of moving averages should first be outlined in greater detail.

1. Since a moving average is a smoothed version of a trend, the average itself becomes an area of support and resistance. Thus, in a rising market reactions in stock prices are often reversed by finding support at the moving-average level. Similarly, a rally in a declining market often meets resistance at a moving average and turns down.

2. Since a moving average is itself a significant juncture point, its violation warns that a change in trend may already have taken place. If the moving average is flat or has already changed direction, its violation by the index is fairly conclusive proof that the previous trend has been reversed.

3. If the violation occurs while the moving average is still proceeding in the direction of the prevailing trend, this development should be treated as a preliminary warning that a trend reversal has taken place. Confirmation should await a flattening or a change in direction in the moving average itself or should be sought from alternative technical sources.

4. Generally speaking, the longer the time span covered by a moving average, the greater is the significance of a crossover signal. A violation of an 18-month moving average, since it is smoothing a very long term trend, has substantially more significance than a crossover of a 30-day moving average.

Choice of Time Span

Moving averages can be constructed for any time period, whether a few days, several weeks, many months, or even years. Choice of the length is very important. For example, if it is assumed that a complete bull and bear cycle lasts for 4 years, a moving average constructed over a period of time greater than 48 months will not reflect the cycle at all, since it smooths out all the fluctuations taking place during this period and will appear more or less as a straight line crossing through the middle of the cycle. On the other hand, a 5-day moving average will catch every minor move in the stock cycle and will also prove to be relatively useless in identifying the actual top and bottom of the overall cycle. Even if the 48-month average were shortened to 24 months and the 5-day average expanded to 4 weeks, for example (see Figure 7.2), use of the crossover signals would still cause the 24-month average to give an agonizingly slow confirmation of a change in trend. The 4-week average would be so sensitive that it would continually give misleading or "whipsaw" signals. Only a moving average that can catch the movement of the actual cycle will provide the optimum tradeoff between lateness and oversensitivity, such as the 10-month moving average in Figure 7.2, example *b*.

The choice of moving average will therefore depend on the type of stock market trend that is to be identified, i.e., a primary or an intermediate trend. For shorter intermediate moves 25- and 30-day moving averages have proved useful, and for longer intermediate moves 10- and 13-week averages seem to offer the best results. For primary trends, experiments with 20-, 30-, and 40-week moving averages from 1897 to 1967 have shown the 40-week period to be the most helpful.[1]

ADVANCED MOVING AVERAGES

One technique which has proved useful yet is not widely used is to advance a moving average. For example in the case of a 25-day MA the actual plot would be made on the 28th or 30th day, and so forth. The advantage of this approach is that it delays the signal somewhat, thereby filtering out occa-

---

[1] William Gordon, *Stock Market Indicators,* Investors Press, Palisades Park, N.J., 1968.

(a)

(b)

FIGURE 7.2   (a) Moving average not centered.
(b) Moving average centered.

sional whipsaws or false signals. In *Profits in the Stock Market* H. M. Gartley[2] calculated that during the period from 1919 to 1933, which covered
almost all kinds of market situations, use of a simple 25-day moving-average
crossover netted 446 Dow points (slightly better than 433 points for the 30-
day moving average and far better than 316 and 216 for 40- and 15-day
moving averages, respectively). However, when the 25-day average was
plotted on the 28th day, crossovers resulted in an increase of 231 points to
677. The 30-day moving average, when advanced 3 days, also produced

[2] Lambert Gann Publishing, Pomeroy, Wash., 1981.

CHART 7.1 Comparison of 40-week moving averages, 1966–1978. Charts 7.1a through 7.1c show the 40-week moving average at work in three different countries. Although cross-overs of each index are subject to whipsaws from time to time, the use of this average is still fairly reliable. Note how the 40-week average is continually being used as a support or resistance level. (a) Dow Jones Industrial Average (for the United States), 1966–1978. (b) Financial Times 500 Index (for the United Kingdom), 1966–1978. (c) German Stock Market (for the West German Federal Republic), 1966–1978.

CHART 7.2   Dow Jones Industrial Average versus 30-week/10-week moving averages.

superior results, with an additional gain of 204 points for a total of 637. Chart 7-3a represents 3 moving averages as calculated by Gartley. Although these moving averages are plotted normally, the whipsaw signals that would have been avoided by moving the MA forward 3 days are shown on the chart.

Although the 25-day MA advanced 3 days may not ultimately prove to be the best combination, the technique of advancing a moving average is clearly one that could be usefully incorporated into the technical approach.

MULTIPLE MOVING AVERAGES

Some techniques of trend determination involve more than one moving average at a time. Signals are given by a shorter-term moving average crossing above or below a longer one. This procedure has the advantage of smoothing the data twice and thereby reducing the possibility of a whipsaw, yet warning of trend changes fairly quickly after they have taken place (see Chart 7.2). Two averages which have been found reliable in determining primary market moves are the 10- and 30-week moving averages, when

15, 30 AND 40 DAY MOVING AVERAGES
OF DOW-JONES AVERAGE OF 30 INDUSTRIAL STOCKS
PLOTTED WITH MINIMUM LEAD
SHOWING
VARIOUS MOVING AVERAGE PHENOMENA

CHART 7.3   (b) Dow Jones Industrial Average, 1946–1951.

used together. For the purpose of simplifying the calculation, the weekly closing price rather than a 5-day average is used.

Signals are given when the 10-week average moves below the 30-week average and when the 30-week average itself is declining. This development warns that the major trend is down. It is not assumed to be reversed until both averages are rising simultaneously, with the 10-week higher than the 30-week moving average. Should the 10-week average rise above the 30-week average while the longer average is still declining (and vice versa for bull markets), a valid signal is not constituted. By definition, these warning signals always occur after the ultimate peak or trough of stock prices and serve as a *confirmation* of a change in trend rather than being actual juncture points in themselves.

Moving averages should *always* be used in conjunction with other indicators, for sometimes the stock market fluctuates in a broad sideways pattern for an extended period of time, resulting in a series of misleading signals. Chart 7.3b, depicting the 1946–1949 bear market, gives an example of such a frustrating period, one in which many misleading crossovers would have been experienced.

WEIGHTED MOVING AVERAGES

As discussed at the beginning of this chapter, a moving average can correctly represent a trend from a statistical point of view only if it is centered. It was also pointed out that centering a moving average delays the signal of a reversal in the trend of the stock index or indicator being measured. One technique for overcoming this problem is to weight the data in favor of the most recent observations. A moving average constructed in this manner is

TABLE 7.2

Date	Index (1)	6 × col. 1 (2)	5 × col. 1 1 week ago (3)	4 × col. 1 2 weeks ago (4)	3 × col. 1 3 weeks ago (5)	2 × col. 1 4 weeks ago (6)	1 × col. 1 5 weeks ago (7)	Total cols. 2–7 (8)	Col. 8 ÷ 21 (9)
Jan. 8	101								
15	100								
22	103								
29	99								
Feb. 5	96								
12	99	594	480	396	309	200	101	2080	99.1
19	95	570	495	384	297	206	100	2052	97.7
26	91	546	475	396	288	198	103	2006	95.5
Mar. 5	93	558	455	380	297	192	99	1981	94.3
12	89	534	465	364	285	198	96	1924	92.5

able to "turn" or reverse direction much more quickly than a simple moving average, which is calculated by treating all the data equally.

There are almost limitless ways in which data can be weighted, but the most widely used method incorporates a technique whereby the period of data is multiplied first by 1, second by 2, third by 3, and so on until the latest week, so that a 6-week weighted moving average is multiplied by 6. The resulting amount for each week is then totaled, but instead of dividing by the number of weeks—in this case 6—the divisor becomes the total of the weights, i.e., $1 + 2 + 3 + 4 + 5 + 6 = 21$. For a 10-week weighted moving average, the sum of the weights would be $1 + 2 + 3 + 4 + 5 + 6 + 7 + 8 + 9 + 10 = 55$. Table 7.2 illustrates how the calculations are made.

Another method is to calculate a simple moving average but in doing so to use the most recent observation twice, thereby doubling its weight. The calculation of a 6-week weighted moving average using this approach and the data from the table above would be as follows:

Week	Index
1	101
2	100
3	103
4	99
5	96
5	96
Total	595

$$\frac{\text{Total}}{\text{Weeks}} = \frac{595}{6} = 99.2$$

The interpretation of a weighted average is different from that of a simple average. In the case of this more sensitive weighted average, a warning of a trend reversal is given by a change in direction of the average rather than a crossover.

EXPONENTIAL MOVING AVERAGES

Weighted moving averages are very useful for the purpose of identifying trend reversals. However, the time-consuming calculations required to construct and maintain such averages greatly detract from their usefulness (unless, of course, a computer is within easy reach). An exponential moving average (EMA) is really a shortcut to obtaining a form of weighted moving average, since an exponential smoothing also gives greater weight to more recent data. In order to construct a 20-week exponential moving average, it is first necessary to calculate a simple 20-week moving average, i.e., the total of 20 weeks' observations divided by 20. In Table 7.3 this has been done for the 20 weeks ending January 1, and the result appears as 99.00 in column 6. (See also Chart 7.4.)

This 20-week average becomes the starting point for the exponential moving average and is then transferred to column 2 for the following week. Next, the entry for the twenty-first week (January 8 in the example above) is compared with the moving average, and the difference is added or subtracted and posted in column 3, i.e., $100 - 99 = 1.0$. This difference is then multiplied by the exponent, which for a 20-week EMA is 0.1. This exponentially treated difference, 1.0×0.1, is then added to the previous week's EMA, and the calculation is repeated each succeeding week. In the example, the exponentially treated difference for January 8 is 0.1, which is added to the previous week's average, 99.0, to obtain an EMA for January 8 of 99.10. This figure in column 6 is then plotted. Figure 7.3 shows an example of a 13-week EMA.

TABLE 7.3

Date	Price (1)	EMA for previous week (2)	Difference (col. 1 − col. 2) (3)	Exponent (4)	Col. 3 × col. 4 +/− (5)	Col. 2 + col. 5 EMA (6)
Jan. 1	...	...	...	...	...	99.00
8	100.00	99.00	1.00	0.1	+0.10	99.10
15	103.00	99.10	3.90	0.1	+0.39	99.49
22	102.00	99.49	2.51	0.1	+0.25	99.74
29	99.00	99.64	(0.64)	0.1	−0.06	99.68

CHART 7.4 Dow Jones Industrial Average, 1930–1937.

If the difference between the new weekly observation and the previous week's EMA is negative, as in the reading 99.00 versus 99.64 for January 29, the exponentially treated difference is subtracted from the previous week's EMA.

The exponent used varies with the time span of the moving average. The correct exponents for various time spans are as follows:

Number of weeks	Exponent
5	0.4
10	0.2
15	0.13
20	0.1
40	0.05
80	0.025

In Table 7.3 the time periods have been described as weekly, but in effect the exponent 0.1 can be used for any measure of 20, whether it is days, weeks, months, years, or an even longer period. Exponents for time periods other than those shown in the table can easily be calculated by dividing 2 by the time span.

For example, a 5-week average will need to be twice as sensitive as a 10-week average, so 2 divided by 5 gives an exponent of 0.4. On the other hand, a 20-week average should be half as sensitive as that for a 10-week period (0.2), so its exponent is halved to 0.1.

If an EMA proves to be too sensitive for the trend being monitored, one solution is to extend its time period. Another is to smooth the EMA by

FIGURE 7.3

another EMA. This method uses an EMA, as calculated above, and repeats the process using a further exponent. There is no reason not to do a third or fourth smoothing, but the ever-present tradeoff between sensitivity and lateness should be borne in mind.

ENVELOPES

It has already been mentioned that moving averages often act as important juncture points in their role as support and resistance areas. The longer the time span of the average, the greater will be its significance in this respect. An expansion of this support and resistance principle involves the drawing of symmetrical lines called "envelopes" parallel to a moving average (see Figure 7.4).

This technique is based on the principle that stock prices fluctuate around a given trend in cyclical movements of reasonably similar proportion. In other words, just as the moving average serves as an important juncture point, so do certain lines drawn parallel to that moving average. Looked at in this way, the moving average is really the center of the trend, and the envelope consists of the points of maximum and minimum divergence from that trend.

FIGURE 7.4

FIGURE 7.5

There is no hard-and-fast rule about the exact position at which the envelope should be drawn, since that can only be discovered on a trial-and-error basis with regard to the volatility of the index being monitored and the time span of the moving average. This process can be expanded, as in Figure 7.5, to include four or more envelopes (i.e., two above and two below the moving average), each drawn at an identical distance from its predecessor.

In this example the envelopes have been plotted at 10 percent intervals, so that if the moving average is at 100, the envelopes would be plotted at 90, 110, etc.

The example using the DJIA between 1972 and 1974 (Chart 7.5) shows that the envelope technique can be very useful from two aspects: (1) developing a "feel" for the overall trend and (2) discerning when a rally or reaction has overextended. It suffers from the disadvantage that there is no certainty that the envelope will prove to be the eventual turning point. This method, like all techniques attempting to forecast the duration of a move, should be used on the basis that if the index reaches a particular envelope, there is a good probability that it will reverse course at that juncture. The

CHART 7.5 Dow Jones Industrial Average, 1972–1974.

actual conclusion will be determined by an assessment of a number of characteristics, of which an envelope juncture is a contributing factor.

SUMMARY

1. One of the basic assumptions of technical analysis is that stocks move in trends. Since major trends comprise many minor fluctuations in prices, a moving average is constructed to aid in the smoothing of data so that the underlying trend is more clearly visible.

2. A simple moving average should be plotted at the halfway point in the time period being monitored (a process known as centering), but since this would involve a time lag during which stock prices could change rapidly and lose much of the potential profit of a move, such an average is plotted at the end of the period in question.

3. This drawback has been largely overcome by the use of moving-average crossovers, which provide warnings of a reversal in trend, and by the use of weighted or exponential moving averages, which are more sensitive to changes in the prevailing trend since they weight data in favor of the most recent periods.

Momentum

The methods of trend determination considered so far have been concerned with an analysis of the movement of an indicator itself through trendlines, price patterns, and moving averages. Although such techniques can be extremely useful, they identify a change in trend *after it has taken place* and are helpful only when a trend reversal is detected at a relatively early stage in its development. On the other hand, using the concept of *momentum* can often warn of latent strength or weakness in the indicator being monitored, usually well ahead of its ultimate peak or trough.

MOMENTUM

The concept of momentum can be understood through a simple example. When a ball is thrown into the air, it begins its trajectory at a very fast pace, i.e., it possesses strong momentum. Gradually the speed with which the ball travels upward becomes distinctly slower, until it finally comes to a temporary standstill before the force of gravity causes it to reverse its course. This slowing-down process, known as a loss of upward momentum, is also a phenomenon of the stock market. If the flight of a ball is equated to a price index of the stock market, the rate of advance in the index begins to slow down noticeably before the ultimate peak in prices is reached.

On the other hand, if a ball is thrown in a room and hits the ceiling while its momentum is still rising, the ball and the momentum will reverse at the same time. Unfortunately, momentum indexes in the stock market are not dissimilar, since sometimes momentum and price peak simultaneously as either a ceiling of selling resistance is met or buying power is temporarily exhausted. In such instances momentum as a lead indicator is not a particularly useful concept, although under such conditions the level of momentum is often as helpful as its direction in assessing the quality of a price trend.

The idea of downward momentum may be better understood by comparing it to a car being pushed over the top of a hill. As the gradient of the hill steepens, the car begins to pick up speed, and finally at the bottom it hits maximum speed. Although its speed decreases, the car continues traveling until it finally comes to a halt. Stock prices in a declining trend act in a similar fashion, since the rate of decline (or loss of momentum) often slows ahead of the final low in stock prices. This is not always the case, since momentum and price sometimes (as at peaks) turn together as prices meet a major level of support. Nevertheless, this concept of momentum leading price occurs sufficiently often to be useful in warning of a potential trend reversal in the indicator or market average which is being monitored.

There are essentially two ways of looking at momentum: as a measure of rate of change, and as a measure of internal market vitality. Rate of change is a more suitable technique for measuring a price average such as the DJIA, while specific measures of internal strength are better applied to monitoring market indicators such as breadth. For the purpose of clarity internal measures of momentum will be referred to as *oscillators,* even though rates of change also oscillate within a prescribed range, and momentum measures of price averages will be described as *rates of change.*

The following discussion describes the construction and application of momentum indexes from the point of view of determining the trend of the index from which the momentum is derived. The significance for the rest of the market of a change in trend of that particular indicator will be examined in Part 2.

RATE OF CHANGE

The simplest method of measuring momentum is to calculate the rate at which a market average changes price over a given period of time. If it is desired, for example, to construct an index measuring a 10-week rate of change, the current price is divided by the price 10 weeks ago. If the latest price is 100 and the price 10 weeks ago was 105, the rate of change (ROC) or momentum index will read 95.2, that is, 100 ÷ 105. The subsequent reading in the index would be calculated by dividing next week's price by the price 9 weeks ago (see Table 8.1). The result is an index that oscillates around a central reference point which marks the level at which the price is unchanged from its reading 10 weeks ago (Figure 8.1). Consequently, if a calculation were being made of the momentum of a market average that did not change price, its momentum index would be represented as a straight line.

TABLE 8.1

Date	DJIA (1)	DJIA 10 weeks ago (2)	10-week rate of change (col. 1 ÷ col. 2) (3)
Jan. 1	985		
8	980		
15	972		
22	975		
29	965		
Feb. 5	967		
12	972		
19	965		
26	974		
Mar. 5	980		
12	965	985	98.0
19	960	980	98.0
26	950	972	97.7
Apr. 2	960	975	98.5
9	965	965	100.0
16	970	967	100.3
23	974	972	100.2
30	980	965	101.6
May 7	985	974	101.1

When a momentum index is above the reference line, the market average which it is measuring is higher than its level 10 weeks ago.

If the momentum index is also rising, it is evident that the difference between the current reading of the market average and its level 10 weeks ago is growing. If a momentum index is above the central line but is declining, the market average is still above its level 10 weeks ago, but the difference between the two readings is shrinking. When the momentum index is below its central line and falling, this indicates that the market average is

FIGURE 8.1

FIGURE 8.2

below its level 10 weeks ago, and the difference between the two is growing. When it is below its central line but rising, the market average is still below its level 10 weeks ago, but its rate of decline is slowing.

In short, a rising rate-of-change index implies a growth in momentum and a falling index a loss of momentum. Rising momentum should be interpreted as a bullish factor, and declining momentum as a bearish one.

There are two methods of scaling a rate-of-change chart. Since the choice does not affect the trend or level of the index, the method used is not important; but because the two alternatives are often found to be confusing, a brief explanation is in order. The first method is the one described above and shown in Figure 8.1, where 100 becomes the central reference point. In the example, 100 (this week's observation) divided by 99 (the observation 10 weeks ago) is plotted as 101, 100 divided by 98 as 102, 100 divided by 102 as 98, and so on.

The alternative is to take the difference between the index and the 100 level and plot the result as a positive or negative number, using a reference line of 0.

In this case, 101 would be plotted as $+1$, 102 as $+2$, 98 as -2, and so on (see Figure 8.2).

OSCILLATORS (INTERNAL STRENGTH)

In measuring price indexes, the rate-of-change method of determining momentum is useful for historical comparative purposes, since it reflects moves of similar proportion in an identical way. On the other hand, this method is not suitable for gauging the vitality of the indicators that monitor internal market structure, such as those that measure volume or breadth, since the construction of such indexes is often started from a purely arbitrary number; under certain circumstances this might require a rate of change to be calculated between a negative and a positive number, which would obviously give a completely false impression of the prevailing trend of momentum.

Rather than unduly complicating matters by trying to cover many different types of oscillators for the various stock market indicators, the discussion at this stage can be confined to the construction of one index, since the basic principles are the same for all. The more important oscillators are examined in Part 2.

Breadth Momentum

Stock market breadth is measured by an *advance/decline line* (A/D line). This line is constructed by cumulating the difference between the number of stocks advancing over those declining within a given period (usually a day or a week). Generally speaking, the advance/decline line rises and falls with the DJIA, but when their paths diverge it is usually a sign that a reversal in trend in the DJIA may be expected. Since the A/D line is a very useful technical indicator, it is obviously important to derive some measurement of its vitality or momentum so that an advance warning of a reversal in its trend can be obtained.

Momentum of breadth is measured by dividing the total of the number of stocks advancing in a given period against the total of the number declining. For a 10-week oscillator the calculations would be as in Table 8.2.

A momentum oscillator constructed in this way is shown in Figure 8.3. There are, of course, a whole variety of indicators that can be derived from these or similar methods (see Chart 8.1). Some of the variations are examined in more detail in Part 2.

TABLE 8.2

Date	No. of stocks advancing (1)	10-week total of col. 1 (2)	No. of stocks declining (3)	10-week total of col. 3 (4)	10-week momentum index (col. 2 ÷ col. 4) (5)
Jan. 2	1346	. . .	447		
9	1807	. . .	165		
16	1479	. . .	412		
23	1451	. . .	419		
30	1335	. . .	547		
Feb. 6	1086	. . .	822		
13	1267	. . .	631		
20	1389	. . .	489		
27	657	. . .	1238		
Mar. 5	844	12661	987	6157	206
12	1048	12363	772	6482	191
19	721	11277	1115	7432	152
26	1126	10924	675	7695	142

FIGURE 8.3

PRINCIPLES AND APPLICATION OF MOMENTUM INDEXES

The following description of the principles and application of momentum indexes applies as well to oscillators (indexes which measure internal market momentum) as it does to the rate-of-change indexes discussed earlier.

The momentum index is usually plotted below the indicator that it is measuring, as in Figure 8.4. The example of the ball, used at the beginning

CHART 8.1 Dow Jones Industrial Average versus 10-day breadth oscillator. The 10-day breadth oscillator shown here is calculated in the same way as a 10-week oscillator (see Table 8.2). Note how the 1978 April–May rally was preceded by declining downward momentum as represented by the fact that the February low in the oscillator was above that of January. This positive divergence between the oscillator and the DJIA itself gave a useful clue to the market's "improving" technical position.

FIGURE 8.4

of the chapter, showed that maximum momentum was obtained fairly close to the point where the ball leaves the hand. Similarly, stock prices usually reach their maximum level of momentum reasonably close to the bear market bottom.

In Figure 8.4 this is shown as point A. If the stock index makes a new high which is confirmed by the momentum index, no indication of technical weakness arises. On the other hand, should the momentum index fail to confirm (point B), a negative divergence is set up between the two indexes, and a warning of a weakening technical structure is given. Usually such discrepancies indicate that prices are likely to undergo a corrective process, which can either be sideways or (more likely) downward. However, an index will sometimes continue upward to a third top accompanied by even greater weakness in the momentum index. Occasionally, the third peak in the momentum index may be higher than the second but still lower than the first. Under either circumstance extreme caution is called for, since this characteristic is a distinct warning that a sharp reversal in price or a long corrective period may soon get under way.

Whenever any divergence between momentum and price occurs, it is essential to wait for a confirmation from the price index that its trend has also been reversed. This confirmation can be achieved by (1) the violation of a simple trendline, as shown in Figure 8.4, (2) the crossover of a moving average, or (3) the completion of a price pattern. This form of insurance is well worth taking, since during a long cyclical advance (such as the 1962– 1966 bull market), it is not unknown for an index to continually lose and regain momentum without suffering a break in trend.

As a general rule, the greater the number of negative divergences, the weaker is the underlying structure, and vice versa. It can be seen that at point C in Figure 8.4 the index moves to a significant new high but the momentum index is barely able to remain above the 100 reference line. Such a situation demands the utmost caution when accompanied by a trend

FIGURE 8.5

break, for it is a sign of extreme technical weakness and is often followed by a very sharp decline. The opposite type of situation in a bear market should be viewed as a very positive characteristic especially if the upward trend break is accompanied by high volume. The more explosive the volume, the more reliable the signal is likely to be.

A good example of price and momentum interaction can be seen in Chart 8.1 (page 110) where the DJIA makes a new low at a time when the momentum index is almost up to the zero level. Although the rally proved to be a bear market correction, it was nonetheless explosive.

The same principles of divergence are also applicable following price declines. In Figure 8.4 the price index makes a new low at point *E*, but the momentum index does not. This evidence of technical strength was later confirmed when the price index rose above its bear market trendline.

When at times the momentum index peaks simultaneously with price (as shown in Figure 8.5), no advance warning is given that a price decline is imminent. Nevertheless, a clue indicating technical weakness is given when a trendline joining the troughs of the momentum index is penetrated on the downside.

As with any trendline construction, judgment is still required to decide the significance of the break based on the principles outlined in Chapter 4. Moreover, the break in momentum should be regarded as an alert, and action should be taken only when it is confirmed by a break in the price trend itself (indicated by line *AA* in Figure 8.5).

Momentum indexes are also capable of tracing out price patterns. Usually these are of the accumulation type, although distribution formations are not uncommon. Because of the shorter lead times normally associated with reversals of falling momentum, a breakout from an accumulation pattern, when accompanied by a reversal in the downward trend of the index itself, is usually a highly reliable indication that a worthwhile move has just begun. Such an example is shown in Figure 8.6.

Another way in which momentum indexes may be useful is with regard to

FIGURE 8.6   **FIGURE 8.7**

their level. Since this type of index is an oscillator fluctuating backward and forward across its 0 to 100 reference line, there are clearly definable limits beyond which it rarely goes (see Figure 8.7).

The actual boundaries will depend on the volatility of the index being monitored and the time period on which the rate-of-change period is based, since the rate of change of an index has a tendency to vary more over a longer period than a shorter one.

In view of these two variables, there is no hard-and-fast rule about what constitutes an unduly high (known as "overbought") or low (known as "oversold") level. This can be determined only with reference to the history of the index being monitored and the maturity of the cycle. For example, when a bull market has just begun there is a far greater tendency for an index to move quickly into overbought territory and remain at very high readings for a considerable period of time. At such points the overbought readings tend to give premature warnings of declines. Consequently, during the early phases of the bull cycle when the market possesses strong momentum, reactions to the oversold level are much more responsive to price reversals, and such readings therefore offer more reliable signals. It is only when the bull market is maturing or during bear phases that overbought levels indicate that a rally is shortly to be aborted. That an index is unable to remain at such high readings for long periods is itself a signal that the bull market is losing momentum.

A further indication of the maturity of a trend is given when the momentum index moves strongly in one direction but the accompanying move in the price index is a much smaller one. Such a development suggests that the price index is tired of moving in the direction of the prevailing trend, for despite a strong push of energy from the momentum index, prices are unable to respond. This phenomenon is illustrated in Figure 8.8.

A further application of momentum techniques is to incorporate two measures on one chart and compare their performance. An example using the West German D-mark with a 13- and a 26-week rate of change is shown in Figure 27.6 (page 360). Typically, both ROC indexes move in the same direction. A warning sign that an important change in trend might be taking place is given when the two series noticeably diverge, as in late 1980, early

Example a   Example b

FIGURE 8.8

1982, and mid-1983. Each occurrence was followed by an important sell-off. For such a development to offer a reliable signal, it seems that the 26-week ROC index should be reaching a new peak or testing an old one while the 13-week ROC index is near or below the 0 reference line.

Selection of Time Span

Choice of the correct time span is important. For longer-term trends a 12-month or 52-week momentum is generally the most reliable, although a 14- or 18-month period can also prove useful. For intermediate trends a 26-week (6-month) and 13-week (3-month) momentum work well, whereas for price movements of even shorter duration 6-week, 30-day, and 10-day momentums are more appropriate.

SMOOTHED MOMENTUM INDEXES

The interpretation of momentum indexes as described above depends to a considerable extent on judgment. One method of reducing this subjectivity is to smooth the rate-of-change index by using a moving average.

Warnings of a probable trend reversal in the price index being monitored would be offered by a reversal in the smoothed momentum index itself (example a, Figure 8.9) or by a penetration of the moving average through a designated level (example b, Figure 8.9). (Also see Figure 8.10.)

The level (see the dashed line) would be determined on a trial-and-error basis by reference to a long historical study of the relationship between the index and the momentum curve. For this purpose any type of moving average can be used, but more timely results have been achieved through the use of a weighted or an exponential average in view of their greater sensitivity (see Chart 8.2).

A further method of filtering out volatility is to construct a momentum index by taking the averages of two or three rates of change and weighting

Example a Example b

FIGURE 8.9

FIGURE 8.10

CHART 8.2 West German stock market averages, 1959–1978. This chart shows the German stock market and a 12-month rate of change. The dashed line is a 14-month EMA of the rate of change. In the past, whenever this EMA has risen above the 110 level and fallen below it, a useful sell signal has resulted.

115

TABLE 8.3

Date	DJIA (1)	6-week rate of change (2)	10-week rate of change (3)	Col. 2 × 6 (4)	Col. 3 × 10 (5)	Col. 4 + col. 5) (6)	Col. 6 ÷ 16 (7)
Jan. 1	900						
8	910						
15	920						
22	918						
29	925						
Feb. 5	950						
12	945	105	. . .	630			
19	936	103	. . .	618			
26	925	101	. . .	606			
Mar. 4	934	102	. . .	612			
11	940	102	104	612	1040	1652	103
18	945	100	104	600	1040	1640	103
25	951	101	103	606	1030	1636	102

them according to their time span. The calculation using the combination of a 6- and a 10-week momentum would be done as in Table 8.3.

A similar momentum index for breadth (or any other indicator measuring internal strength) can also be achieved by combining the ratios of two or more different time periods.

Since these momentum indexes using several periods are still relatively volatile, a moving-average smoothing is normally still necessary. Chart 8.3 indicates how effective such an index can be. In this case the smoothing is a 10-month weighted average of 11- and 14-month rates of change of DJIA monthly closing prices. For timing purposes, this index has been found useful for market bottoms rather than tops, so the momentum curve takes on significance only when it falls below the 0 reference line and then rises.

A further variation on constructing a smoothed momentum index is to take the rate of change of a moving average of a price index itself. This method reverses the process described above, for instead of constructing a rate of change and then smoothing the resulting momentum index, the price index itself is first smoothed with a moving average, and a rate of change is taken of that smoothing.

INDEX TO TREND

A final form of momentum index is obtained by dividing a price index by a moving average of that index. Since the moving average represents the trend

CHART 8.3 Long-term price momentum indicator, 1960–1975. This momentum indicator has a long history of successful buy signals and is plotted up to December 1975 on this chart. It turned up in the following month and successfully confirmed the 1974–1976 bull market. (SOURCE: *Derived from data developed by E. S. C. Coppock, Trendex Research, San Antonio, Tex.*)

1. Buy 12/30/60 – DJIA 615   3. Buy 3/31/67 – DJIA 865
2. Buy 12/31/62 – DJIA 652   4. Buy 8/31/70 – DJIA 764

of the index being monitored, the resultant momentum indicator shows how fast the index is advancing or declining in relation to that trend.

This is really a horizontal representation of the envelope analysis discussed in Chapter 7. Examples *a* and *b* in Figure 8.11 show these two approaches for the same index. The upper and lower envelopes are both drawn at a level that is 10 percent from the actual moving average, so that when the price index touches the 100 line it is really at the same level as the moving average. When the momentum index is at 110, the price index is 10 percent above its average, and so on.

While this index portrays essentially the same information as the envelope analysis, in many ways it can better illustrate subtle changes in the latent strength or weakness of the price index being monitored.

Example *a*   Example *b*

FIGURE 8.11

SUMMARY

1. The concept of momentum, which measures the rate at which prices rise or fall, gives useful indications of latent strength or weakness in a price trend. This is because prices usually rise at their fastest pace well ahead of their peak and normally decline at their greatest speed before their ultimate low.

2. Markets usually spend more time in a rising than a falling phase, so that this lead characteristic is usually greater in bull markets than in bear markets.

3. Since momentum in the vast majority of cases either leads or coincides with price reversals in the trend of the index from which it has been constructed, this concept is useful as supplementary confirmation.

4. Under certain circumstances the level of momentum can also be used to predict a reversal in the price trend itself.

9

Point and Figure Charting

POINT AND FIGURE CHARTS VERSUS BAR CHARTS

Point and figure charts differ from bar charts in two important ways. First, bar charts are plotted at specific time intervals regardless of whether there is any change in price. A new plot on a point and figure chart, on the other hand, is made only when the price changes by a given amount. Point and figure charts are concerned only with measuring price, whereas bar charts measure both price (on the vertical axis) and time (on the horizontal axis).

The second major difference is that bar charts record every change in price for the period they are measuring, but point and figure charts ignore all price movements that are smaller than a specified amount. For example, if a box is set at price movements of 5 points for the DJIA, only price changes in excess of 5 points will be recorded, and smaller fluctuations will not appear.

CONSTRUCTION OF POINT AND FIGURE CHARTS

Point and figure charts are constructed using combinations of x's and 0's, known as "boxes." The x shows that prices are moving up, the 0 that they are moving down. Once the amount of historical data to be plotted has been

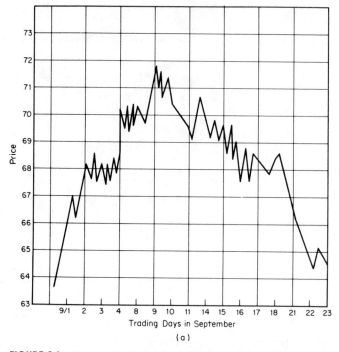

FIGURE 9.1   [SOURCE: *Martin J. Pring (ed.)*, The McGraw-Hill Handbook of Commodities and Futures, *McGraw-Hill, New York, 1985, p. 50-5.*]

established, there are two important decisions to be made before a chart can be constructed.

First, the size of each box must be determined. For individual stocks it is common practice to use a 1-point unit or box for issues trading above $20 and a ½-point unit for lower-priced stocks. However, for very long term charts or for averages consisting of much higher numbers, it is more convenient to use 5-, 10-, or even 20-point boxes. As the box size is decreased, the detail of price movement graphically displayed is increased, and vice versa. In following the price action of a stock or market over many years, it is more convenient to use a relatively large box since small boxes will make the chart unduly large and unmanageable. Often it is a good idea to maintain two or three different versions, just as daily, weekly, and monthly bar charts may be plotted.

The second decision is whether to use a regular point and figure formula or to use a reversal chart (which should not be confused with a "reversal pattern"). The straight point and figure chart is plotted just as the data are recorded. If the price moves from 64 to 65, five 0's will be plotted on a 0.20¢-point chart as in Figure 9.1*b*. If the price reverses from 67 to 66, five 0's

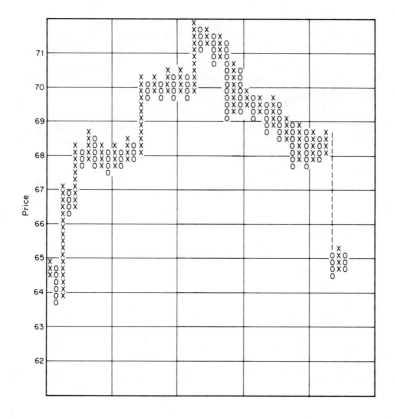

(b)

will be posted. Reversal charts, on the other hand, follow a predetermined rule: *A new series of x's or 0's cannot begin until prices have moved by a specified amount in the opposite direction to the prevailing trend.* The use of the reversal technique therefore helps to reduce misleading or whipsaw signals, and to greatly compress the size of the chart so that more data can be plotted.

The construction of ½-point charts, 5- or 10-point charts, or charts by any other measure is identical to the above method except that a new box can be posted only when the price has moved by the degree specified, that is, by ½ point, 5 points, or 10 points, respectively. Since only price is recorded it could take several days or even weeks before a new box is plotted. Hence a common practice is to record dates either at the foot of the chart or in the boxes at the appropriate points. A combination of both date locations is used for longer-term charts. For example, the year is recorded at the bottom of the chart against the column for which the first posting of that year was

Bottoms | Tops

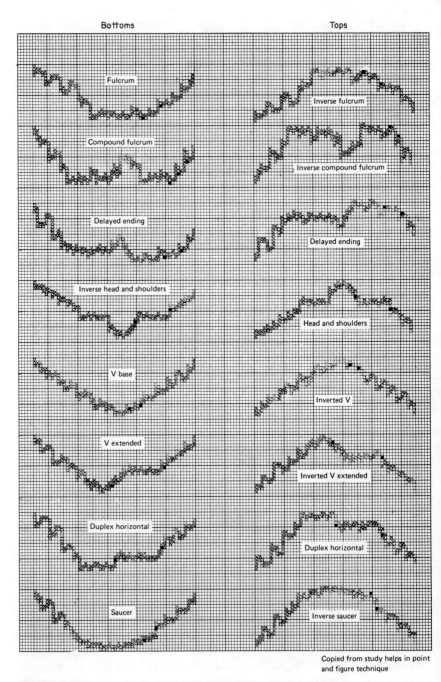

Copied from study helps in point
and figure technique

FIGURE 9.2 [SOURCE: Study Helps in Point and Figure Technique.]

CHART 9.1 Gold price $5 and $2 reversals. These two charts show the gold price plotted on $5 and $2 reversals. The trendlines are self-explanatory. Note that the $5 chart captures 10 years of trading history very concisely. On the other hand, the 2-point reversal chart, which covers March–November 1982, offers far better detail.

(SOURCE: *Chart Analysis Ltd., London, England.*)

made, and the beginning of each month is recorded in a box using the number of the month—1 for January, 2 for February, etc.

The decision about unit size (and thus the degree of price change required to trigger a new column of 0's or x's) is essentially based on personal judgment. It is determined by the price range and degree of volatility of the indicator, stock, or market under consideration. Reducing the size of the units (figures) increases the detail of the price movement portrayed. Making the unit larger expands the base of data which can be included but limits the number of fluctuations which can be illustrated. (See Chart 9.1.) Following a market with bar or line charts on a daily, weekly, or monthly basis corresponds to keeping several point and figure charts using various unit sizes.

Point and figure charts are plotted on arithmetically ruled cross-section paper, with 8, 10, or 12 squares to the inch. Occasionally point and figure charts are constructed on semilogarithmic or ratio scale charting paper.

Data published in the financial press covering the high, low, and close for specific stocks are not suitable for accurate point and figure charts. For example, if a $15 stock has an intraday price range of $1½, it is impossible to know for point and figure purposes the actual course of the stock from 14½ to 16. It could have risen from 14½ to 16 in one move, which for a ½-point chart would have been represented by three rising x's. Alternatively it might have moved from 14½ to 15½, back to 14½, and then to 16, which would have resulted in two x's, two 0's, then a column of three x's. The character of the rally has a very important bearing on the appearance of a point and figure chart.

When dealing with data published in this form, it is better to use larger units so that intraday fluctuations do not distort the chart unduly. If more detail is required, the data should be purchased from a source which publishes intraday price movements.

Accepted rules for plotting point and figure data where the actual prices on the tape are not known are as follows:

1. If the opening price is closer to the high than the low, assume that the course of prices is open, high, low, close.

2. If the opening price is closer to the low, assume open, low, high, close.

3. If the opening price is also the high, assume open, high, low, close.

4. If the opening price is also the low, assume open, low, high, close.

5. If the opening price is the low and the closing price the high, assume open, low, close, high.

6. If the opening price is the high for the day and the close is the lowest price, assume open, high, close, low.

INTERPRETING POINT AND FIGURE CHARTS

General

Since point and figure charts do not include volume, moving averages, or time, price action is the only element to be examined.

In this respect the basic principles of bar chart analysis are applied. There are certain disadvantages to using point and figure charts; for example, key reversal days, islands, gaps, and other such formations do not show up. On the other hand, if properly constructed, these charts represent all important price swings even on an intraday basis. They effectively emphasize important support and resistance areas; for example, on a weekly bar chart a single bar representing a weekly price action can take up only one line. However, if there was considerable volatility during the week in which support and resistance were each tested 3 or 4 times, this would most likely show up on a point and figure chart as a congestion area. As a result the importance of these levels would be drawn to the attention of the technician, who would then be in a good position to interpret the significance of any breakout which might develop.

Point and figure patterns are similar in nature to those of price patterns and may be of the continuation or reversal type. The most common ones are shown in Figure 9.2. Head-and-shoulders and inverse head-and-shoulders patterns, double tops and bottoms, rounding tops and bottoms, etc., can easily be recognized as the point and figure equivalent of regular bar or close-only price formations, discussed earlier. Most of the price patterns shown in Figure 9.2 are explained in Chapter 4.

The Count

The essential difference between price projections based on point and figure charts and those based on bar or close-only charts is that the measuring formula of point and figure charts is derived from a horizontal rather than a vertical count. As discussed in Chapter 4, the minimum downside projection from a head-and-shoulders top is derived by projecting downward the vertical distance from the top of the head to the neckline. In point and figure charting the *width* of the pattern is used as the projecting mechanism from the breakout. No one, to my knowledge, has so far satisfactorily explained why this principle appears to work. It seems to be based on the idea that lateral and vertical movements are proportional to each other on a point and figure chart. In other words, the more times a stock or market has undergone price swings within two given levels (as dictated by the price pattern), the greater the *ultimate* move is likely to be once the breakout has taken place. On a point and figure chart the dimensions of the consolidation or reversal

FIGURE 9.3 [SOURCE: Martin J. Pring, The McGraw-Hill Handbook of Commodities and Futures, McGraw-Hill, New York, 1985, p. 48-5.]

pattern can be easily discerned by adding up the number of boxes and projecting that number downward or upward depending on which way prices break out.

The essential problem with the count method is that formations with irregular outlines can generate confusion about where the count should begin. The best approach is to select an important horizontal line in the formation, measure across it, and add (or subtract) the number of boxes in the line to (or from) the level of the line.

Price projections for point and figure formations are by no means 100 percent accurate in all situations. In general, upside projections are likely to be exceeded in bull markets, and downside projections surpassed in bear markets. Projections which are made counter to the prevailing trend have a *tendency* not to be achieved—for example, a downside projection in a bull market.

Trendlines on Point and Figure Charts

It is possible to construct down trendlines on point and figure charts by joining a series of declining peaks. Up trendlines are drawn by connecting a series of rising lows, and horizontal trendlines are created by joining identical support or resistance levels. The same principles of interpretation discussed in Chapter 6 apply to trendlines drawn on point and figure charts. The trendline takes its significance from a combination of length, angle of descent or ascent, and the number of times it has been touched. Misleading or whipsaw signals occur occasionally, but if a carefully chosen reversal amount is used as a filter in the construction of the chart, such whipsaws can be kept to a minimum. Another possibility is to draw a parallel line one box above (or below) the actual trendline and use this as the signal to buy (or sell). Although some timeliness is clearly lost with this type of approach, it does offer some protection from misleading price moves.

SUMMARY

1. Point and figure charts measure only one dimension: time.
2. They are constructed from columns of x's and 0's, known as figures, which represent a specified predetermined price movement.
3. Point and figure charts emphasize the number of price swings which take place within a given congestion area.
4. Point and figure charts are interpreted similarly to bar charts, the main exception being the measuring formula which is achieved by the principle of the count.

10

Miscellaneous Techniques for Determining Trends

Two of the techniques discussed in this chapter, namely, the concepts of *support and resistance* and of *proportion,* are concerned with estimating the possible extent or duration of a trend, in contrast to most of the indicators previously examined, which attempt to confirm a change in trend after it has already occurred. Such techniques should be used only as an indication of the *probable* extent of the move, however, not as the basis of an actual forecast, as there is no known method of predicting the duration of a market trend.

The third concept considered in this chapter is that of *relative strength*. This is a method which helps to determine the quality of a trend of an index by comparing it with the trend of another index—usually "the market," as measured by the Dow Jones Industrial Average.

Declining relative strength after a long upmove is regarded as a sign of weakness, while improving relative strength after a substantial decline is interpreted as a sign of strength. Since some indexes have a habit of leading the DJIA, changes in the trend of their relative strength offer a good preliminary indication of a reversal in the trend of the index itself.

SUPPORT AND RESISTANCE

The concept of support and resistance has already been mentioned, but it warrants further consideration. Support has been defined as "buying, actual or potential, sufficient in volume to halt a downtrend in prices for an appreciable period" and resistance as "selling, actual or potential, sufficient in volume to satisfy all bids and hence stop prices from going higher for a time."[1]

A support zone represents a *concentration* of demand, and a resistance zone a *concentration* of supply. The word "concentration" is emphasized since supply and demand are always in balance, but it is their relative strength or concentration which determines trends.

The reasons for the occurrence of areas of support and resistance and some methods of detecting them in advance are best illustrated by the use of a simple example.

At the beginning of Figure 10.1 the market is in a downtrend. The bear market is interrupted by a consolidation pattern (rectangle), from which prices ultimately break down. The index reaches its low and then after a brief period of consolidation mounts a rally. The rally is halted at the dashed line, which is at the same level as the lower end of the rectangle. People who bought during the period when the rectangle was being formed have all lost money up to this point, and many of them are keen to liquidate their positions and "break even." Consequently there is a concentration of supply at this level, transforming what was formerly a level of support to one of resistance. Such levels are often formed at a round number such as 10, 100, or 50, since these represent easy psychological points at which investors can make investment decisions.

Returning to the example, prices then fall off slightly and mount another assault on the resistance level, but still more stock is put up for sale. Finally prices and volume pick up, and the resistance is overcome as the available supply at this level is absorbed.

The first rule in assessing the importance of a support or resistance zone therefore relates to the amount of stock that changed hands in that area. The greater the activity, the more significant the zone.

The next level of resistance in Figure 10.1 is around the level of the "panic" bottom (line *BB*) of the previous bear market. The price is forced back at this point since the combination of an overextended rally and a substantial level of resistance is too overpowering.

In this instance the attempt of the index to climb through the resistance level can be compared to the efforts of a man who, having just finished a 10-

---

[1] Robert D. Edwards and John Magee, *Technical Analysis of Stock Trends,* John Magee, Springfield, Mass., 1957, p. 211.

FIGURE 10.1

mile run, tries unsuccessfully to push open a heavy concrete trapdoor. The trapdoor would have proved difficult at the best of times, but after such violent physical exercise the man is forced to rest before making another attempt. The same principle can be applied to the market in that a long, steep climb in price is similar to the 10-mile run, and the resistance level resembles the trapdoor. Consequently, a second rule for assessing the significance of a support or resistance zone is to assess the speed and extent of the previous move.

The more overextended the previous price swing is, the less resistance/ support that is required to halt it.

Reference to Figure 10.1 shows that the index, having unsuccessfully mounted an assault on the resistance level at *BB*, falls back to the first level at *AA*, which now returns to its previous role of support. This reversal in role arises from the experiences of the investors concerned. In the first place, some who bought at the bear market low may have decided to take profits at *AA*, i.e., $10, and have been so frustrated by subsequently watching the stock rise to $20 that they have decided to repurchase if it ever returns to $10 again. Similarly, an investor who bought at $10 previously and sold at $20 may wish to repeat this shrewd maneuver.

The third rule for establishing the potency of a support or resistance zone is to examine the amount of time that has elapsed between the formation of the original congestion and the nature of general market developments in the meantime. A supply which is 6 months old has greater potency than one established 10 or 20 years previously. Even so, it is almost uncanny how support and resistance levels repeat their effectiveness time and time again even when separated by many years.

The process described above is concerned with decisions on the buying and selling of stocks, but the principle of support and resistance applies equally well to the market averages, since they are themselves constructed from a number of stocks.

PROPORTION

The law of motion states that for every action there is a reaction. Since the stock market as reflected in the price trends of stocks is really the measurement of crowd psychology in motion, it is also subject to the law. In earlier chapters it was pointed out that at certain times the stock market moves in simple proportion with the prevailing trend or directly against it. The measuring implications of price patterns, trendlines, moving averages, and envelopes are embodiments of this concept of proportion in practice.

Just as support and resistance levels can help give an idea of just where a trend in stock prices may be temporarily halted or reversed, so may the principles of proportion, but these principles go much farther.

When an index is exploring new, all-time high ground, there is no indication of where a resistance level may occur, since there is no record of one. Consequently, the use of the concept of proportion offers a guide to where a move may terminate.

Perhaps the best-known principle of proportion is the 50 percent rule. Many bear markets, as measured by the DJIA for instance, have cut prices by half. For instance the 1901–1903, 1907, 1919–1921, and 1937–1938 bear markets recorded declines of 46, 49, 47, and 50 percent, respectively. The first leg of the 1929–1932 bear market ended in October 1929 at 195, just over half the September high. Sometimes the halfway mark in an advance represents the point of balance, often giving a clue to the ultimate extent of the move in question or, alternatively, indicating an important juncture point for the return move. Thus, between 1970 and 1973 the market advanced from 628 to 1067. The halfway point in that rise was 848, or approximately the same level at which the first stage of the 1973–1974 bear market ended.

By the same token, rising markets often find resistance after doubling from a low; the first rally from 40 to 81 in the 1932–1937 bull market was a double.

In effect, the 50 percent mark falls halfway between the one-third to two-thirds retracement described in Chapter 2 on Dow theory. These one-third and two-thirds proportions can be widely observed in the stock market and also serve as support or resistance points.

Ratio scale charts are most helpful in determining such points, since moves of identical proportion can easily be projected up and down.

The principle of proportion can also be applied to stocks. The example in Chart 10.1a shows General Motors' habit of rising in proportions of about 50 percent. In downmoves this results in a 33 percent decline from high to low. The 55 and 35 percent proportions and multiples thereof tend to act as pivotal points for support and resistance areas. Thus the 1974 low of about 32 when multiplied by 150 percent results in an objective of just over 65.

CHART 10.1a   General Motors 50 percent swings.

(SOURCE: *Securities Research, Boston, Mass.*)

The 65 area proved to be one of strong support in 1976 and 1977 and one of resistance in 1978 and 1979.

It is not possible to project which proportion will result from a specific move. However, these swings occur with sufficient consistency to offer possible reversal points at both peaks and troughs. If general market conditions and additional technical analysis of the stock also appear to be consistent, there is a good chance that the projections based on this approach may prove accurate. Forecasts using only this method should not be undertaken. Experimentation will show that each stock has a character of its own, some lending themselves more readily to this approach, others not at all.

SPEED RESISTANCE LINES

This concept incorporates the one-third and two-thirds proportions, but instead of using them as a base for a probable price objective, uses them in conjunction with the speed of an advance or a decline.

During a downward reaction from a price rise, an index may be expected to find support when it reaches a line which is advancing at either two-thirds or one-third of the rate of advance from the previous trough to the previous

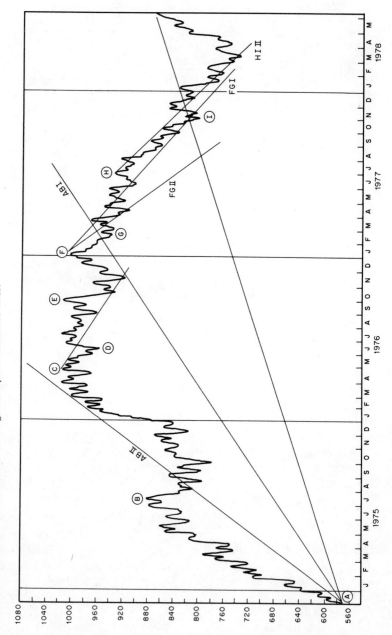

CHART 10.1*b* Dow Jones Industrial Average and speed resistance lines.

134

FIGURE 10.2

peak. This is illustrated in Figure 10.2. In examples a and b, A marks the trough and B the peak. The advance from A to B is 100 points and takes 100 days, so that the speed of the advance is 1 point per day. A ⅓-speed resistance line will advance at one-third of that rate (that is, ⅓ point per day), and a ⅔ line will move at ⅔ point per day.

A rally or decline is measured from the extreme intraday high or low and not the closing price. In order to construct a ⅓ speed resistance line from example a it is necessary to add 33 points (i.e., one-third of the 100-point advance) to the price at A and plot this point directly under B. In this case A is 100 points, so a plot is made at 133 under B. This point is then joined to A and the line extended to the right-hand portion of the graph. Similarly, the ⅔ line joins A and the 166 level on the same date as B. If the chart were plotted on a ratio scale, the task would be much easier. All that would be required (as example b shows) would be a line joining A and B. The angle of ascent is then recorded, in this case 30 degrees. Two lines at one-third (10

Example a

Example b

FIGURE 10.3

degrees) and two-thirds (20 degrees) of this angle are then drawn. Figure 10.3 illustrates the same process for a declining market.

Once constructed, the speed resistance lines act as important support and resistance areas.

More specifically, the application of these lines is based on the following rules:

1. A reaction following a rally will find support at the ⅔-speed resistance line. If this line is violated, the support should be found at the ⅓-speed resistance line. Should the index fall below its ⅓ line, the probabilities indicate that the rising move has been completed and that the index will decline to a new low, possibly below that upon which the speed resistance lines were based.

2. If the index holds at the ⅓ line, a resistance to further price advance may be expected at the ⅔ line. If the index moves above the ⅔ line, a new high is likely to be recorded.

3. If the index violates its ⅓ line and then rallies again, it will find resistance to that rally at the ⅓ line.

4. Rules 1 through 3 apply in reverse for a declining market.

Chart 10.1*b* shows the application of these rules in the marketplace.

RELATIVE STRENGTH

Most market averages rise and fall in concert with the general market, and under such conditions no warnings are being given of a probable reversal in their trend. It is only when the market, as measured by the DJIA, makes a new high or low unaccompanied by an index that a signal is given. This discrepancy, known as a divergence, is a useful technique for discovering when various market sectors are moving "out of gear" with the DJIA.

A more subtle approach to the principle of divergence is the concept of *relative strength*. Relative strength is obtained by dividing the price of one index by another. Usually the divisor is a measurement of "the market," for example, the DJIA or the Standard and Poor's 500.[2] When calculated in this way, a rising relative-strength line denotes that the index in question is performing better than the market, and a declining line indicates that it is being outperformed by the market.

Relative strength (RS) moves in trends just as stock prices do, and the reversal of these relative-strength movements has significance for the particular index concerned.

Relative strength is more normally used for the purpose of deciding *what* stock to buy, for it is obviously best to choose one that is likely to outperform the market. For the purpose of assessing the overall technical position of the market, RS is still a useful concept when applied to certain market averages, since there are several indexes (such as the Utilities) that traditionally lead the DJIA. An assessment of the quality of their RS trends is therefore helpful in determining the overall technical strength of such averages.

Interpretation of trends in relative strength is subject to exactly the same principles as the identification of the trends of the price indexes themselves. An analysis of an RS line, therefore, involves the use of trendlines, moving averages, price patterns, support and resistance, momentum, etc.

When an index and its relative strength are both rising and it appears that

---

[2] Unless otherwise indicated, the relative strengths of all U.S. stock indexes in this book are calculated against the DJIA.

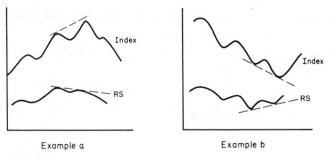

Example a   Example b

FIGURE 10.4

the relative-strength trend is about to reverse, a warning is given of a possible reversal in the trend of the index itself, since the trend of relative strength typically reverses *ahead* of the trend in the index. During a declining trend, a firming of the relative-strength line indicates a position of growing technical strength. Since the lead time given by such signals varies, it is very important to await a confirmation by a similar trend reversal in the index itself. On the other hand, if the RS were being used to monitor a position in a particular stock, a reversal in RS might justify the sale of that particular stock in favor of another one with a rising relative strength trend. However, it would still be important to identify the major trend in the market itself, since a stock with a rising RS could still be falling in price if the rate of decline in the market were even sharper.

The use of the level of the RS index in conjunction with that of the price index itself can also be helpful. In Figure 10.4 it can be seen that the price index rises in a series of three ascending peaks.

The first two of these tops are also confirmed by a new high in the RS line, but the third is not. This represents a negative divergence and is a powerful indication that the positive trend in the index itself is likely to be reversed soon (also see Chart 10.2). Example *b* in Figure 10.4 shows a similar situation, but this time at a market bottom, where a new low in the price index is not confirmed by the RS line. This situation is known as a positive divergence and offers a bullish undertone.

Volume can also be included in this analysis, since an index or stock which is moving up in price on higher volume should be viewed with suspicion if the trend in RS is moving in the opposite direction. A divergence between RS and price volume indicates that although there may be tremendous enthusiasm for a stock (or index), as measured by expanding volume, this high level of activity is still insufficient to permit the index to rise as fast as the market itself.

The concept of RS can be applied to almost any market situation. For example, if a switch between one stock and another were under considera-

CHART 10.2 Dow Jones Transportation Average versus relative strength, 1966–1977. This chart of the Dow Jones Transportation Average and its relative strength shows how in early 1969 both the average and its relative strength broke down from their bull market trendlines, thereby signaling a decline. The same characteristics occurred at the end of 1971.

tion, a quick calculation of the RS between the two would indicate the trend between them. The trend in gold bullion is often compared with that of gold shares, or the U.S. stock market with that of the United Kingdom or Japan. The variations are almost limitless, but the principles associated with the determination of the trend remain identical.

Putting the Techniques Together:

An Analysis of the Dow Jones Utility Average, 1962-1969

The Dow Jones Utility Average was first constructed in 1929. It did not record its secular bottom in 1932, as was the case with most of the other indexes, but its low was delayed until April 1942. From that level (10.42) the index rose irregularly for 23 years until April 1965, at which point it reached an all-time high of 164.39; it then proceeded to lose nearly 100 points in the next 9 years (see Chart 11.1). An examination of the period between 1962 and 1969 is valuable since it covers the culmination of the secular advance and its associated distribution as well as several intervening cycles.

In May 1962 the average was at 99.8, which represented the closing low of a 7-month bear market. At this particular juncture there was nothing to suggest that a reversal in trend had taken place. The first significant signs appeared several months after the bottom. At this point the downtrend in the index (trendline AA in Chart 11.2) had been reversed, and the index had crossed above its 40-week moving average. These two signals confirmed the

CHART 11.1 Dow Jones Utility Average, 1929–1978.

——— monthly index
- - - 9 – month moving average

(SOURCE: Pring Market Review.)

CHART 11.2 Dow Jones Utility Weekly Average, 1959–1978, and 40-week moving average (with weighted momentum index).

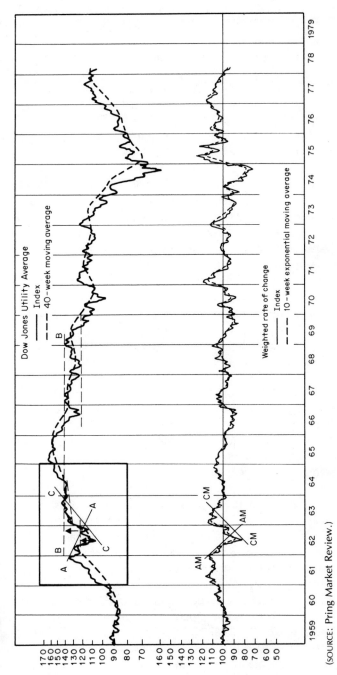

(SOURCE: Pring Market Review.)

reversal in the downtrend of the weighted momentum index that had taken place earlier (line AM/AM). This rate-of-change index was constructed by combining 6-, 13-, and 26-week rate-of-change indexes and weighting them according to their respective time periods. These positive signs were also accompanied by the completion of a double bottom by the Utility Average. Since the second decline occurred on lower volume than the first, the breakout to a new recovery high in December indicated that higher prices could be expected.

The average continued to rally until it reached the upside price objective indicated by the double bottom. This level, represented by line BB on the chart, proved to be a major resistance level in the 1963–1964 period and later in 1967 and 1969 as well. During the 12 months following the break-out, the initial bull market trendline CC remained intact, and the average also remained above its 40-week moving average. In late 1963, both the trendline CC and the moving average were violated. This development, combined with the two declining peaks and the break in trend of the momentum index (line CM/CM), suggested that further upside potential in the average would be difficult to achieve. Indeed, the index did not decisively break above the September 1963 high for almost a year.

This break in trend was followed by a long sideways movement. The most significant development during this period was the formation of a head-and-shoulders top between 1963 and 1964. This is shown in more detail in the boxed area of Chart 11.2. The pattern was almost completed, but instead of breaking below the neckline, the index broke above its 40-week moving average and began a sharp advance. This type of move is typical of a potential distribution pattern that is never completed. While the ensuing move is usually long and explosively sharp, the formation of the distribution pattern indicates some form of underlying weakness even though it fails. As it happened, the late 1964 advance was to prove to be the last before the significant 1965 peak.

It should be noted that while the late 1963 break in trend indicated that some form of consolidation was likely, at no time did the 14-month expo-nential average shown on Chart 11.3 threaten to reverse direction in a way that would have thrown doubt on the entire primary movement. Further reference to Chart 11.3 shows that the early 1964 decline offered a useful benchmark for the construction of a significant bull market trendline (line AA, Chart 11.3) by joining this point with the 1962 bottom. It was an important one, since it lasted a long time (2 years) and rose at a fairly shallow angle. Although this particular bull market had another 2 years to run, the average time span for a primary advance is about 2 years, so a trendline of this type that remains intact for 2 years represents a relatively long period. Its violation would therefore give a strong signal that the overall trend from 1962 had been reversed. In actual fact, the downward penetra-

CHART 11.3 Dow Jones Utility Monthly Average, 1959–1978 (with 14-month exponential average), and 12-month rate of change (with 14-month exponential average of 12-month rate of change).

(SOURCE: Pring Market Review.)

145

CHART 11.4 Dow Jones Utility Average relative strength, 1959–1978.

Relative strength of Dow Jones Utility Average
— monthly index
– – 14-month exponential moving average

12 – month rate of change
— monthly index
– – 14-month exponential moving average

(SOURCE: Pring Market Review.)

tion of this line occurred in early 1965 just after the peak. Further signs of weakness at this point can be seen from the rather dramatic deterioration in relative strength (see Chart 11.4) that had begun in 1963.

The 12-month momentum index (see Chart 11.3) had also recorded a negative divergence, since it did not confirm the 1965 top in the Utility Average itself.

By late 1965 the technical position had deteriorated even more dramatically. First, from a cyclical point of view the 14-month exponential moving average shown on Chart 11.3 had turned down, and the Utility Average index had also crossed below this important moving average. The weakening position of the momentum index was also apparent, as the index itself had broken its uptrend established by the 1962 and early 1964 bottoms (line AM/AM). Moreover, the 14-month exponential moving average of this rate-of-change index had also turned down.

From a longer-term point of view, the most significant development was the fact that the 12-month momentum index had made a series of three declining peaks in 1961, 1963, and 1965. This showed that throughout this period the Utility Average was gradually losing its vitality. As long as the trend in the average itself continued to be positive, there was no danger of falling prices, but by late 1965 the important trendline (BB, Chart 11.3) joining the 1960 and 1962 bottoms was decisively penetrated on the downside. While no distribution patterns were evident at this point, the break in this important trendline accompanied by a long-term deterioration in the momentum index and relative strength indicated that the progress of the Utility Average was going to be constrained for a considerable period.

The cyclical decline that began in mid-1965 bottomed out in late 1966. The ensuing bull market was a rather weak one and essentially proved to be a 3-year period of consolidation. In effect the Utility Average, as illustrated by Chart 11.2, was forming a rectangle. By the time the 1969–1970 bear market was under way, it became apparent that the Utility Average had been forming an 8½-year head-and-shoulders distribution pattern between 1961 and 1969 (Chart 11.3). The completion of this pattern was confirmed when the average broke below its 1968 low in the fall of 1969.

It is worth noting that throughout the 1966–1969 period when the rectangle was being formed, the long-term trend of the Utility Average's relative strength, shown in Chart 11.4, was in a sharp downtrend. The break in the secular uptrend of the average (shown on Chart 11.1), which occurred in 1967, gave an additional bearish warning that the ensuing period would be one of substantial constraint for the Utility Average. This indeed proved to be the case, as the average proceeded to lose over 50 percent of its value in the ensuing 5 years.

PART 2

Market Structure

12

Price: The Major Averages

Price is the most logical starting point for any attempt to analyze the strength of the overall market structure.

There is no ideal index that represents the movement of "the market." Although the majority of stocks move together in the same direction most of the time, there is rarely a period when specific stocks or several groups of stocks are not moving contrary to the general direction of the trend. There are basically two methods of measuring the general level of stock prices. The first, known as an *unweighted index,* takes a mean average of the prices of a wide base of stocks; the second also takes an average of the prices of a number of stocks, but in this case the prices are weighted by the outstanding capitalization (i.e., number and market value of shares) of each company. The first method monitors the movement of the vast majority of listed stocks, but since the second method gives a greater weight to the larger companies, movements in a market average constructed in this way more fairly represent changes in the value of the nation's portfolios. For this reason, and because such averages can be compiled from stocks representing public participation, market leadership, and industry importance, weighted averages are usually used as the best proxy for "the market."

In addition, several price indexes have been developed which measure various segments of the market and whose interrelationship can offer useful clues about the market's overall technical condition. Chapter 2 dealt in detail with the relationship between the Dow Jones Industrial Average and

Transportation Average, but there are many other useful indexes—such as the Utility Average and unweighted indexes as well as a few bellwether stocks. These indexes are examined below in the context of their contribution to the market's overall technical structure.

COMPOSITE MARKET INDEXES

The Dow Jones Industrial Average is the most widely followed stock market index in the world. It is constructed by totaling the prices of 30 stocks and dividing the total by a divisor. The divisor, which is published regularly in *The Wall Street Journal* and *Barron's,* is changed from time to time because of stock splits, stock dividends, and changes in the composition of the average. Strictly speaking, it is not a "composite" index, since it does not include such industries as banks, transportation, and utilities. Yet the capitalization of the Dow Jones Industrial stocks is equivalent to approximately 25 to 30 percent of the outstanding capitalization on the New York Stock Exchange (NYSE), and it has normally proved to be a reliable indicator of the general movement of the market. The original reason for including a relatively small number of stocks in an average was convenience, since years ago the averages had to be laboriously calculated by hand. With the advent of the computer, the calculation of a much more comprehensive sample became possible.

One of the drawbacks of this method of construction is that if a stock increases in price and is not split, its influence on the average will become substantially greater, especially if many of the other Dow stocks are growing and splitting at the same time. In spite of this and other drawbacks, the Dow has over the years acted fairly consistently with many of the more widely capitalized market averages.

The Standard and Poor's Composite, which comprises 500 stocks representing well over 90 percent of the NYSE market value, is another widely followed bellwether average. It is calculated by multiplying the price of each share by the number of shares outstanding, totaling the value of each company, and reducing the answer to an index number.

Most of the time the DJIA and the S&P 500 both move in the same direction, but there are times when a new high or low is achieved in one index but not the other. Such occasions often warn of a reversal in trend for the overall market. Generally speaking, the greater the divergence, the greater the ensuing move in the opposite direction is likely to be. Reference to Chart 12.1a shows that in late 1968 the S&P 500 reached a new all-time high, unlike the DJIA, which was not able to surpass its 1966 peak. This development helped to signal a bear market that was to wipe nearly 40 percent off the value of both averages. On the other hand, the 1973–1974

CHART 12.1a Key market averages, 1965–1978.

(SOURCE: *Securities Research Co., a Division of United Business Service Co.*)

CHART 12.1b Wilshire 5000 Equity Index: 100 months.

(SOURCE: *Dominion Securities Ames Graphics, Trend and Cycle Department.*)

bear market was completed with a double bottom. In the case of the DJIA the second bottom in December 1974 was lower than the October one, yet the S&P 500 failed to confirm the new low in the DJIA. In the space of the next 2 years the DJIA rose by some 80 percent. This is also shown on Chart 12.1a.

The New York Stock Exchange compiles an all-encompassing index called the NYSE Composite. In a sense it represents the ideal average, since its value is based on the capitalization of all shares on the exchange. Its movements are very similar to those of the DJIA and the S&P 500. Nevertheless, divergences between the trends of these three averages offer additional confirmation of changes in the overall technical structure.

The most encompassing indicator of all is the Wilshire 5000 Equity Index since it represents the value-weighted total, in billions of dollars, of all actively traded common stocks in the United States. Conceptually this is the indicator that should be used for monitoring trends of the overall market, but because of the lethargy of the investment community and the obvious vested interest of the sponsors of the other popular averages it has not received the widespread recognition which it justly deserves. The Wilshire 5000 is shown in Chart 12.1b.

Chart 14.5 (page 186) shows a complete history of the DJIA from 1790 to 1976. In reality this is not a 200-year record of the Dow Jones Industrials, since from time to time (through mergers or takeovers, for example) new stocks have been substituted. In the late nineteenth century the index was made up of 12 stocks; this was changed to 20 in 1916 and 30 in 1928. Since records of the original 12 stocks are unavailable for most of the last century, the index portrayed in Chart 14.5 comprises at least two different indexes which have been spliced together to maintain some form of continuity. Consequently, while the interpretation of the actual level of the index in these earlier years should be treated with some caution, the timing and size of the various cyclical swings can be regarded as more reliable.

The average has been plotted on ratio scale, so price movements of identical vertical distance are also of the same proportion. While the wild gyrations of the market in recent years appear substantial to those who have been investing during this period, it is apparent on the chart that such movements have so far been relatively mild by historical standards.

The DJIA is the most widely followed proxy for "the market," so an analysis of the other indexes and indicators described in this and the ensuing chapters is really geared to projecting the performance of the DJIA. Many of the techniques already described in Part 1 are useful for identifying trends in the DJIA itself. The charts in Chapter 3 offered several illustrations of the use of price pattern analysis with the DJIA. Chart 12.2, which portrays the monthly swings in this average from 1929 to 1977, indicates how the reversal or cyclical bull markets can be indicated by the drawing of a simple trendline joining the bear market low with the trough of the first major reaction. This simple technique signaled the termination of nine bull markets at relatively early stages. The 1942–1946 primary uptrend would initially have been broken in 1943, since it was too steep to be maintained. The violation of the 1962–1966 line was late, but it foreshadowed an extended period of consolidation which was later confirmed by a downward penetration of the line joining the 1932 and 1942 bottoms in 1969. Finally, note how these lines, once violated, have become resistance levels to further price advance. This is especially marked for the 1942–1943 and 1962–1966 advances.

CHART 12.2 Long-term Dow showing important bull-market trendlines.

Monthly index
9 – month moving average

Trendlines can also be drawn for bear markets, and these are shown on Chart 12.3. Although this technique provides a reasonable indication of a reversal in trend, some degree of subjectivity and judgment is necessary in the interpretive process. For example, the relatively shallow declining trend in the 1957, 1962, and 1973–1974 bear markets resulted in some unreasonably late signals. In cases where it is obvious that a trendline is going to be "late," it is better to disregard it and fall back on another technique. In the three cases outlined above, for instance, the completion of price patterns could have been used to discern a reversal in trend.

THE DJIA AND MOVING AVERAGES

When experimenting with a moving average from the point of view of trend determination, it is necessary first to assess the type of cycle to be considered. As explained earlier, for example, the 4-year stock market cycle has corresponded with the United States business cycle for many decades. Since the stock market is greatly influenced by business cycle developments, this 4-year (or to place it more exactly, 41-month) cycle is of great significance in trend determination. Consequently, the choice of a moving average to detect such swings is limited to anything less than the full period, i.e., 41 months, since a moving average covering this whole time span would smooth out the complete cycle and theoretically become a straight line. In practice the moving average does fluctuate, since the cycle is rarely limited exactly to its average 41 months and varies in magnitude of price change. Through trial and error it has been found that a 9-month (or 40-week) moving average (approximately a quarter of the time span of the ideal cycle) is the most useful.

In his book *The Stock Market Indicators,* William Gordon calculated that between 1897 and 1967, 29 buy and sell signals were given for the DJIA, using a 40-week crossover as a signal.[1] The average gain for all bull signals (i.e., between the buy and sell signals) was 27 percent, and the average change from sell signals was 4 percent. For investors who had used the buy signals to purchase stocks, nine of the signals would have resulted in some losses, although none greater than 7 percent, while gains were significantly higher. By comparison similar research using a 30-week moving average, also considered by technicians to be a useful average, revealed an average gain for buy signals during this period of 19 percent.

---

[1] Investors Press, Palisades, N.J., 1968. The actual rule used for buy signals was as follows: "If the 200-day (40-week) average line flattens out following a previous decline, or is advancing and the price of the stock penetrates that average line on the upside, this comprises a major buying signal." The opposite conditions were used for "sell" signals.

CHART 12.3 Long-term Dow showing important bear market trendlines.

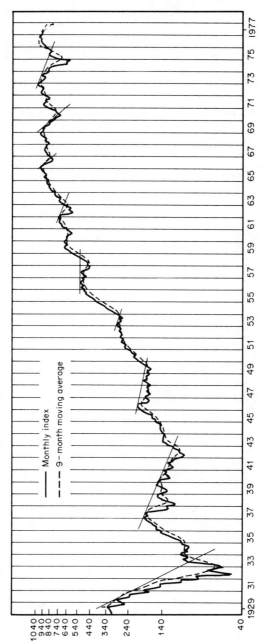

CHART 12.4   Dow Jones Industrial Average versus 4-, 13-, and 50-week moving averages. This system was devised by Richard Russell. Buying (and selling) "alerts" are provided when the 4-week average crosses above (or below) the 13-week average. Major signals are given when the 13-week average crosses above (or below) the 50-week average. To quote Russell: "By construction these signals have to come fairly early in a major and extended market move. Since true primary movements tend to be protracted both in duration and extent they are usually signaled in ample time and extent by the 13- and 50-week moving averages."

(SOURCE: *Courtesy of Dow Theory, Inc.*)

For intermediate swings in the DJIA, crossovers of 13-week and 10-week averages have proved to be useful benchmarks, but naturally a moving average covering such a brief time span can result in many misleading whipsaws and is therefore less reliable than the 40-week average. For even shorter swings a 30-day (6-week) moving average works well, although some technicians prefer a 25-day average. Finally, the use of multiple moving averages is described in Chapter 7—in this case the 30-week/10-week relationship for the DJIA, which has been a reliable indicator.

A simpler technique for identifying intermediate trends is to use a 13-week rate of change of the DJIA in conjunction with trends in the level of the average itself. The technique used in Chart 12.5 involves the drawing of trendlines for both the weekly closing price of the Dow and its 13-week momentum. When a break in one index is confirmed by the other, a reversal in the prevailing trend usually takes place. Such signals are illustrated in the chart by the use of arrows. This type of analysis should be supported where appropriate with price pattern analysis for the DJIA and with other techniques utilizing the momentum principles described in Chapter 8. Although the method does not always work well, whenever there are clearly definable

CHART 12.5 Dow Jones Industrial Average versus 13-week momentum.

(SOURCE: Pring Market Review.)

trendlines that have been touched three or more times, the conclusions drawn from this technique are usually extremely reliable. A less subjective alternative is to use a moving-average crossover for the DJIA and either a change in direction of a smoothed rate of change for the momentum index or its penetration of a predetermined level. Such a combination is shown on Chart 12.6, which incorporates a 14-month exponential moving average for the DJIA and a 14-month exponential moving average for a 12-month rate-of-change index.

THE DOW JONES TRANSPORTATION AVERAGE

The Transportation Average was formerly known as the Rail Average before it incorporated other forms of transportation, such as airline and trucking stocks. Originally the Rail Average was devised to reflect the transportation of goods. In the last part of the nineteenth century and the early part of the twentieth century, rail was the dominant form of transportation, so an average composed solely of rails represented a good proxy for transportation stocks. In 1970 the Rail Average was expanded to embrace other transportation segments, and the index was renamed the Transportation Average.

The Transportation Average is basically affected by two factors, volume of business and changes in interest rates. First, as a business recovery gets

CHART 12.6   Dow Jones Industrial Average versus 12-month rate of change. Most of the time a reversal in the 14-month EMA of the DJIA, when confirmed by a similar exponential smoothing for the 12-month rate of change, resulted in a reliable signal that the new trend will be perpetuated for some time. The experience in 1971, when both moving averages turned down for a short period, is a fine reminder, however, that even the best indicators can give misleading signals at times.

(SOURCE: Pring Market Review.)

under way, inventories are low and raw materials are needed to initiate production. Transportation volume picks up, and investors anticipating such a trend bid up the price of transportation shares. Similarly, at business peaks companies typically overbuild their stocks, and when sales start to fall they reduce their requirements for raw materials. Under such circumstances transportation volume falls sharply, and the stock market reacts accordingly. Second, transport companies tend to be relatively more heavily financed with debt than industrials. Because of the leverage of this heavy debt structure, their earnings are also more sensitive to changes in interest rates and business conditions than those of most industrial companies. As a result, the Transportation index quite often leads the Industrial index at important juncture points.

The importance of the Dow theory rule concerning confirmation now takes on added weight, since a move by the producer stocks (the Industrials) really has to be associated with an increased volume of transportation to be valid, that is, with a comparable move by the Transports. Similarly, increased business for the transport stocks is likely to be of temporary

CHART 12.7 Transports and relative strength.

significance if the industrial companies fail to follow through with a rise in sales and production levels. The longer-term cycles of the Transportation Average and the Industrial Average are more or less the same as a result of their close association with business conditions. The techniques and choice of time spans for moving averages, rates of change, etc., are therefore similar to those described above for the Industrials.

One principle which is not normally used for the Industrials but can be applied to the Transports is that of relative strength. This technique is particularly useful during periods of nonconfirmation between the two averages, when RS can offer a useful clue as to how the discrepancy will be resolved. One such example occurred in early 1974 and is shown in Chart 12.7. The DJIA made an impressive advance in January 1974, reacted in early February, then rose strongly to a new recovery high in March. The relative strength for the Transports, which had been extremely strong up to this point, topped out in early March, and by the time the Industrials made their second peak, the Transports' RS had crossed below its 13-week moving average. The 13-week momentum index for the RS, having peaked in January, was also falling sharply during this period. The conclusion that would have been drawn from an analysis of the RS trend at that time would have placed a low probability on the Transports' confirming the March recovery high in the Industrials.

THE UTILITY AVERAGE

The Dow Jones Utility Average comprises 15 utility stocks drawn from electric utilities, gas pipelines, telephone companies, etc. This average has historically proved to be one of the most reliable barometers of the industrials, because utility stocks are extremely sensitive to changes in interest rates. Interest rate changes are important to utility stocks from two aspects. First, because utility companies require substantial amounts of capital, they are usually highly financed with debt relative to equity. As interest rates rise, the cost of renewing existing debt and raising additional money increases, so that profits are reduced. When interest rates fall, these conditions are reversed and profits rise. Second, utility companies generally pay out most of their earnings in the form of dividends, so that utility stocks are normally bought just as much for their yield as for their potential capital gain. When interest rates rise, bonds—which are also bought for their yield—fall in price, rendering them relatively more attractive than utilities. As a result, investors are tempted to sell utility stocks and buy bonds. When interest rates fall, the money returns once again to utility stocks, which then rise in price.

Since changes in the trend of interest rates usually begin before those of the stock market, the Utility Average more often than not leads the DJIA at both market tops and market bottoms.

Generally speaking, when the Utility Average flattens out after an advance or moves down while the Industrials continue to advance, or when the Utilities, after a decline, refuse to confirm a new low in the Industrials, this is usually a sign of an imminent change in trend for the Industrials. Thus at the 1937, 1946, 1953, 1966, 1968, and 1973 bull market peaks the Utilities led the Industrials. Conversely, at the 1942, 1949, 1953, 1962, 1966, and 1974 bottoms the Utilities made their bear market lows ahead of the Industrials. At most major juncture points the Utilities coincided with the Industrials, and occasionally, as at the 1970 bottom and the 1976 top, the Utilities lagged.

NYSE FINANCIAL INDEX

The New York Stock Exchange publishes a series of indexes in addition to the NYSE Composite. They are the NYSE Industrials, the NYSE Transportation, and the NYSE Financial, which are all constructed by weighting a series of component stocks and reducing the total to an index. The Financial Index has been singled out since it, too, is a very interest-sensitive indicator; this is because it is constructed using organizations such as banks, savings and loan institutions, and insurance companies, whose profits are greatly influenced by changes in interest rates. Unfortunately, because records of this NYSE index extend back only to the 1960s, its characteristics cannot really be put to the test with some of the other averages, for which the records extend over much longer periods. The Financial Index is shown in Chart 12.8.

THE UNWEIGHTED INDEXES

An unweighted index is calculated by simply adding up the prices of a number of stocks and dividing the total by that number. The resulting average is therefore one weighted by price rather than by capitalization. The history of these indexes is relatively short because of the laborious task of compilation before the use of the computer. The two most widely followed are the Value Line Composite and the Indicator Digest Average unweighted index. These indexes are shown in Chart 12.9. Since their construction is based on more or less the same stocks, their performance over the years has been similar.

Unweighted indexes are useful since they closely represent the price of the "average" stock often found in individual portfolios—as opposed to the blue chips, to which institutional investment is more oriented. Unweighted indexes are also helpful in gaining an understanding of the market's technical structure, since they have a tendency to lead the market (i.e., the DJIA) at market tops. A show of good relative strength by the unweighted indexes at a time of sustained weakness in the major averages often signifies that when the decline is over a significant rally will follow. Such a development occurred in 1978 when the Value Line index made its low in late 1977 several months ahead of the DJIA. The Value Line Composite Index is also shown in Figure 13.12b. The performance of these unweighted indicators is almost identical to that of the weekly advance/decline line (see Chart 17.1, page 223). The relationship between the broad market and the DJIA is discussed in Chapter 17.

GENERAL MOTORS

It has been claimed that "what is good for General Motors is good for America," and the record for the last 50 years or so certainly bears out this

CHART 12.8 Various measures of the NYSE Financial Index. This chart shows how the drawing of simple trendlines when used in conjunction with relative strength analysis can offer useful clues as to reversals in trend of a price index—in this case the daily average of the NYSE Financial Index.

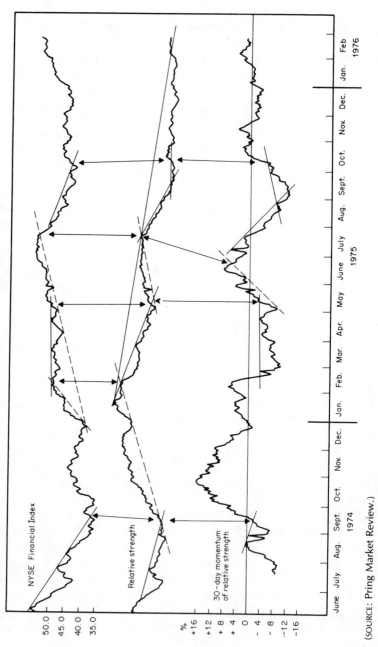

NYSE Financial Index

Relative strength

30-day momentum
of relative strength

%
+16
+12
+ 8
+ 4
0
- 4
- 8
-12
-16

50.0
45.0
40.0
35.0

June July Aug. Sept. Oct. Nov. Dec. Jan. Feb. Mar. Apr. May June July Aug. Sept. Oct. Nov. Dec. Jan. Feb.
1974   1975   1976

(SOURCE: Pring Market Review.)

CHART 12.9   Dow Jones Industrial Average versus the Value Line Composite and Indicator Digest Average.

(SOURCE: *Courtesy of Securities Research Co., a Division of United Business Service Co.*)

statement as far as the stock market is concerned, for GM is a bellwether stock par excellence.

General Motors has hundreds and thousands of employees and over 1 million shareholders, and its business is very sensitive to credit conditions. It is the largest auto manufacturer in the country, and one in six of American jobs is either directly or indirectly dependent on the auto industry.

As a result, GM tends to rise and fall in concert with the trend of the DJIA or the S&P 500 most of the time. At market tops GM usually leads the market, so that a new high in the DJIA which is unconfirmed by GM is a warning signal of a reversal in trend. On the other hand, GM is not so helpful at market bottoms since it usually lags the market. The long-term chart of GM (Chart 12.10a) shows this quite clearly. It is also worth noting the huge head and shoulders formed between 1928 and 1929 as well as the right-angled broadening top between 1964 and 1966. The completion of both these long-term distribution patterns led to substantial declines in the stock.

Proponents of GM have developed a useful principle. Known as the 4-

CHART 12.10a Market profile of General Motors, 1924–1935, 1948–1975.

CHART 12.10b Dow Jones Industrial Average versus General Motors Corporation stock, 1966–1978.

month rule (although some analysts prefer a 19- to 21-week rule), it states that if in a bull market General Motors fails to make a new high within 4 calendar months (for example, February 27 to June 27, or March 31 to July 31) of its previous peak, the bullish trend of the market has reversed or is just about to do so. Similarly, during a market decline if GM fails to make a new low within 4 months of its previous trough, a reversal in the downward trend of the market has already taken place or is just about to occur. The GM rule is not infallible, but its record is extremely good.

Price: Group Rotation

INTRODUCTION

The position of the three key financial markets—debt, equity, and gold—was considered in Chapter 1 in relation to the business cycle. It was pointed out that there were certain periods when these markets were all moving in concert and other periods when they were going in different directions, depending on the maturity of the business cycle. It will be recalled that deflationary forces predominate during the early stages of the cycle whereas inflationary pressures come to the fore only as the recovery matures. Since no business cycle ever repeats itself exactly, the leads and lags between the peaks and troughs of the various financial markets differ from cycle to cycle. In spite of this drawback the concept of the chronological development of the debt, equity, and gold cycles works quite well in practice.

This chapter takes the concept of cycles one step further by categorizing the various industry groups according to their sensitivity to deflationary or inflationary forces, i.e., leading or lagging characteristics. Unfortunately, this categorization is far from an exact process since equities rise and fall not only in reaction to the outlook for profits but also, what is more important, in response to investor attitudes to those profits. Since interest rates are a significant, but not necessarily dominant, influence on the profits of interest-sensitive stocks, it follows that the price performance of certain interest-sensitive issues may from time to time become unlatched or independent of the price movements in the debt markets. Similarly, it is possible for the economy to be very strong and for overall levels of industry profit to be rising dramatically and yet for a particular industry group, which would normally be thriving at such a stage of the economic recovery, to be in a position of chronic overcapacity. The result is poor profit margins and a dramatically reduced overall level of earnings.

There are therefore a number of fundamental factors which can develop from time to time to preclude a specific group from performing as might normally be expected in the industry rotation cycle. Most industry groups can be conveniently characterized into leading, coincident, and lagging, based on historical performance. An additional caveat is that there are a substantial number that do not easily fit into this picture.

In spite of such drawbacks, the theory of group rotation serves two useful functions. First, it can provide a framework within which to assess the maturity of a primary trend. For example, if there is technical evidence that the stock market is deeply oversold when the primary trend is signaling a reversal from bearish to bullish, it would be very useful to know that some of the groups which normally lead market turns have failed to confirm new lows made by the market averages. In a situation where the overall technical picture was indicating weakness at a major bull market peak, it would also be important to know that leading industry groups had made their highs some weeks or months before and that the most recent rally was led by industry groups which typically lag the stock market cycle.

Second, the group rotation theory can act as a guide in the purchase or sale of specific equities. This aspect is discussed in greater detail in Chapter 25.

THE CONCEPT OF GROUP ROTATION

Since most stocks are moving up most of the time during a bull market, it follows that the majority make their bear market lows around the same time as the averages. When utilities are described as a leading group and steels as a lagging group, the implication is not necessarily that utilities reach their lows ahead of the low in the DJIA and steels bottom out well after utilities. This may be the case or it may not. What is more likely to happen is that utilities, being interest-sensitive, will put on their best performance *relative to the market* around the beginning of the cycle. Similarly, steels might advance in sympathy with the averages during the early stages of the bull market, but their best relative performance *has a tendency* to occur during the later stages of a bull market or the early phases of a bear market.

The sine curve on Figure 13.1 represents growth and contraction of the economy under a typical business cycle. The dashed line reflects intermediate rallies and reactions of the stock market during a typical cycle. The peaks and troughs of the other financial markets are also shown. The debt markets typically make their lows (i.e., interest rates reach their cyclical

——— Economic activity

— — — Stock market prices

FIGURE 13.1

peaks) after the recession has been under way for some months. The stock market, which essentially discounts profits, makes its low about 3 to 6 months before the low in economic activity, whereas the gold market, which discounts inflation, usually comes to life only several months after the recovery has set in. Since the leads and lags vary in each cycle, it should again be emphasized that this approach should be used as a framework, not a mechanical extrapolation.

The overall market consists of a plethora of stock groups which are a reflection of the companies making up the various segments of the economy. The economy, as defined by an aggregate measure such as GNP, is either rising or falling at any one time. However, there are very few periods when all segments of the economy are rising or falling simultaneously. This is because the economy is not one homogeneous unit but an aggregate of a number of different parts. Some industries respond better to deflationary conditions and the early stages of the productive cycle; others are more prosperous under inflationary conditions which predominate at the tail end of the business cycle.

Economic recoveries are typically led by consumer spending spearheaded by the housing industry. As interest rates fall during a recession, demand for housing gradually picks up. Hence home building and some building and construction stocks can be considered leading groups.

In anticipation of a consumer spending improvement, retail stores, restaurants, cosmetics, tobacco, and so forth also show leading tendencies, as do certain interest-sensitive areas such as telephone and electric utilities; insurance, savings and loans; and consumer finance companies. As the recovery continues, inventories, which were cut dramatically during the recession, become depleted. Manufacturing industry groups, which might be classified as coincident, respond by beginning to improve in price or relative strength. Finally, as manufacturing productive capacity is used up during the final stages of the recovery, stock groups associated with capital spending such as steels, some chemicals, and mines have a tendency to emerge as market leaders.

A further influence on the group rotation cycle is confidence. As a bull market emerges, caution declines. During the initial stage of a bull market, emphasis is placed on prudence. Stocks with good balance sheets and high yields begin a period of superior relative strength. As the cycle progresses, the rotation turns to more speculative issues of little intrinsic value. Even though the peak in speculative issues usually leads that of the major averages, their most rapid and volatile period of advance typically occurs in the final or third leg of a bull market.

Some groups are not readily classifiable in terms of the productive process. Air transport, which goes through sharp cyclical swings, is a case in point. This industry average either coincides or lags slightly at bear market lows but is almost always one of the first groups to turn down before a peak. This could be because the group is sensitive to interest rates and energy prices, both of which have a tendency to rise at the end of the business cycle. On the other hand, drug stocks as a group have a distinct tendency to put in their best relative performance at the tail end of the bull market and in this respect should be regarded as a lagging group. At market bottoms they also have a lagging tendency (in terms of relative strength), although this is far less marked than at market tops.

It is also worth noting that the group rotation process has a tendency to work during intermediate-term rallies and reactions as well as cyclical ones.

SOME EXAMPLES

Chart 13.1 shows three industry groups—utilities, household furnishings, and aluminum—which are examples of leading, coincident, and lagging groups, respectively. The upward- and downward-pointing arrows represent bull market peaks and troughs. The chart shows that these groups act consistently with what might be expected most of the time, since the actual group, its relative strength line, or both reflect their leading, lagging, or coincident tendencies. It is also apparent that on several occasions these characteristics do not fit neatly into the theory because of investors' attitudes toward the fundamentals. An unusual occurrence of this nature can often be useful in warning of a major turn in the industry's fortunes. For example, in 1953 and 1970 the Utility index RS line reached its cyclical peak *ahead* of the bear market low. Normally such a development occurs 6 to 18 months after a bull market has begun. In each instance the utility average underperformed in the ensuing bull market. In the 1953–1956 bull trend, the average did in

CHART 13.1 Leading, coincident, and lagging groups. (a) Dow Jones Utilities.

(SOURCE: *Securities Research Co., a Division of United Business Service Co.*)

174

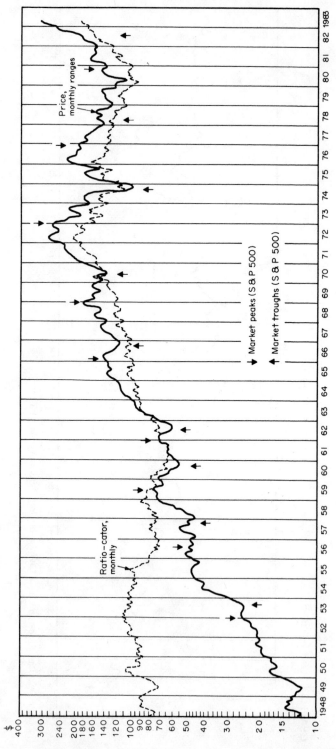

CHART 13.1 Leading, coincident, and lagging groups. (b) Standard & Poor's Household Furnishings & Appliances Index.

CHART 13.1 Leading, coincident, and lagging groups. (c) Standard & Poor's Aluminum Index.

175

fact rise because this was an extremely powerful advance. However, in the 1970–1974 cycle, the index put on its worst price performance since the 1930s.

In an opposite sense the utility average relative strength reached its low slightly *ahead* of the 1956 bull market high. Although there were some intermediate periods of weakness the next 9 years proved to be one of the best periods ever for the average. Under such circumstances, although the action of the RS line is useful in forecasting the group itself, it also warns that the group, its RS line, or both are likely to offer confusing signals vis-à-vis group rotation analysis.

The coincident nature of the Household Furnishings and Appliance Index can best be seen by comparing the actual peaks and troughs of the index itself to the peaks and troughs in the market. In the two instances, 1973 and 1976, where Household Furnishings and Appliances led the actual market peak by more than 6 months, i.e., deviated from its normal coincident role, the index suffered its two worst bear markets in the postwar period.

The S&P Aluminum group offers some other useful examples. In 1953 the RS index bottomed out ahead of the bear market low and was actually making a 2-year high 1 month later. For a leading group such as the utilities, this would be quite normal, but for a lagging group such as aluminum, it was clearly something out of the ordinary. As Chart 13.1c shows, the ensuing rally was the best one in the postwar period. Similarly, at the 1956 and 1959 peaks the uncharacteristic softness of the Aluminum index, its RS, or both would have provided a useful warning of a weaker than normal bear market, since this is the juncture at which superior relative strength should have been expected.

SUMMARY

1. During the stock market cycle there is a distinct pattern of industry group rotation. Interest-sensitive groups have a tendency to lead at peaks and troughs, whereas those profits which are helped by increases in capital spending or price inflation generally lag the overall market.

2. Sometimes significant changes in the fundamentals of an industry will cause a group to be uncharacteristically strong or weak during a specific cycle. It is therefore better to monitor a spectrum of groups rather than to use one specific group as a proxy for the leaders.

3. An understanding of the industry group rotation cycle is helpful both in assessing the maturity of a primary trend and for the purpose of stock selection.

14

Time: Longer-Term Cycles

Time is represented on the horizontal axis of most technical charts, so it is normally used in conjunction with the other three dimensions of psychology involved in determining trends in the stock market which are measured on the vertical axis. On the other hand, time is often assessed independently through the analysis of cycles.

So far in this book, discussions of the importance of time have been related to the dependence of the significance of a reversal in a stock market trend upon the length of time needed for the completion of distribution or accumulation. In other words, the longer the period, the greater the ensuing move in the opposite direction is likely to be. Removal of the speculative excesses of a trend will require a commensurately large corrective movement, just as the discipline of a long period of accumulation provides a sound base from which a substantial and lengthy advance can take place. Although the very long 8-year bull market between 1921 and 1929 was interrupted from time to time with corrective reactions, the substantial increase in stock prices during this period resulted in the development of a considerable amount of excess confidence which could only be erased by a sharp and lengthy decline. Similarly, the 1966 stock market peak, which was preceded by 24 years of basically rising prices, was followed by a long period of consolidation involving widely swinging stock prices. When adjusted for inflation, stock prices peaked in 1965 and have since undergone an extremely severe bear market comparable to the 1929–1932 debacle. This is shown in Chart B.2 in Appendix B (page 388).

Time, therefore, is concerned with *adjustment,* for the longer a trend takes to complete, the greater is the psychological acceptance of that trend,

177

and the greater will be the necessity for stock prices to move in the opposite direction and adjust accordingly. In a rising market investors become accustomed to rising prices, so that each reaction is reviewed as temporary. When the trend finally has reversed and the first bear market rally takes place, the majority are convinced that this too is a temporary reaction and that the bull trend is being renewed. As prices work their way lower in a bear market, the adjustment becomes more neutral because the majority of investors forsake their expectations of a rising market and look for prices to move sideways for a time. Finally, the adjustment pendulum switches completely to the other (bearish) side as investors watch prices slip even farther and then become overly pessimistic. At this point sufficient time and downside price action have elapsed to complete this adjustment process, and stocks are then in a position to embark on a new bull market.

Time has been viewed here in an emotional context, in the recognition that it takes time for investors to adjust to unrealized expectations. It is important for the trader or investor to realize also that time is deeply bound up with the business cycle. This is because a strong and lengthy recovery such as that between 1921 and 1929 breeds confidence not only among investors but also among businesspeople, who tend to become inefficient and overextended as a result of a long period of prosperity. The ensuing contraction in business conditions needed to wipe out such distortions is thus more severe, so that stock prices suffer the double influence of (1) losing their intrinsic value due to the decline in business conditions and (2) being revalued downward from the unrealistically high levels during the period of prosperity. The reverse set of circumstances will apply following a long market decline. This idea of a reaction commensurate with the previous action is known as the *principle of proportionality*.

Measuring time as an independent variable is a complicated process, since prices move in periodic fluctuations known as cycles. These cycles can operate for periods ranging from a few days to many decades. At any given moment a number of these cycles are operating simultaneously, and since they are exerting different forces at different times, the interaction of their changing relationships has the effect of distorting the timing of a particular cycle. The most dominant of the larger cycles is the so-called 4-year cycle, which has a nominal or average length between troughs of 41 months. It corresponds to the business cycle which is reflected in primary bull and bear movements in the stock market. Since several other cycles are all acting at the same time but with different influences, the length of the 4-year cycle has varied from 36 to 54 months.

Cycles are represented on a chart in the form of a sine wave, as in Figure 14.1. These curves are usually based on a rate-of-change index which is then smoothed to iron out misleading fluctuations. Since it occurs only rarely that two cycles are identical in length, an average or *nominal* period is

FIGURE 14.1

FIGURE 14.2

calculated, and this theoretical time span is used as a basis for future forecasting.

In Figure 14.2 this idealized cycle is represented by the dashed line and
the actual cycle by the solid line. The arrows indicate the peaks and troughs
of the idealized cycle. In actual fact the price trend will rarely reverse
exactly at the theoretical point, especially at peaks, where there is often a
long lead time. Nevertheless these theoretical points provide a useful guide.

There are three other important principles concerned with cycle analysis
in addition to those of proportionality and nominality discussed above. The
first is the *principle of commonality,* which states that cyclicality of similar
duration exists in the price action of all stocks, indexes, and markets. This
means that a 4-year cycle exists not only for the stock market itself but also
for each individual stock and for foreign stock markets as well. The second
principle, that of *variation,* states that while stocks go through similar cycles,
the price magnitudes and durations of these nominal cycles will be different
because of fundamental and psychological considerations. In other words,
whereas all stocks, indexes, and markets go through a similar cycle, the
timing of both their peaks and their troughs differs, and so does the size of
their price fluctuations. For example, the interest-sensitive and cyclical (basic industry) stocks go through a similar cycle, but because interest-sensitive
stocks (such as utilities) lead the market, cyclicals (such as steel groups)
generally lag behind them. This is shown in Figure 14.3.

This principle is also illustrated in Chart 14.1, which shows the interaction of financial series during a typical business cycle.

FIGURE 14.3

CHART 14.1 Typical cycles with financial series in percentages of their averages: a mechanistic approach to business cycles.

(SOURCE: *L. Ayres, Cleveland Trust Company, 1939.*)

Similarly, the interest-sensitive issues may rise by 80 percent from the trough to the peak of their cycle, where the cyclicals advance by only 20 percent.

Each rising part of a cycle usually consists of three stages, which correspond to the three phases described in the Dow theory. It is normal for prices to reach a new cyclical high as each stage unfolds, but sometimes this does not happen. Such a development, known as a magnitude failure, is a distinct sign of weakness. It normally results from poor underlying fundamentals for the stock group or index concerned, so that the cycle in effect actually misses a beat. By the same token, strong underlying fundamentals can give rise to a fourth stage in which prices have an additional upward leg. Often this final upward surge is associated with an extended period of declining interest rates. Such strong underlying conditions will normally develop when the 4-year cycle is occurring in conjunction with the peak of

FIGURE 14.4

longer-term cycles such as the Kondratieff (50- to 54-year) and Juglar (9.2-year) cycles, which are discussed below.

The third principle is *summation* (or summed cyclicality, as it is sometimes known). Summation is really the combination of a number of cycles into one. The result is an idealized cycle such as that shown in Figure 14.4.

For any time series trend such as that of the stock market, there are four influences at any one time—secular, cyclical, seasonal, and random. For the purpose of analyzing primary bull and bear markets, the cyclical trend is the starting point. Specifically, this is the 4-year or Kitchin cycle. The secular influence is a very long term one that embraces many 4-year cycles. From a stock market point of view, the longest "secular cycle" is the 50- to 54-year cycle known as the Kondratieff wave (after the Russian economist Nicolai Kondratieff). Two other important cycles in excess of 4 years have also been noted, namely the 9.2-year and 18⅓-year cycles. These time periods are not long enough to be defined as secular, but nevertheless they are observable and have an influence on the duration and timing of the 4-year cyclical trend.

Chart 14.2a, reproduced from Joseph Schumpeter's book,[1] combines the effect of three observable business cycles into one curve. In effect, it shows the summation principle using three longer-term cycles: the 50- to 54-year (Kondratieff), the 9.2-year, and the 41-month (Kitchin) cycles. The model is not intended to be an exact prediction of business conditions and stock prices, but rather to indicate the interaction of the shorter cycles with the longer ones. By comparing this model with that in Chart 14.5 it can be seen that the long upmove dating from about 1942 to about 1974 was associated with rising stock prices interrupted by relatively mild cyclical corrections.

Since the underlying force of this model is concerned with the 54-year Kondratieff wave, that will be a good starting point.

KONDRATIEFF WAVE

The 54-year wave is named after a little-known Russian economist who observed in 1926 that the United States had undergone three long economic

---

[1] Joseph Schumpeter, *Business Cycles*, McGraw-Hill, New York, 1939.

CHART 14.2a   Schumpeter's model of the nineteenth-century business cycle.

CHART 14.2b   The twentieth-century business cycle and crisis points (calculated path).

(SOURCE: *T. J. Zimmerman, Geschichte der theoretischen Volkswirtschafts-lehrs, in an unpublished paper by P. E. Erdman.*)

waves, each lasting between 50 and 54 years.[2] It is worth noting that while only three such cycles have been recorded for the United States, E. H. Phelps Brown and Sheila Hopkins of the London School of Economics have noted a regular recurrence of 50- to 52-year cycles of prices in the United Kingdom, between 1271 and 1954, with the crest for the current cycle projected for the 1974–1978 period. The same cycle has been observed in interest rates, as shown in Chart 14.4b.

Kondratieff used wholesale prices as the focal point of his observations, as shown in Chart 14.3. He noted that each wave had three phases: an upwave, lasting about 20 years, a transition or plateau period of 7 to 10 years, and a downwave again of about 20 years. Kondratieff observed that each upwave was associated with rising prices, the plateau with stable

[2] The cycle was also noted by Professor Jevons in the second half of the nineteenth century.

prices, and the downwave with declining prices. He also noted that a war was associated with both the beginning and the end of each upwave.

At the start of a cycle, business conditions are very depressed, and since there is considerable excess capacity of plant and machinery, people prefer to save money out of fear rather than invest it. The war at the bottom of the downwave, known as the trough war (see Chart 14.3), acts as a catalyst to get the economy moving again. In view of the tremendous economic slack in the system, this war is not associated with inflation. As time progresses, each cyclical upwave becomes stronger and stronger; confidence returns and business once again reaches full production capacity. Since price inflation is almost absent, rates of interest are very low, so that credit is both abundant and cheap. During this phase businesses not only replace old plant and equipment but also invest in new capacity, thereby improving productivity and creating wealth. This up phase is usually associated with some new technological development, such as canals in the 1820s and 1830s, railroads in the mid-nineteenth century, automobiles in the 1920s, and electronics in the 1960s. As the upwave progresses, distortions arising from overinvestment (which was caused by the long cycle interrupted by mild recessions) begin to develop in the economy, leading to social tensions and economic instability. A common characteristic around this period, known as the peak, is a war accentuating these distortions. This is true of the peaks of 1814, 1864, and 1914.

The above description is important since it is possible to understand the cyclical movements of the market only if they are put into perspective by their position in relation to the longer-term waves (see Chart 14.5). For example, during the up phase and its associated mild recessions, it would be reasonable to expect mild and brief bear markets. During the relatively stable plateau period the possibility of a very strong bull market exists (e.g., 1820, 1860, and 1920), and in the down phase there may be a series of very sharp and devastating bear markets. The interpretation of the technical indicators should be adjusted accordingly. For example, whereas a normal time span for a bear market might be 12 months during the up phase, with the annual rate of monthly price change being limited to a − 20 percent reading, the standards should be different during the Kondratieff downwave, when each business cycle becomes weaker and weaker. Under such conditions, bear markets would be expected to last for considerably more time and be far more devastating. A study and appreciation of the Kondratieff cycle is therefore a fine example of why stock market predictions based on the experience of only the two or three previous cycles are likely to prove unfounded. Since the Kondratieff wave has occurred only three times and each time the conditions have been different, this cycle should be used as a framework from which a better understanding of the forces at work can be derived, rather than as a basis for unqualified prediction.

CHART 14.3 The Kondratieff wave, based on annual averages with a ratio scale of 1967 = 100.

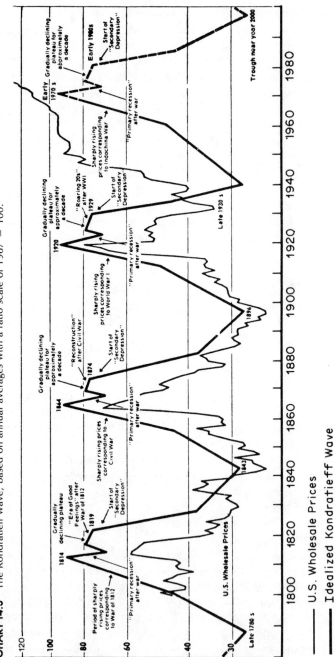

U.S. Wholesale Prices

Idealized Kondratieff Wave

(SOURCE: The Media General Financial Weekly, June 3, 1974.)

CHART 14-4a Index numbers of 1780–1925 commodity prices (1901–1910 = 100).

CHART 14.4b Interest rates for the United Kingdom and France, 1815–1925.

(SOURCE: *N. D. Kondratieff*, The Long Waves of Economic Life.)

THE 18-YEAR CYCLE

Normally the amplitude of a cycle is a function of its duration, i.e., the longer the cycle the bigger the swing.

The 18-year (or, more accurately, the 18⅓-year) cycle has occurred fairly reliably in stock market prices since the beginning of the nineteenth century. Greater credibility is given to this cycle through the observation that it has occurred in several other situations, such as real estate activity, loans and discounts, and financial panics.

Chart 14.6 shows a 3-year centered moving average of common stock

CHART 14.5 United States stock prices, 1790–1976, showing "Kondratieff" bull markets (annual mean monthly averages). The Foundation for the Study of Cycles has spliced together the following series: 1790–1831 Bank & Insurance Companies; 1831–1854 Cleveland Trust Rail Stocks; 1854–1871 Clement-Burgess Composite Index; 1871–1897 Cowles Index of Industrial Stocks; 1897–1974 Dow Jones Industrial Averages. The shaded areas represent the plateau period in the Kondratieff cycle.

CHART 14.6 The 18⅓-year cycle of stock prices, 1840–1974 (3-year centered moving average).

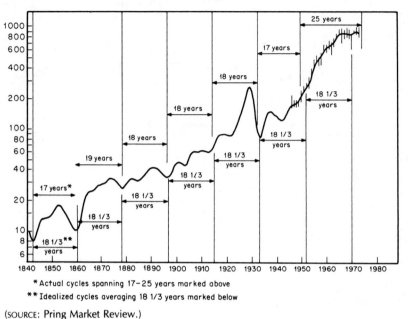

* Actual cycles spanning 17–25 years marked above
** Idealized cycles averaging 18 1/3 years marked below

(SOURCE: Pring Market Review.)

prices from 1840 to 1974. The use of this average helps to smooth the trend and isolate more clearly the long-term picture. The occurrence of the beginning of the 18-year cycle at major market bottoms is self-evident.

The 3-year moving average bottomed out in 1970 and is due to complete its cycle around 1988.

While a period of 18⅓ years represents the average cycle, actual cyclical lows can vary 2 to 3 years either way. These troughs are marked on the chart above the 3-year moving average. The increase in government interference in the economy resulting from the Keynesian revolution and the postwar commitment to full employment appears to have had two effects on the most recent cycle (i.e., 1952–1970). First, it has stretched the cycle out from 18 to 25 years (1949–1974), and second, it has prolonged the upward phase. This is especially noticeable for the 1949 low, which on a 3-year moving average hardly shows as a trough.

The 18-year cycle fits in well with the Kondratieff picture, since three such cycles form one Kondratieff wave. In the last two Kondratieffs, when the upwave part of the 18-year cycle coincided with the plateau period, an explosive bull market and only a mild correction took place.

Since 1840, the 18-year cycle has operated fairly consistently. Except for

CHART 14.7 The 9.2-year cycle in stock prices, 1830–1946.

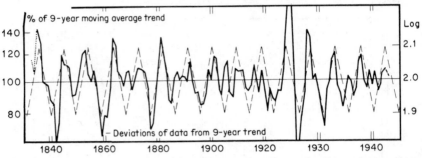

(SOURCE: *From Edward R. Dewey,* Cycles: The Mysterious Forces that Trigger Events, *Hawthorne Books, New York, 1971. Reproduced by permission of the Foundation for the Study of Cycles.*)

the prolonged nature of the last cycle, there are really no grounds for suspecting that this 18-year periodicity no longer exists.

THE 9.2-YEAR CYCLE AND THE DECENNIAL PATTERN

Chart 14.7 represents the 9.2-year cycle in stock prices from 1830–1946. The dashed lines represent the ideal cycle if stock prices had reversed exactly on schedule, and the solid line portrays the actual annual average as a percentage of its 9-year moving-average trend.

The cycle has reproduced 14 times since 1834, and according to the Bartels test of probability, it could not occur by chance more than once in 5000 times. Further evidence of the significance of this cycle is given by observation of the 9.2-year periodicity in other phenomena as unrelated as pig iron prices and the thickness of tree rings.

One problem of using the technique portrayed in the chart is that the annual average is expressed as a percentage of a centered 9-year moving average. This means that the trend is not known until 4 years after the fact, so that there is always a 4-year lag in learning whether the 9.2-year cycle is still operating. Nevertheless, if the theoretical crest in 1965.4 is used as a base and the 9.2 years are subtracted all the way back to 1919, the peaks of the 9.2-year cycle correspond fairly closely with major stock market tops. Unfortunately, one of the most recent theoretical peaks occurred in mid-1974, almost at the bottom of the 1973–1974 bear market, and represents the worst "signal" since 1947. However, the 1983 peak was right on target.

One interesting characteristic of the 9-year cycle that is probably of greater forecasting significance is the so-called decennial pattern.

CHART 14.8 The decennial patterns of industrial stock prices.

(SOURCE: *Courtesy of Anametrics, Inc., New York City.*)

CHART 14.9   Average of nine decades, 1881–1970.

(SOURCE: *Courtesy of Anametrics, Inc., New York City.*)

This pattern was first noted by Edgar Lawrence Smith, who observed that when the stock market was divided into 10-year segments and these segments were charted parallel to one another, a comparison showed that years ending in the same digit appeared to have similar characteristics.[3] This is represented in Chart 14.8. Thus, years ending in a 5 (1965, 1975, etc.), an 8, and a 9 tend to be consistently good years for investing, while the seventh and tenth years often show weakness. These characteristics are better illustrated in Chart 14.9, which shows the average of the nine decades from 1881–1970.

Smith could find no explanation for this repeating cycle, although in a later book he tried to connect it with human response to weather and sunspot changes.[4]

THE 41-MONTH (4-YEAR) CYCLE

One interesting observation made by Smith was that the decennial pattern appeared to "contain three separate cycles in a decade, each one lasting for approximately forty months." This is most interesting, as it ties in with the so-called 4-year cycle of stock prices. More precisely, the 4-year cycle is a 40.68-month (41-month) cycle. It has been present in stock prices

---

[3]*Tides in the Affairs of Men: An Approach to the Appraisal of Economic Change*, Macmillan, Toronto, 1939.
[4]*Common Stocks and Business Cycles*, William Frederick Press, New York, 1959.

CHART 14.10α The 41-month rhythm in stock prices, 1868–1945.

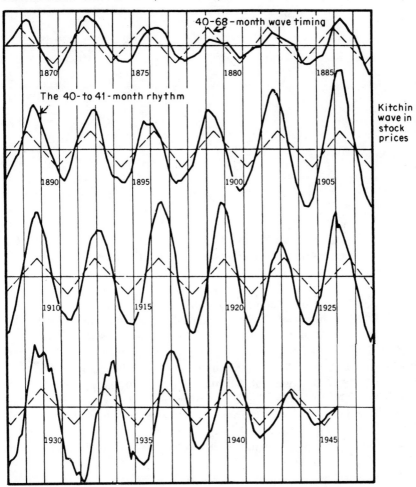

(SOURCE: *Edward R. Dewey, Cycles: The Mysterious Forces that Trigger Events, Hawthorne Books, New York, 1971. Courtesy of the Foundation for the Study of Cycles.*)

CHART 14.10b The "reversed" cycle from 1946.

(SOURCE: *Courtesy of the Foundation for the Study of Cycles.*)

CHART 14.11a   Four-year cycle in the postwar period for the United States.

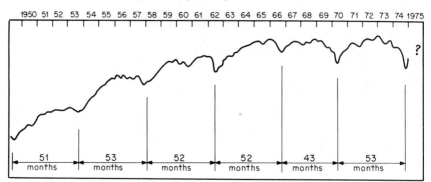

(SOURCE: Edward R. Dewey, Cycles: The Mysterious Forces that Trigger Events, Hawthorne Books, New York, 1971.)

since 1871. Around 1923 Professor Joseph Kitchin was also able to show a cycle of 41 months in bank clearings, wholesale prices, and interest rates in the United States and United Kingdom. This cycle has since carried his name.

The Kitchin cycle applied to stock prices is illustrated in Chart 14.10. Between 1871 and 1946 it has occurred 22 times with almost uncanny consistency. Then in 1946, as Edward Dewey describes it, "Almost as if some giant hand had reached down and pushed it, the cycle stumbled, and by the time it had regained its equilibrium it was marching completely out of step from the ideal cadence it had maintained for so many years."[5]

Not only did the cycle reverse, it also extended to an average period of about 50 months, as shown in Chart 14.11a. The average of the last six bull phases since 1949 has been 28.7 months, and the corresponding bear phase has lasted 22.1 months. A similar situation applies to the United Kingdom (see Chart 14.11b).

This reversal and extension in the Kitchin wave is a fine example of how a cycle that has appeared for a long time to be working consistently can suddenly, for no apparent reason, become totally distorted. Once again, the fact that a particular indicator or cycle has operated successfully in the past is not in itself a guarantee that it will continue to do so, although probability may favor it.

SEASONAL PATTERN

There is a distinct seasonal pattern of stock prices which tends to repeat year after year. Stocks seem to have a winter decline, a spring rise, a late-second-

[5]Cycles: The Mysterious Forces that Trigger Events, Hawthorne Books, New York, 1971.

CHART 14.11b Four-year cycle in the postwar period for the United Kingdom.

Average post war
bull market: +99.3%

Average post war
bear market: −38%

(SOURCE: The London Daily Mail, Financial Times.)

CHART 14.12 Market probability chart: the chances of the market's rising on any trading day of the year; based on the number of times the market rose on a particular trading day (shows the usual number of trading days in each month, Saturdays, Sundays, and holidays excluded) during the period May 1952–April 1971.

Shows the usual number of trading days in each month (Saturdays, Sundays, and holidays excluded)

(SOURCE: Stock Traders Almanac, *Hirsch Organization, Old Tappan, N.J.*)

quarter decline, a summer rally, and a fall decline. The year end witnesses a rally which usually extends into January. Stocks purchased in October have a high probability of appreciating if held for a 3- or 6-month period.

Apart from seasonal changes in the weather which affect economic activity and investor psychology, there are also some seasonal patterns in financial activities. For example, July and January are heavy months for dividend disbursement, retail trade around the year-end (Christmas) period is the strongest of the year, and so on.

Chart 14.12 represents the seasonal tendency of the stock market to rise in any given month. The probabilities were calculated over the 73-year period from 1900–1973. As can be seen, January is normally the strongest month of the year and May the weakest. All movements are relative, since a month with a strong tendency will be accentuated in a bull market and vice versa.

Generally if the market rises in the first 5 days of January it is likely to maintain the rise during the month. And if the market rises in January, it tends to end the year at a higher level than it started at.

Time: Practical Identification of Cycles

This chapter discusses some of the basic principles of cyclic analysis, and with the help of examples describes some simple techniques to aid in their identification.

CYCLES DEFINED

The term "cycle" will be used here to mean an observable price pattern or movement that occurs with some degree of regularity in a specific time interval. A market, stock, or indicator that is observed to have a relatively consistent price low at 6-week intervals is said to have a 6-week cycle. That successive lows are higher or lower than their predecessors is of no importance in determining the cycle. What is significant is that there is a clearly definable low point every 6 weeks, separated from its predecessor by a high point known as the "cycle high." Figure 15.1 shows some possible examples.

Figure 15.1 also shows that while cycle lows occur at approximately 6-week intervals, cycle highs vary. Occasionally they arrive early, as at point A, sometimes they occur in the middle of the cycle, as at point B, but they may also appear late, as at point C. Generally when the cycle high develops shortly after the cycle low it implies that the upward part of the cycle is weak and that the overall strength of the cycle lies on the downside. Such a

FIGURE 15.1

situation normally results in the next cycle low being below that of the previous cycle. Similarly, a cycle high that is "late" in arriving, i.e., that arrives well after the halfway period, normally indicates a strong cycle, the implication being that the cycle low will be above that of its predecessor. For any market or stock a number of different cycles can be observed, some long and some short in duration. The task of the technician is not to identify as many as possible but to isolate the most dominant and reliable.

There are several principles that should be borne in mind, as follows:

1. The longer the cycle, the greater the amplitude in price is likely to be, e.g., a 10-week cycle will have far greater trading significance than a 10-hour cycle.

2. It follows from principle 1 that the larger the cycle, the greater the significance of the low.

3. The larger the number of cycles reaching a low at around the same time, the stronger the ensuing price movement is likely to be.

4. In a rising trend the cycle high has a tendency to "translate to the right," i.e., to occur after the halfway point of the cycle. The same principle holds in reverse for bear markets, i.e., there is a tendency for the cycle high to translate to the left.

5. It is possible to observe cyclic highs that occur at regular time intervals.

6. A projected cyclic high or low may develop in the opposite way to that anticipated. In such cases the cycle is said to be "inverted."

METHODS OF DETECTION

Many mathematical techniques have been used in the process of trying to identify cycles. Fourier analysis, for example, isolates the existence of various cycles by length, amplitude, phase, etc. Systematic reconnaissance is a technique that tests for periods requested. The result is a periodgram that shows the most dominant cycles. Although such techniques can be useful, they have the tendency to make technical analysis appear to be an exact science, which it very definitely is not. Since such approaches fall outside the scope of this book, the curious reader is referred to the Bibliography. This chapter will be confined to three methods of cycle identification: deviation from trend, momentum, and simple observation.

Deviation from Trend

This method takes a series of data and divides each period by a moving average. The period under observation therefore represents the deviation, and the moving average the trend. In cycles analysis, it is normal to center the moving average (for an explanation of centering, see Chapter 7) for the purpose of achieving the calculation.

It will be recalled from Chapter 7 that since a moving average is designed to reflect the underlying price trend it should really be plotted halfway along its span. This is true because the "average" price occurs halfway through the observation period, e.g., in the seventh week for a 13-week moving average. However, changes in direction of the moving average usually occur far too late for the purpose of identifying trend reversals to offer timely signals. For this reason technicians normally use a moving-average crossover for generating signals. In cycles identification, only historical data are used, and so this disadvantage is not important. The moving-average deviation is therefore calculated by dividing the period in question by the midpoint of the moving average. In other words, the price observation for February 27 is divided by a 13-week moving average as calculated on April 18, i.e., the moving average is "moved" back 7 weeks. The result is then plotted as an oscillator which clearly points up the cyclical high and low points.

It is then a relatively simple task to see whether there are any consistent time periods which separate these points. One method is to note down the time differences between all the cycle lows (and highs) and see which ones come up most frequently. Since moving averages smooth out all cycles within their time span, it is important to experiment with several averages in order to identify as many cycles as possible. The more reliable ones should then be incorporated into the analysis.

Momentum

A simpler method of cycle identification is to calculate a momentum oscillator such as a rate of change and smooth it by an appropriate moving average determined by trial and error. This approach will bring out the underlying rhythm in the price movement, just as a deviation-from-trend calculation does. It is doubtful whether the momentum approach alone can be successfully used for cycle identification, but certainly, when used in conjunction with the technique of simple price observation discussed below, it can prove to be an invaluable confirmation of cyclic reliability.

Figure 16.8 (page 217) shows the NYSE Composite daily close plotted against the 8-day Most Active indicator. In the 1977–1978 period this indicator appeared to be going through a regular 4- to 5-week cycle, as indicated on the chart by the upward-sloping arrows.

The position of a momentum index can also be useful in warning of potential cyclic inversions, i.e., where a projected cyclic low might turn out to be a cyclic high and vice versa. For example, if the observed data projected that a cyclic low would likely develop around a specific date, yet the momentum indicator being used in conjunction with this study was at or coming down from an overbought level, the strong suggestion would be that the low was going to invert to a high.

Simple Observation

The easiest method of identifying cycles is to take a price chart and observe two or three major lows which appear to be relatively equidistant. Then pencil in the projections for that particular cycle.[1] If a substantial proportion of those projections result in either highs or lows, it is a good idea to mark them up with a colored pencil. If most projections result in failure the cycle should be abandoned and a new one sought. A cycle high occurring at any of these points should be treated as a successful projection since the first objective of cycle analysis is to determine potential turning points. Once a reliable cycle has been established, the second step is to look at all the important cycle lows which are "unexplained" by the first cycle and try to "explain" them by discovering another cycle. The chances are that the second cycle will not only fit some of the unexplained lows but will also occur at or near some of the cycle lows previously established. This is very important since one of the principles of cycles analysis is that the greater the number of cycles making a low around a certain time, the stronger the ensuing move is likely to be. Such knowledge *must* be used in conjunction with other technical evidence, but if that too is offering a green light, the odds of a significant upwave will be enhanced.

The exercise for cycle bottoms discussed above may also be done for cycle highs; an example is given in Chart 15.1.

COMBINING A CYCLE OF HIGHS AND LOWS: AN EXAMPLE

The final part of the exercise is to try to combine certain cyclical high and low points into a projected cycle. Chart 15.1 shows this approach using

---

[1] A unique tool called "The Ehrlich Cycle Finder" greatly facilitates this process. The International Institute for Economic Research, Inc., Washington Depot, Conn.

CHART 15.1 U.S. Treasury bonds 8⅜ percent, 1995/2000, and a 30-day rate of change.

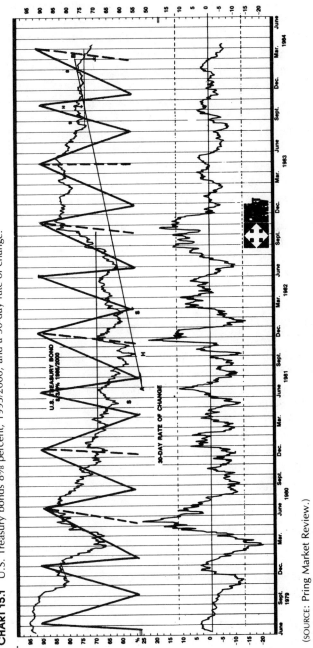

(SOURCE: Pring Market Review.)

daily prices for the U.S. Treasury 8⅜ of 1995/2000. The arrows above and below the bond price point up a fairly reliable pattern for both cyclic highs at approximately 24-week intervals and lows at approximately 18-week intervals. The next step is to join some of these points in order to construct an overall, idealized cycle wave. Since the cycles of lows and highs are of unequal length, the periods between the cyclic lows and highs (i.e., the upwaves and downwaves) vary in duration. Because of this variance, a cycle low can occur before the next cycle high. Such a situation arose in December 1980. This low was followed by a very brief but sharp rally. In November 1982 the cyclic low occurred very close to the October high, but the price went sideways rather than rallying. A valuable clue that this was going to take place was given by the 30-day rate-of-change index which was at an extremely overbought condition; in addition, that the two cycle points occurred at around the same time suggested that a major turning point was at hand. This did in fact prove to be the case since the November high represented the top of the 1981–1982 bull market.

It should not be assumed that a reliable combination of cycles as shown in Chart 15.1 will always work out. For example, the July–August 1980 low was accompanied by a deeply oversold condition, yet a worthwhile rally failed to materialize.

One of the advantages of combining high and low cycles is that it is possible to obtain some idea of how long a rally or reaction might last. For example, the proximity of the May 1982 high to the June low suggested a short reaction, whereas the somewhat longer period between the May low and the projected November high indicated a rally of somewhat longer duration than average. Again, it should be emphasized that it is important to combine the interpretation of cyclic analysis with the position of an important rate-of-change index. For example, the high and low cycle points occurred very close together in April 1983, suggesting that a major move was at hand. The rate-of-change index was not offering a clear-cut signal about the direction of the impending move. If anything, the moderately overbought level suggested the move would be down. This in fact proved to be the case but only after a marginal new high had been set. This cycle is portrayed in Chart 15.1 by a dashed line because the April peak and August low seem to better reflect the actual course of prices.

Not all examples work out quite so accurately as that shown on Chart 15.1. Readers are cautioned not to try and make a cycle "work." If it does not fit naturally and easily, the chances are that it does not exist or is likely to be highly unreliable and should therefore not be used.

SUMMARY

1. Recurring cycles, both of low points and high points, can be observed from charts of financial markets.

2. A cyclic turning point obtains its significance both from the time interval between cycles and from the number of cycles that are turning at the same time.

3. Cycle lows and highs which recur at regular intervals may be connected to form an idealized complete cycle.

4. Suspected cycles which do not easily fall into a consistently recurring pattern should not be made to "work" and should be discarded.

16

Volume

Knowledge of the principle that volume goes with the price trend is a useful confirmation of price action, but the study of volume is even more helpful since volume often leads the trend of prices, thereby offering an advance warning of a potential price trend reversal. Before the various methods of volume measurement are examined, the general observations made earlier will be briefly reviewed.

1. A price rise accompanied by expanding volume is a normal market characteristic and carries no implications of a potential trend reversal.

2. A rally which reaches a new (price) high on expanding volume but which has an overall level of activity that is lower than the previous rally is suspect and warns of a potential trend reversal (see Figure 16.1, example a).

3. A rally which develops on contracting volume is suspect and warns of a potential trend reversal in price (see Figure 16.1, example b).

4. Sometimes both price and volume expand slowly, gradually working into an exponential rise with a final blow-off stage. Following this development, both volume and price fall off equally sharply. This represents an exhaustion move and is a characteristic of a trend reversal. The significance of the reversal will depend upon the extent of the previous advance and the degree of volume expansion (Figure 16.1, example c).

5. A market which rises on expanding volume is a perfectly normal phenomenon and by itself has no warning implications of a trend reversal.

6. When prices advance following a long decline and then react to a level at or above the previous trough, it is a bullish sign if the volume on the secondary trough is lower than the volume on the first (Figure 16.1, example d).

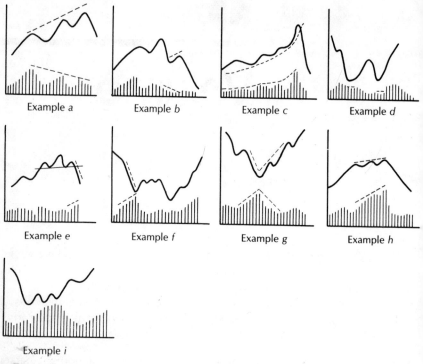

Example a

Example b

Example c

Example d

Example e

Example f

Example g

Example h

Example i

FIGURE 16.1

7. A downside breakout from a price pattern, trendline, or moving average that occurs on heavy volume is a bearish sign which emphasizes the reversal in trend (Figure 16.1, example e).

8. A selling climax occurs when prices fall for a considerable time at an accelerating pace accompanied by expanding volume. Following a selling climax, prices may be expected to rise, and the low established at the time of the climax is unlikely to be violated for a considerable time. Termination of a bear market is often, but not always, accompanied by a selling climax (Figure 16.1, examples f and g).

9. When the market has been rising for many months, an anemic price rise (Figure 16.1, example h) accompanied by high volume indicates churning action and is a bearish factor. Following a decline, heavy volume with little price change is indicative of accumulation and is normally a bullish factor (Figure 16.1, example i).

VOLUME LEADS PRICE

In his book *The Stock Market Indicators* William Gordon noted that, between 1877 and 1966, "In 84 percent of the bull markets the volume high

CHART 16.1 Annual rate of change of Dow Jones Industrial Average versus annual rate of change of New York Stock Exchange volume (3-month average).

(SOURCES: (1) Dow Jones Industrial Averages, (2) New York Stock Exchange 3-month averages. Courtesy of The Bank Credit Analyst.)

did not occur at the price peak but some months before."[1] Of the 18 bull markets, two uptrends ended with volume and price reaching a peak simultaneously (January 1906 and March–November 1916), and in one uptrend (October 1919) volume lagged by a month. The lead time of volume in the remaining 15 cycles was from 2 months (April 1901 and December 1965) to 24 months (January 1951). The average for all cycles was 9 months. My own research shows that between 1966 and 1983 volume has consistently continued to lead major price peaks.

Since volume is a relative concept, i.e., the level of volume is compared to that of a recent period in order to determine its level, it is usually measured on a rate-of-change basis, although some analysts prefer to use moving averages of the actual volume figures.

Chart 16.1 shows the annual rate of price change for the DJIA and an annual rate of change of a 3-month total of volume. In most instances the rate of change of volume led that of price, especially at market bottoms. This method of portraying volume suffers from the fact that the movements are jagged, and it is therefore difficult to interpret when a reversal in trend has taken place. Chart 16.2 attempts to surmount this problem by smoothing the data. The technique used is an annual rate of change of a 6-month total of volume. The resulting index is then smoothed by a 14-month exponential moving average. The price index is a 12-month rate of change smoothed by a 12-month weighted average. When used together the two series are very useful.

First, the volume curve has an almost consistent tendency to peak out

---

[1] Investors Press, Palisades Park, N.J., 1968.

CHART 16.2 Long-term volume/price relationships.

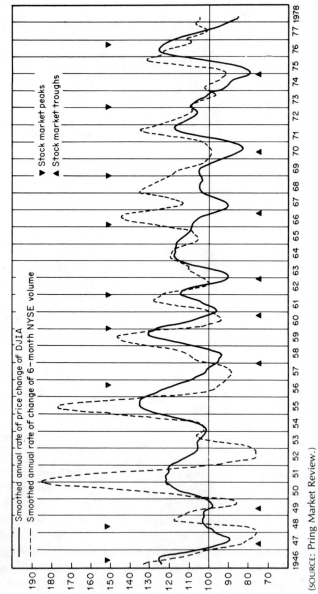

——— Smoothed annual rate of price change of DJIA
– – – Smoothed annual rate of change of 6–month NYSE volume

▼ Stock market peaks
▲ Stock market troughs

1946 47 48 49 50 51 52 53 54 55 56 57 58 59 60 61 62 63 64 65 66 67 68 69 70 71 72 73 74 75 76 77 1978

190
180
170
160
150
140
130
120
110
100
90
80
70

(SOURCE: Pring Market Review.)

CHART 16.3   New York Stock Exchange weekly advance/decline line versus volume momentum indicator.

(SOURCE: Pring Market Review.)

ahead of price during both bull and bear phases. Second, when the price index is above its zero reference line and is falling, but volume is rising (e.g., 1966, 1969, and to a lesser extent late 1976), the expanding activity appears to be indicative of distribution and should be interpreted as a very bearish factor once the rally has terminated. Third, in view of the long lead times at market tops given by both price and volume, the use of the two indexes for precise timing purposes is best employed at major bottoms. Reference to Chart 16.2 shows that a reversal in one curve unaccompanied by a reversal in the other at market bottoms would have given a premature signal at the end of 1973 and 1977, where volume turned up ahead of price. Consequently, it is wiser to await a signal from both, even though this may occur at slightly higher levels.

The monitoring of intermediate market trends involves the use of a rate of change covering a much shorter time span. Chart 16.3 shows a 25-day rate of change of a 25-day moving average of NYSE volume. There is a useful relationship between the 25-day cycles of volume and the corresponding cycle in the DJIA itself, but it should be remembered that a specific time span will be a useful market indicator only as long as the implied cycle in the market itself is still in force. In other words, most of the time the market rises and falls on a fairly consistent basis—for example, 4 years for a cyclical movement, 13 to 26 weeks on an intermediate basis. The moment price movements diverge significantly from these set movements, indicators based on these cycles will fail to operate successfully. For example, the 1970–1974 cycle was a textbook case of the 4-year cycle in operation. However, the rate-of-change indicators used to successfully signal the peak of this cycle would have been extremely early in forecasting the termination of the 1921–1929, 1942–1946, and 1962–1966 bull market peaks. Because intermediate movements are less consistent in either recurrence or magnitude than primary movements, they are far more difficult to predict.

UPSIDE/DOWNSIDE VOLUME

Measures of upside/downside volume try to separate the volume in advancing and declining stocks. Use of this technique makes it possible to determine in a subtle way whether distribution or accumulation is taking place.

The widespread publishing of these statistics has been available only since 1965, so the history of indicators based on such data is relatively short. The daily volume of advancing and declining stocks on the NYSE is printed in *The Wall Street Journal;* slightly more comprehensive coverage is given in *Barron's.*

Upside/downside volume is measured basically in two ways.

The first is an index known as an *upside/downside volume line,* constructed by cumulating the difference between the daily plurality of the volume of advancing and declining stocks. Since an index of this type is always started from an arbitrary number, it is a good idea to begin with a fairly large one; otherwise there is the possibility that if the market declines sharply for a period, the upside/downside line will become negative, thereby unduly complicating the calculations. If a starting total of 500 million shares were assumed, the line would be constructed as shown in Table 16.1.

These statistics are not published on a weekly or monthly basis, so longer-term analysis should be undertaken by recording the value of the line at the end of each Friday, or taking an average of Friday readings for a monthly plot. From these weekly or monthly observations the appropriate moving average can then be constructed.

It is normal for the upside/downside line to rise during market advances

TABLE 16.1

Date	Volume of advancing stocks, in millions	Volume of declining stocks, in millions	Difference	Upside/downside line
Jan. 1	10.1	5.1	+5.0	505.0
2	12.0	6.0	+6.0	511.0
3	15.5	15.5	0.0	511.0
4	15.0	10.0	+5.0	516.0
5	11.1	12.0	−0.9	515.1

and to fall during declines. When the line fails to confirm a new high (or low) in the price indexes, it warns of a potential trend reversal. The basic principles of trend determination discussed in Part 1 may be applied to the upside/downside line in order to better assess the technical position of this index.

When a market is advancing in an irregular fashion, with successively higher rallies interrupted by a series of rising troughs, the upside/downside line should be doing the same. Such action is indicating that the volume of advancing issues is expanding on rallies and contracting during declines. When this trend of the normal price/volume relationship is broken, a warning is given that one of two things is happening. Either upside volume is failing to expand sufficiently, or volume during the decline has begun to expand excessively on the downside. Both are bearish factors. The upside/downside line is particularly useful where prices may be rising to new highs and overall volume is expanding. In such a case, if the volume of declining stocks is rising in relation to that of advancing stocks, this will show up in either a slower rate of advance in the upside/downside line or an actual decline. A hypothetical example of this condition is shown in Figure 16.2.

The upside/downside line from 1972 to 1976 is shown in Chart 16.4. Major peaks and troughs in the DJIA are illustrated by the triangles plotted above and below the line. The initial period covered by the chart occurred

FIGURE 16.2

CHART 16.4   Upside/downside volume, 1973–1976.

(SOURCE: Pring Market Review.)

during the 1972–1974 bear market. It can be seen that the upside/downside line had already turned down by the time the DJIA made its bull market peak in January 1973. The final run-up by the Dow beginning in November 1972 therefore marked the first bear market rally of the upside/downside line itself. The overall downtrend in this index remained intact until early 1975, at which time a reversal was indicated by both a decisive upside penetration of its bear market trendline and the successful completion of and breakout from a double bottom formation.

Chart 16.5a shows the actual daily plottings of the line with a 30-day moving average for this critical period. During November the sharp downtrend which began in the previous March was broken on the upside and confirmed the crossover of the 30-day moving average which had already taken place in the middle of October. A comparison of Charts 16.4 and 16.5a illustrates well the principle that the significance of a trendline is determined by its length and steepness. This penetration of the bear market trendline in Chart 16.4 signaled the end of the bear market, yet the trendline (AA) in the daily chart which covered the March–October 1974 period, because it was so much steeper and shorter, only signaled the end of the intermediate decline. It can also be seen how the extension of this inter-mediate trendline became a level of support for the upside/downside line in late November and December. The violation of trendline AB and the deci-sive downside penetration of the 30-day moving average were both useful in signaling that a peak in the DJIA had been reached in mid-July. In view of the steepness and brevity of this sharp uptrend, the breakdown merely sig-naled that an intermediate top had been reached, so that following a 3-month correction the line was able to resume its primary advance.

The second method of measuring upside/downside volume is to plot a moving average of upside volume and another moving average of downside

CHART 16.5a   Upside/downside volume, 1974–1975 (closer view).

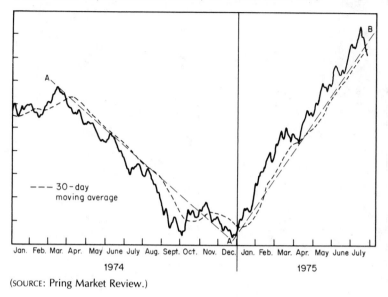

(SOURCE: Pring Market Review.)

volume on the same chart in the form of an oscillator. When a crossover occurs it is often a valid sign that the overall trend in the market has also reversed. Clearly, the size of the moving averages used in the calculation has a bearing on the significance of any given signal. An example using a 10-day moving average is shown in Chart 16.5b. Even though such signals have offered excellent buying opportunities, there have been many instances of whipsaws. The indicator on Chart 16.5c attempts to get around this problem by using a moving average calculated over a longer 10-week period. The method of calculation is also slightly different since it uses the formula V/T and D/T where V = upside volume, D = downside volume, and T = total volume.

BIG-BLOCK ACTIVITY

Large volume in a stock or the market has attracted the attention of many technicians and stimulated the development of indicators that can measure big-block activity. Technical research has been heavily concentrated in this area not only because of the emotional appeal of such indicators, but also because it is felt that the large-block traders, i.e., institutions, can have a tremendous effect on market prices through their buying (or selling) power. The ability of an investor (or, for that matter, most technicians) to monitor

CHART 16.5b Upside/downside volume 10-day moving average.

(SOURCE: *Trendline, a division of Standard & Poor's Corporation.*)

214

CHART 16.5c Upside/downside volume 30-day moving average.

(SOURCE: Pring Market Review)

such activity is limited, since such statistics are not recorded in the popular press. Even the advisory services that do publish such indexes do not have a long historical record from which reliable conclusions can be drawn.

Consequently, most interpretation of block activity is confined to institutional brokerage reports and advisory services. One of the most useful of the block-activity indicators published by the advisory services is that developed by Don Worden.[2] This indicator is constructed by taking the ratio of blocks (i.e., transactions in excess of 100,000 shares) where the price was higher than the previous sale (known as an uptick) and those where it was

[2]Worden Tape Reading Studies, Fort Lauderdale, Fla.

CHART 16.6 Worden $100,000 indexes versus Dow Jones Industrial Average, 1976–1977.

(SOURCE: *Courtesy of Worden Tape Reading Studies, Fort Lauderdale, Fla.*)

CHART 16.7 New York Stock Exchange Composite versus the 30-Day Most Active indicator.

lower (a downtick). Various moving averages of these ratios are then calculated and plotted as oscillators. Worden's big-block ratios and the DJIA for 1976 and 1977 are shown in Chart 16.6. The relationships are self-evident, and it can be seen that the various ratios rise and fall with the market as they move from "overbought" to "oversold" levels.

MOST ACTIVE STOCKS

To investors who wish to monitor big-block activity, the most active stocks represent a viable alternative. Statistics on the most active stocks are published in the popular press on both a daily and a weekly basis. Usually the

CHART 16.8 New York Stock Exchange Composite versus 8-Day Most Active indicator.

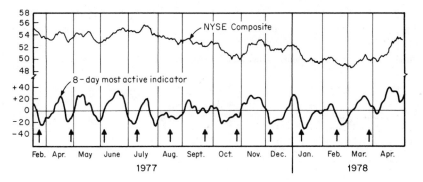

20 most active NYSE issues are recorded, but results do not seem to differ significantly whether 10, 15, or 20 issues are used. Active stocks are worth monitoring since they not only reflect the actions of institutions but also account for some 20 to 25 percent of total NYSE volume. Since the net price changes of such issues are recorded, it is possible to derive an indicator that can confirm movements in the upside/downside line.

The indicators derived from most active statistics are similar to those derived from upside/downside data. Chart 16.7 shows an oscillator constructed by taking a 30-day moving total of the net difference between the 10 most active advancing and declining stocks. The calculation is made by totaling the number of the 10 most active stocks each day that advance and those that decline. Sometimes the 15 or 20 most actives are used as a basis for the indicator, but results do not differ appreciably. In order to obtain the 30-day oscillator, the number of advancing stocks over the 30-day period is then totaled. The same calculation is made for the declining stocks, and one total is taken from the other. If the number of advancing stocks over the 30-day period is greater than the number of those declining, the oscillator will have a reading above zero, and vice versa. As new data are received each day they are added to the two totals, and the data for the 31st previous day are deleted. The resulting index appears to be useful for confirming intermediate advances and declines as it crosses above and below its zero reference line. Although the history of this indicator is relatively short, it has already achieved an impressive track record. In order to reduce the possibility of whipsaws it is a good idea to wait for the index to cross its zero reference line more decisively. An alternative method is to construct an oscillator in a similar manner but using weekly data, i.e., the 10, 15, or 20 most active stocks based on weekly volume.

Shorter-term market movements can be indicated by using a shorter time span; in Chart 16.8 an 8-day total has been used.

CHART 16.9   Dow Jones Industrial Average versus the 20 most active stocks. This chart shows a cumulative A/D line of the 20 most active stocks combined with a 6-week oscillator. Note that neither the A/D line nor its oscillator confirmed the December 1974 low in the Dow.

(SOURCE: *Courtesy of Juncture Recognition, Pompano Beach, Fla.*)

The second method of using the most active stocks is to take a cumulative difference between the number of stocks advancing each day and those declining. The result is an index which is not dissimilar to the upside/downside line. Although most of the time these two indicators move in concert, it is well worth keeping up both series since the junctures when their courses differ are often most informative about a potential reversal in the overall market trend. (See Chart 16.9.)

17

Breadth

The degree to which the vast majority of issues are participating in any stock market move is measured by indicators of breadth. Breadth therefore monitors the extent of a market trend. Generally speaking, the fewer the number of issues that are moving with the trend, the greater the probability of an imminent reversal in that trend.

The concept of breadth can probably be best explained using a military analogy. In Figure 17.1, lines *AA* and *BB* mark military lines of defense drawn up during a battle. It might be possible for a few units to cross over from *AA* to *BB*, but the chances are that the *BB* line will hold unless an all-out effort is made. In example *a*, the two units represented by the arrows are quickly repulsed. In example *b*, on the other hand, the assault is successful since many units are taking part, and army B is forced to retreat to a new line of defense at B_1.

A narrowly advancing stock market can be compared to example *a*, where it *looks* initially as though the move through the line of defense (in stock market terms, a *resistance level*) is going to be successful, but because the move is accompanied by such little support, the overall price trend is soon reversed. In the military analogy, even if the two units had successfully assaulted the *BB* defense, it would not be long before army B would have overpowered them, for the further they advanced without broad support, the more vulnerable they would have become to a counteroffensive by army B.

The same is true of the stock market, for the longer a price trend is maintained without a follow-up by the broad market, the more vulnerable is the advance.

At market bottoms breadth is not such a useful concept for determining major reversals, since the majority of stocks usually coincide with or lag behind the major indexes. On those few occasions when breadth reverses its downtrend before the averages, it can be a useful indicator of market bot-

FIGURE 17.1

toms. For the moment, attention will be concentrated on the reason why the broad market *normally* leads the averages at market tops. The word "normally" is used because, in the vast majority of cases, the broad list of stocks does peak out ahead of the DJIA; this rule is not invariable, however, so it should not be assumed that the technical structure is necessarily sound just because market breadth is strong.

ADVANCE/DECLINE LINE

The most widely used indicator of market breadth is an *advance/decline line*. This indicator is constructed by taking a cumulative total of the difference (plurality) of the number of NYSE issues advancing over those declining in a particular period (usually a day or a week). Similar indexes may be constructed for the American Exchange, or from the over-the-counter issues. Because the number of issues listed on the NYSE has expanded since breadth records were first kept, an A/D line constructed from a simple plurality of advancing over declining issues gives a greater weighting to more recent years. For the purpose of long-term comparisons it is better to take a ratio of advances versus declines, or a ratio of (advances/declines) ÷ the number of unchanged issues, rather than limiting the calculation to a simple plurality.

One of the most useful measurements of breadth is a cumulative running total of the formula $\sqrt{A/u - D/u}$, where A = the number of stocks advancing, D = the number declining, and u = the number unchanged. Since it is not mathematically possible to calculate a square root of a negative answer, i.e., when the number of declining stocks is greater than the number of those advancing, the D and A are reversed in such cases, so that the formula becomes $\sqrt{D/u - A/u}$. The resulting answer is then subtracted from the cumulative total, as opposed to the answer in the earlier formula, which is added. Table 17.1 illustrates this calculation.

Inclusion of the number of unchanged issues is useful, because at certain points a more reliable advance warning of an imminent trend reversal in the A/D line can be given. This is because the more dynamic the move in either direction, the greater the tendency for the number of unchanged stocks to

TABLE 17.1

Date	Issues traded (1)	Ad-vances (2)	De-clines (3)	Un-changed (4)	Ad-vances ÷ un-changed (5)	De-clines ÷ un-changed (6)	Col. 5 − col. 6 (7)	√Col. 7 (8)	Cumu-lative A/D line (9)
Jan. 7	2129	989	919	221	448	416	32	5.7	2475.6
14	2103	782	1073	248	315	433	−118	−10.9	2464.7
21	2120	966	901	253	382	356	26	5.1	2469.8
28	2103	835	1036	232	360	447	−87	−9.3	2460.5
Feb. 4	2089	910	905	274	332	330	2	1.4	2461.9
11	2090	702	1145	243	289	471	−18.2	−13.5	2448.4
18	2093	938	886	269	349	329	20	4.5	2452.9
25	2080	593	1227	260	228	472	244	−15.6	2437.3

diminish. Consequently, by giving some weight to the number of unchanged in the formula, it is possible to assess a slowdown in momentum of the A/D line at an earlier date, since an expanding number of unchanged issues will have the tendency to restrain extreme movements.

The A/D line normally rises and falls in sympathy with the DJIA, but at market peaks it usually peaks ahead of the senior average. There appear to be three basic reasons why this is so.

1. The market as a whole discounts the business cycle and normally reaches its bull market peak 6 to 9 months before the economy tops out. Since the peak in business activity is itself preceded by a deterioration of certain leading sectors, such as consumer spending and construction, it is logical to expect that the stocks representing these sectors will also peak out ahead of the general market.

2. Many of the stocks listed on the NYSE, such as preferreds and utilities, are sensitive to changes in interest rates. Since sharply rising interest rates are a phenomenon of a rapidly maturing business cycle, they usually begin to rise before the stock market has reached its peak.

3. Poorer-quality stocks offer the largest gains, but they are also representative of smaller, less well managed companies that are more vulnerable to reduced earnings (and even bankruptcy) during a recession. On the other hand, since blue-chip stocks normally have good credit ratings, reasonable yields, and sound underlying assets, they are typically the last stocks to be sold by investors during a bull market.

Since the DJIA and other market averages are almost wholly composed of larger companies which are normally in better financial shape, these popular averages continue to advance well after the broad market has peaked out.

Divergences between the A/D line and the DJIA at primary peaks are the most significant ones, but divergences also occur at intermediate tops; because they are generally much smaller than those occurring at primary peaks, the portent of intermediate divergences is usually less ominous. One of the basic principles of the breadth/price relationship is that the longer and greater the divergence, the deeper and more substantial the implied decline is likely to be. For example, Chart 17.1 shows that the weekly A/D line peaked in March 1971, almost 2 years ahead of the DJIA, a very long period by historical standards. The ensuing bear market was the most severe since the Depression. On the other hand, the absence of a divergence does not necessarily mean that a steep bear market cannot take place, as the experience of the December 1968 top indicates. This is also shown in Chart 17.1.

Positive divergences develop at market bottoms where the A/D line refuses to confirm a new low in the Dow. The most significant divergence of this nature occurred in the 1939–1942 period. The DJIA (as shown in Chart 17.2) made a series of lower peaks and troughs between 1939 and 1941, while the A/D line refused to confirm. Finally, in the middle of 1941 the A/D line made a post-1932 recovery high unaccompanied by the DJIA. The immediate result of this discrepancy was a sharp sell-off into the spring of 1942 by both indicators, but even then the A/D line held well above its 1938 bottom, unlike the DJIA. The final low in April 1942 was followed by the best bull market on record (in terms of breadth). This positive action by the broad market is unusual, for typically at market bottoms the A/D line either coincides with or lags behind the low in the DJIA and has no forecasting significance until its downtrend reversal is signaled by a breakout from a price pattern, a trendline, or a moving-average crossover, for example.

Chart 17.1 shows the A/D line and its 10-week oscillator. The oscillator is constructed by taking a 10-week moving average of the $\sqrt{A/u} - D/u$ formula. A comparison of the two indicators illustrates the principle of divergence, as evidenced by declining peaks of momentum and rising peaks in the A/D line itself. These discrepancies are shown by the dashed lines just above the two indexes. It is not possible to know at the time how high the A/D line will extend, only that the technical position (indicated by the declining peaks in the 10-week momentum) is deteriorating. The best method of determining when the A/D line has made its final advance is to wait for a downside trendline penetration or a moving-average crossover to confirm the action of the momentum index. Normally, as shown on Chart 17.1, the A/D line will sell off quite sharply following a combination of such trend breaks, but sometimes an extended sideways fluctuation results as the A/D line struggles to regain some momentum. The same principle can also be applied during bear markets, when signals are triggered as a series of higher

CHART 17.1 Dow Jones Industrials and the weekly advance/decline line.

(SOURCE: Pring Market Review.)

CHART 17.2 Dow Jones Industrials and the long-term advance/decline line.

40-week moving average of advance/decline ratio

Dow Jones Industrial Average closing weekly price each month

Advance/decline line

40-week moving average of advance/decline ratio

(SOURCE: Pring Market Review.)

troughs in the oscillator and lower lows in the A/D line are confirmed by a break in the negative trend of the A/D line itself.

Advance/decline lines have been constructed for most of the world's stock markets, and the same principles of divergence between breadth and the market average seem to apply. The only exception appears to be the Japanese market, where the line seems to have a permanent downward bias and is of relatively little forecasting value.

Advance/decline lines can also be constructed for gold (see Chapter 26), currencies (see Chapter 27), and commodities (see Chapter 28).

INDUSTRY BREADTH

An alternate method of measuring breadth is to calculate an A/D line for a number of industry groups. Several organizations publish such data, but those published in *Barron's* will be discussed here since they are the most accessible to the general public. Each week *Barron's* publishes data on 35 industry groups. The industry A/D line is calculated by cumulating the difference between those groups that advanced during the week and those that declined. Indexes that remain unchanged are ignored. Some technicians prefer to omit gold, since it is considered to be a countercyclical industry. Whether the results are meaningfully changed as a result of this exclusion is doubtful.

The principle behind the interpretation of the industry A/D line is similar to that of the A/D line itself in that a reversal of the prevailing market trend is likely whenever a divergence occurs between it and the DJIA. The industry A/D line is therefore a very useful indicator from the point of view of confirming a trend in the broader A/D line.

The industry group index has a distinct advantage over the A/D line in that it does not include preferred shares and is therefore less interest-sensitive than the A/D line. Normally, as discussed above, interest rates start to rise before the eventual peak in the stock market, so that the inclusion of a substantial amount of interest-sensitive stocks in the A/D line aids the leading characteristics of this index. However, there have been some occasions where interest rates have been stable or falling during the initial phases of a bear market. In late 1929 and 1930, for instance, interest rates fell by half while stocks also plunged. Similarly, in 1939–1941 interest rates hardly changed at all, yet the DJIA fell. For this reason the industry A/D line usually gives a more accurate reading of what is actually going on in the marketplace than the A/D line itself. Consequently, when the A/D line and the DJIA disagree, the A/D line normally wins. On the few occasions when the industry A/D line and the A/D line diverge, it is the industry A/D line that usually portrays the eventual outcome.

CHART 17.3   Industry line versus 13-week momentum index. Note the bullish positive divergence between the 13-week momentum, which made a decisive bear market low in mid-1974, and the index itself, which almost made a new low in December. The position was reversed in mid-1975, as the July high in the A/D line was not confirmed by the 13-week index.

(SOURCE: *Barron's 35 Industry Groups*. Pring Market Review.)

The industry A/D line is useful (1) from the point of view of the divergences which may arise between it and other averages and (2) through an analysis of the quality of its own trend, performed using the trend determination techniques discussed in Part 1.

Chart 17.3 shows the industry A/D line. The 1974 bottom is of particular interest since the industry line did not confirm the December low in the DJIA. Moreover, in 1976 the industry line peaked out in February, while the DJIA made its bull market high in September. By this time, however, the industry A/D line had begun to warn of impending trouble, as it had already traced out a series of declining peaks. Following this divergence the DJIA lost 20 percent in the ensuing 12 months. It is also worthwhile to compare the industry A/D line in this 1976–1977 period with the weekly A/D line shown in Chart 17.1. As noted earlier, the industry line topped out in February 1976, but the A/D line itself reached its bull market high a long time afterwards.

Industry breadth can also be used to construct a rate-of-change indicator. As discussed earlier (see Chapter 8), a rate-of-change index based on these data may be used, but only to compare two periods in which the level of the indicator has not altered appreciably. Such an index is also shown in Chart 17.3.

The alternate method of constructing a momentum index is to take a total of the net advances over declines for a specific period, such as 10 or 13 weeks, and plot the result. This is illustrated in Table 17.2 for a 10-week oscillator and is also shown in Chart 17.1. The movement of the industry A/D line in Chart 17.4 differs at some points from that shown in Chart 17.3 because of a slightly different construction.

PERCENTAGE OF STOCKS IN POSITIVE TRENDS

Another useful technique for analyzing stock market breadth is to construct an index based on the number of stocks that may be classified as being in a positive trend. There are basically three ways in which this can be achieved.

1. Stocks in Positive Trends

This method involves the classification of stocks according to whether they are in a positive or a negative trend. A stock is considered to be in an uptrend when it rallies following a decline, reacts, and then rallies to a new high above the previous rally peak. This is shown in Figure 17.2, example a, at point X. An uptrend is assumed to exist until a previous trough is penetrated on the downside, as in Figure 17.2, example b, shown as point Y. Once the number of stocks in an uptrend has been determined, the percentage as a total in the sample is taken and the result plotted. These data are calculated and published by Chartcraft.[1] Chart 17.5 shows this method and similar data for the DJIA stocks and various industry groups. Since this indicator is an oscillator type, its interpretation should be based on the rules

[1]Chartcraft Ltd., Larchmont, N.Y.

TABLE 17.2

Date	No. of groups advancing (1)	No. of groups declining (2)	Col. 1 ÷ col. 2 (3)	10-week total of col. 3 (4)
Jan. 1	1	32	− 31	
8	10	25	− 15	
15	25	10	+ 15	
22	17	18	− 1	
29	12	22	− 10	
Feb. 1	35	0	+ 35	
8	10	25	− 15	
15	20	15	+ 5	
22	5	30	− 25	
Mar. 1	10	25	− 15	− 57
8	18	17	+ 1	− 25
15	12	21	− 9	− 19
22	27	8	+ 19	− 15

and principles established in Chapter 8. It can be seen that the index measuring the percentage of stocks in an uptrend was making a series of declining peaks throughout 1971 and 1972, a period when the DJIA was in a rising trend.

2. Percentage of Stocks Over a Moving Average

This method involves the calculation of a specific moving average for a wide number of stocks and then of the percentage of that number that is above the average. The longer the time span chosen for the moving average, the less sensitive the oscillator will be.

Chart 17.7 shows the percentage of the 600 or so stocks monitored by Trendline above their 200-day (30-week) moving average. The data have been smoothed by a 5-week simple moving average to iron out misleading fluctuations.

This indicator usually moves in the same way as the positive trend index discussed above. During the period under consideration, a juncture point worthy of note occurred during the December 1974 low, when the trough in the 200-day indicator was well above that of October. This compares with a marginally higher one for the NYSE Composite Index and one that was lower in the case of the DJIA (shown above the 200-day indicator).

It should also be noted that when this index reaches an extreme of 90 to

CHART 17.4 NYSE Composite and three measures of breadth.

(SOURCE: Pring Market Review.)

100 percent or 10 to 15 percent, it is not necessarily indicating that a sharp reversal is imminent, but it *is* pointing out that a substantial proportion of the prevailing move has already taken place. Once the indicator reaches such extremes and starts to reverse its direction, the probabilities favor an immediate reversal in the trend of the market itself. At the beginning of a bull market it is not unknown for this index to remain at a high level for a considerable period of time, as in early 1975, but as the cycle matures, high readings become difficult to reach and maintain. A series of declining peaks in this index is a clear sign that a primary bull market is rapidly running out of steam.

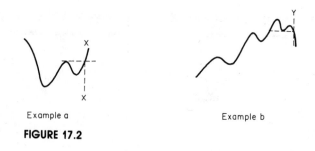

Example a   Example b

FIGURE 17.2

CHART 17.5 Percentage of all stocks, Dow stocks, and industry groups in positive trends.

(SOURCE: *Courtesy of Dow Theory Letters, Inc., La Jolla, Calif., based on data provided by Chartcraft Ltd.*)

3. Percentage of Stocks with Positive Momentum (Diffusion Indexes)

This type of index is calculated by using rate-of-change techniques on either a wide number of stocks or a number of industry indexes, such as Barron's 35 Groups. Indicators calculated in this way are known as *diffusion indexes*. Two such examples are shown in Chart 17.8. These indicators are based on the percentage of Standard & Poor's Industry Groups that are above their level 8 weeks and 3 months ago; they are published by *The Money Manager*

CHART 17.6 Dow Jones Industrial Average versus Over-200-Day Moving Average Ratio, 1970–1975.

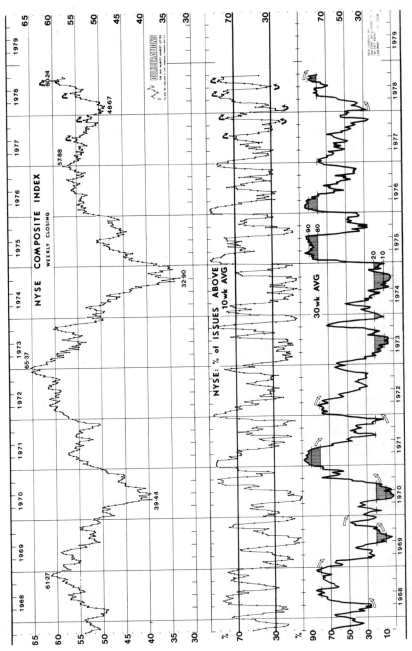

(SOURCE: Deliberations, *Toronto, Ontario, Canada*.)

231

CHART 17.7   New York Stock Exchange Composite and two breadth ratios; two alternative methods of portraying the percentage of stocks above their moving averages. The data were calculated by Chartcraft Ltd. and plotted by the innovative Canadian technician Ian McAvity. The 10-week ratio is useful for identifying intermediate peaks and troughs, while the 30-week average is more useful for determining cyclical bottoms and tops.

(SOURCE: Trendline Daily Basis Charts.)

(a weekly publication for institutional investors). The shaded areas on Chart 17.8a indicate periods of economic recession. Chart 17.9 shows an alternate method of portraying group momentum published by the *Bank Credit Analyst*. These indexes should be interpreted in the same way as any momentum indicator.

HIGH-LOW FIGURES

The popular press publishes daily and weekly figures for stocks reaching new highs and new lows. These "statistics" relate to the number of stocks making new highs or lows in a calendar year. In order to retain some continuity, the year is not "changed" until the following March, so that January and February figures cover 13- and 14-month periods, respectively. More recently, figures covering a 52-week period, as opposed to a calendar year, have been published by *The Wall Street Journal*. In theory, these new figures should offer a much more accurate reflection of the market's technical structure.

There are various methods of measuring the high-low figures. Some tech-

CHART 17.8a Standard & Poor's 500 Stock Index versus Money Manager 3-Month Diffusion Index

CHART 17.8b Standard & Poor's 500 Stock Index versus Money Manager 8-Week Diffusion Index

(SOURCE *Courtesy of* Money Manager.)

CHART 17.9 Dow Jones Industrial Average Annual Rate of Change versus *The Bank Credit Analyst* Stock Market Group Momentum Index

(SOURCE: (1) *Dow Jones Industrials*. (2) *Twenty-five S&P groups. Courtesy of* The Bank Credit Analyst.)

CHART 17.10 Daily Advance/Decline Line versus the 5-Day High/Low Differential. A classic signal of improving technical strength was given in December 1974 when the DJIA fell below its October low. The high/low had fallen to its lowest level in September, thereby pointing up that the majority of stocks were in better technical shape than the DJIA. Between March and July the reverse situation occurred as the DJIA made new highs unaccompanied by an expanding high/low differential. This suggested a weakening technical structure, so that once the A/D line had violated the trendline joining the April–May and June bottoms, an intermediate reaction got underway.

CHART 17.11   S&P Composite and three measures of momentum.

(SOURCE: Pring Market Review.)

nicians prefer to take a moving average of the two series, others a moving average of the net difference between highs and lows. The basic principle is that a rising market over a period of time should be accompanied by a healthy, but not necessarily rising, number of net new highs. When the DJIA continues to make a series of higher peaks following a long advance, and the net number of new highs is tracing out a series of declining peaks, this is a warning of potential trouble. Similarly, in a bear market a new low in the DJIA which is not accompanied by an expanding number of net new lows should be looked at in a favorable light.

Basically, the first example is indicating that while the DJIA is rising, the technical picture is gradually weakening as successive peaks are accompanied by fewer and fewer stocks making breakouts (new highs) from price patterns. Since the net number of new highs also takes into consideration stocks making new lows, the higher peaks in the DJIA may also be accompanied by a larger number of stocks reaching new lows. The reverse, of course, is true at bottoms, where a declining number of stocks reaching new lows implies fewer downside breakouts and therefore a greater number of stocks resisting the downtrend in the major averages, which is clearly a positive sign (see Chart 17.10).

An alternative method of calculating high-low data is shown in Chart 17.11, where a 6-week moving average of net weekly new highs has been plotted against the DJIA. This is a particularly good indicator for identifying major turning points. For example, when the DJIA was making a new low in early 1978 the high-low indicator refused to confirm. Similarly, in 1983 the DJIA made a series of consecutive lows which began in September 1981, whereas the high-low index was making a series of ascending lows. The reverse situation occurred at the 1973 market peak since the high-low indicator had peaked out 2 years before.

PART 3

Interest Rates and the Stock Market

Why Interest Rates Affect the Stock Market

Changes in interest rates affect the stock market for three basic reasons. First, fluctuations in the price charged for money influence the earnings or profits that companies are able to make and therefore the price which investors are willing to pay for stocks. Second, movements in interest rates alter the relationships between competing financial assets, of which the bond market/stock market relationship is the most important. Third, a substantial number of equities are purchased on borrowed money (known as margin debt), so that changes in the cost of carrying that debt (i.e., the interest rate) influence the desirability of holding such stock. Since significant changes in interest rates usually lead stock prices, it is important to understand and identify reversals in their cyclical trend, but first an examination of the cause-and-effect relationship between interest rates and the stock market is worth close scrutiny.

THE EFFECT OF INTEREST RATE CHANGES ON CORPORATE PROFITS

The primary motivation for buying or selling equities is that investors as a group consider stocks to be over- or undervalued in relation to the outlook for corporate profits and the future flow of dividends. Since interest rates affect company earnings, fluctuations in their level are clearly of importance to the trend of profits.

Interest rates affect profits in two ways. First, since almost all companies borrow money to finance either plant and equipment or inventory (or both), the cost of money, i.e., the interest rate they pay, is of great importance. Second, since many of the sales which each company produces are in turn financed by borrowing, the level of interest rates has a great deal of influence on the willingness of customers to make the additional purchases. One of the most outstanding examples is the automobile business, in which both producers and consumers are very heavily financed. Other examples are the utilities and transportation industries, which tend to be large borrowers because of the tremendous capital they require. The construction industry is also highly leveraged, so that the housing market is sensitive to interest rates.

Falling interest rates are normally good for business and profits, while rising interest rates, after a point, have the effect of hurting profits and adversely affecting stock prices.

INTEREST RATES AND COMPETING FINANCIAL ASSETS

As well as influencing corporate sales and profits, interest rate changes also alter the attractiveness of various investment vehicles among themselves. The most significant relationship is that of stocks to bonds. For example, if at any given point investors judge stocks and bonds to be equally attractive, their investment posture will remain unchanged, other things being equal. However, if interest rates rise, it will be possible to obtain a better rate of return on bonds than was offered before. Consequently there will be a flow of money at the margin out of stocks into bonds. Stocks will then fall in value until the relationship is perceived by investors to be more in balance.

The full effect of interest rate changes on any particular stock group will depend upon the yield being obtained combined with the prospects for profit growth. Most sensitive will be the preferred shares, which are primarily held for their dividends and which do not generally permit their owners to participate in corporate profit growth. Second, while some growth in profits may be expected from utility companies, this growth is substantially influenced by regulation, so dividends are a relatively more important factor rendering the shares sensitive to interest rate changes. On the other hand, companies in a dynamic stage of growth are usually financed from corporate earnings and for this reason pay smaller dividends. These stocks are less affected by fluctuations in the cost of money since they are purchased in anticipation of fast profit growth and future yield rather than an immediate dividend return.

INTEREST RATES AND MARGIN DEBT

Margin debt is money loaned by brokers on the basis of securities pledged as collateral. Normally this money is used for the acquisition of equities, but sometimes margin debt is used for purchases of consumer items, such as automobiles. The effect of rising interest rates on both forms of margin debt is similar in that rising rates raise the cost of carrying the debt and make it less attractive to carry. There is therefore a reluctance on the part of investors to take on additional debt as its cost rises, and at some point, when the service charges become excessive, stocks are liquidated and the debt is paid off. Thus, rising interest rates have the effect of increasing the supply of stock put up for sale and thereby pushing prices down.

The relationship between interest rates and bond prices and the calculation of bond yields will now be examined.

BOND YIELDS

When a bond is brought to market by a borrower, it is issued at a fixed interest rate (coupon) which is paid over a predetermined period. At the end of this period, the issuer agrees to repay the face amount. Since bonds are normally issued in denominations of $1000 (known as par), this figure usually represents the amount to be repaid at the end of the (loan) period. Bond prices are quoted in percentage terms, so that par ($1000) is expressed as 100. Normally bonds are issued and redeemed at par; however, the issue price is sometimes at a discount, i.e., less than 100, and occasionally at a premium, i.e., over 100.

While it is usual for a bond to be issued and redeemed at 100, over the life of the bond its price can fluctuate quite widely since interest rate levels are continually changing. Assume that a 20-year bond was issued with an 8 percent interest rate (coupon) at par (i.e., 100); if interest rates rose to 9 percent, the bond at 8 percent would be difficult to sell, because investors would be unwilling to purchase the 8 percent bond while their money could earn a superior rate of return at 9 percent. The only way in which the 8 percent bondholder can find a buyer is to accept a lower price that will compensate a prospective purchaser for the 1 percent differential in interest rates. The new owner will then earn 8 percent in interest with some capital appreciation. When spread over the remaining life of the bond, this capital appreciation will be equivalent to the 1 percent loss in interest. This combination of coupon rate and averaged capital appreciation is known as the *yield.* If interest rates decline, the process is reversed, and the 8 percent bond becomes more attractive in relation to prevailing rates, so that its price rises.

The longer the maturity of the bond, the greater will be the fluctuation in its price for any given change in the general level of interest rates. The reason is that a more substantial adjustment in the price of the bond is necessary to compensate for the differential in the prevailing interest rates and the coupon for a longer maturity.

As interest rates rise bond prices fall, and when interest rates fall bond prices rise. Looked at in this way, it is easier to understand the relationship between the bond and stock markets. For this reason, most of the charts in this and subsequent chapters will use interest rates or yields plotted inversely, i.e., upside down, so that a falling line will indicate declining bond prices (i.e., declining debt markets), and vice versa.

THE STRUCTURE OF THE DEBT MARKETS

The debt markets can be broken down into two main areas known as the *short end* and the *long end.* The short end, more commonly known as the money market, relates to interest rates charged for loans up to 1 year in maturity. Normally, movements at the short end lead those at the longer end, since short rates are more sensitive to trends in business conditions and changes in Federal Reserve policy. Money-market instruments are issued by governments of all kinds and by all types of corporations.

The "long end" of the market consists of bonds issued for a period of at least 15 years. There are, of course, a myriad of bonds issued for periods of between 1 and 15 years which fall between these definitions. Also, once a 25-year bond has been in existence for 20 years, it trades on the same basis as a bond issued for 5 years.

The bond market (i.e., the long end) has three main sectors, which are classified as to issuer. These are the U.S. government sector; the tax-exempt sector (i.e., state and local governments); and the corporate sector. The financial status of the tax-exempt and corporate sectors varies from issuer to issuer, and the practice of rating each bond for quality of credit has therefore become widespread.

The best possible credit rating is known as AAA; next in order are AA, A, BAA, BA, BB, etc. The better the quality of a bond, the lower the risk that investors undertake, so the lower the interest rate that is needed to compensate them. The credit of the U.S. federal government is higher than that of any other issuer, so it can sell bonds at a relatively low interest rate. The tax-exempt sector (i.e., bonds issued by state and local governments) is able to issue bonds with the lowest rates of all in view of the favored tax treatment assigned to the holders of such issues.

Most of the time, price trends of the various sectors will be similar, but at major cyclical turns some will lag behind others in view of the differing demand and supply conditions in each sector.

DEBT AND EQUITY MARKETS

At cyclical peaks, debt markets typically top out ahead of the equity market. The lead characteristics and degree of deterioration of bond prices differ from cycle to cycle. Short-term rates usually start to move up first, followed later by long-term rates. There are no hard-and-fast rules that relate the size of the ensuing equity decline to the time period separating the peaks of bond and equity prices. Thus in 1959 short- and long-term rates peaked 18 and 17 months, respectively, ahead of the bull market high in the Dow. This compared with 11 months and 1 month for the 1973 bull market peak. While the deterioration in the bond and money markets was sharper and longer in the 1959 period, the Dow, on a monthly average basis, declined only 13 percent compared with 42 percent in the 1973–1974 bear market. The significant point is that every cyclical stock market peak in this century was preceded by, or has coincided with, a peak in both the long and short ends of the bond market.

A further characteristic of cyclical peaks is that higher-quality bonds (such as Treasury or AAA corporate bonds) decline in price ahead of poorer-quality issues such as BAA-rated bonds. This has been true of nearly every cyclical turning point since 1919. This lead characteristic of high-quality bonds results from two factors. First, in the latter stages of an economic expansion, private-sector demand for financing accelerates. Commercial banks, the largest institutional holders of government securities, are the lenders of last resort to private borrowers. As the demand for financing accelerates against a less accommodative central bank posture, banks step up their sales of these and other high-grade investments and reinvest the money in more profitable bank loans. A ripple effect is then set off, both down the yield curve itself and also to lower-quality issues. At the same time these pressures are pushing yields on high-quality bonds upward, and are also reflecting buoyant business conditions which encourage investors to become less cautious. Consequently, investors are willing to overlook the relatively conservative yields on high-quality bonds in favor of the more rewarding lower-rated debt instruments; thus, for a temporary period, these bonds are rising while high-quality bonds are falling.

At cyclical bottoms these relationships are similar, in that good-quality bonds lead both debt instruments and equities that are of poorer quality. The

CHART 18.1   Interest rates at cyclical stock market troughs.

Months from trough in stock prices

Months from trough in stock prices

(SOURCE: Pring Market Review.)

lead characteristics of the debt markets are not quite so pronounced as at cyclical peaks, and occasionally bond and stock prices trough out simultaneously.

The trend of interest rates is therefore a useful benchmark for identifying stock market bottoms.

Chart 18.1 shows the cyclical stock market troughs since 1919 that have been associated with tight monetary conditions. The monthly average of stock prices is represented on the top line, with the yields of 4- to 6-month commercial paper and AAA corporate long-term bonds shown underneath. The respective yields have been plotted inversely so that they correspond with the trend of equity and bond prices.

Reference to the chart shows that in every case either one or both yield curves bottomed out ahead of stock prices. This relationship between debt and equity markets may be traced back through the early nineteenth century, and it can be shown that virtually every major cyclical stock market bottom was preceded by strength in one or both areas of the debt market. In most cases where this relationship did not hold, the ensuing rise in stock prices proved to be spurious, and more often than not prices eventually moved well below the previous low.

That interest rates have begun a declining phase is not a sufficient condition in itself to justify the purchase of equities. For example, in the 1919–1921 bear market, bond prices reached their lowest point in June 1920, 14 months ahead of, or 27 percent above, the final stock market bottom in August 1921. An even more dramatic example occurred during the 1929–1932 debacle when money market yields reached their highs in October 1929. Over the next 3 years the discount rate was cut in half, but stock prices lost 85 percent of their October 1929 value. The reason for such excessively long lead times was that these periods were associated with a great deal of debt liquidation and many bankruptcies. Even the sharp reduction in interest rates was not sufficient to encourage consumers and businesses to spend, as is the normal cyclical experience. Although falling interest rates are not by themselves a sufficient reason to expect that stock prices will reverse their cyclical decline, they are a necessary one. On the other hand, a continued trend of rising rates has in the past proved to be bearish.

The principles of trend determination appear to apply equally well to the bond market as to the stock market. In fact, trends in bond prices are in many ways easier to identify, since the bulk of the transactions in bonds are made on the basis of money flows caused by a need to finance and an ability to purchase. Consequently, while emotions are still important from the point of view of determining the short-term trends of bond prices, money flow is responsible for a far smoother cyclical trend than is the case with equities.

Short-Term Interest Rates

Short-term interest rates are more sensitive to business conditions than long-term rates. This is because decisions to change inventories, for which a substantial amount of short-term money is required, are made much more quickly than decisions to purchase plant and equipment, which form the basis for long-term credit demands. The Federal Reserve, in its management of monetary policy, is also better able to influence short-term rates than bonds at the longer end. For these reasons changes in short-term rates usually precede changes in long-term rates.

The key short-term interest rate that should be monitored is the Federal Funds rate. At any particular point in time, banks are required to hold a certain level of reserves with the Federal Reserve in relation to their deposits. Some banks will find themselves with a surplus of reserves over the required amount, and others will have a deficiency. The practice has evolved of surplus-holding banks lending to deficient ones, so that the latter can meet their reserve requirements. The Federal Funds rate is simply the rate of interest charged for these loans. Through various techniques, the Federal Reserve is able to control the amount of reserves in the banking system, and it is therefore able to influence the Federal Funds rate. The trend in the Federal Funds rate is therefore a good indication of the direction of monetary policy and financial pressures in the system as well as a guide to the future course of short-term rates in general.

Chart 19.1 shows one technique that has proved useful in determining

CHART 19.1 Federal Funds rate and 13-week momentum.

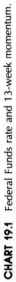

(SOURCE: Pring Market Review.)

248

the intermediate movements in the Federal Funds rate. A reversal in the trend of the rate is signaled when the Federal Funds rate crosses over its 10-week moving average (dashed line) and this is confirmed by the momentum index (13-week rate of change) crossing its zero reference line in the same direction. The trend is assumed to be in existence until both indexes signal a reversal. For instance, at the beginning of 1970 the prevailing trend was down. It appeared to be reversed when the Federal Funds rate crossed above its 10-week average, but this was not confirmed by the momentum index, which remained below its zero reference line. It was not until 1971 that the two indexes confirmed each other and a valid warning of a reversal was given.

The earlier discussion pointed out that changes in the trend of short-term interest rates typically lead changes in equity prices but that the relationship was fairly imprecise because of the variation in lead times. A more reliable relationship can be obtained if the rate of change of short-term interest rates is related to stock prices.

For example, Chart 19.2 shows that between 1971 and 1975 moving-average crossovers in the Federal Funds rate combined with trend reversals in the 13-week momentum index have been useful in forecasting future trend reversals of an intermediate nature in the DJIA. At this point a word of caution is in order, since the relationship between interest rates and the stock market is usually less precise than is indicated in the chart. Consequently it should not be assumed that any change in the Federal Funds rate will necessarily affect the stock market to an equal degree. This relationship should be regarded as an important but *not infallible* indicator of future stock market trends.

Another technique for measuring the importance of the rate of change of interest rates can be seen from Chart 19.3, which shows the Value Line composite with its 13-week ROC index and a 13-week ROC index of the yield on 4- to 6-month commercial paper. The latter indicator has been plotted *inversely* to correspond with stock prices. The arrows relate to periods when the commercial paper yield has risen by 20 percent over a 13-week period, i.e., when the inversely plotted index has fallen to the 120 percent level. The degree of decline has varied, but for the 10 signals shown on the chart the average was 20 percent. Rising rates usually result in greater damage during a bear market. The decline is normally well under way by the time the index has fallen to the 120 percent level. However, it is worth noting that a 20 percent rise in yields over a 13-week period was sufficient to kill even the most powerful rallies during the 1969–1983 period.

FOUR- TO SIX-MONTH COMMERCIAL PAPER

Another key short-term interest rate, one with a long historical record, is that charged for 4- to 6-month prime (i.e., best-quality) commercial paper. From

CHART 19.2   Federal Funds rate versus Dow Jones Industrial Average.

(SOURCE: Pring Market Review.)

time to time corporations have a substantial amount of surplus cash which will be available for a relatively brief period. Other corporations find themselves in need of money. Normally the two corporations would lend each other money through the intermediacy of a bank. The practice has evolved of bypassing the banks and acting through an investment dealer, who is paid considerably less than the bank. Consequently both borrower and lender are able to obtain more favorable terms. This form of debt is known as commercial paper. The monitoring of commercial paper rates is very useful, since these interest rates give a good indication of financial pressures and trends of short-term interest rates in the private sector.

There are of course many techniques that can be used to determine the change in trend of the commercial paper rate, but one that has been found most useful from the point of view of confirming reversals in cyclical movements is shown in Chart 19.4.

CHART 19.3 Value Line composite index and two measures of momentum.

(SOURCE: Pring Market Review.)

The solid line represents the rate itself, the dashed line an 18-month weighted moving average. Signals are given when the moving average changes direction. An 18-month time span has proved to be useful in determining the cyclical trend of short-term interest rates, since it smooths out whipsaws (such as the 1971 rise) yet retains sufficient sensitivity to respond fairly quickly to changes in longer-term trends. In the 64-year period between 1919 and 1983, a reversal in the downward movement of this moving average, following a cyclical decline in short-term rates, has with only two exceptions confirmed that a cyclical rise in rates was under way. The two exceptions occurred in 1931 and 1933, when the discount rate was temporarily raised and then lowered in response to specific crises.

CHART 19.4 Commercial paper rate, 1955–1978.

TREASURY BILLS

Another money market rate that should be monitored is the yield on 3-month Treasury bills. Treasury bills are short-term debt instruments (i.e., 3-month to 1-year) issued by the U.S. government. The bills are redeemed at face value when they mature but pay no interest. The holder obtains his return by purchasing these bills at a discount (i.e., a price below the face value), which compensates for the loss of interest. Unlike the purchaser of commercial paper who earns an income, a Treasury-bill holder really receives a guaranteed capital gain from the investment. It is possible to calculate the rate of return on a Treasury bill by relating the capital gain to the time remaining to maturity. Treasury bills are usually quoted on a yield basis, so that their rate of return can be compared with that of other short-term instruments. A Treasury-bill yield is shown in Chart 20.1 (page 258). Most of the time the rate on 90-day Treasury bills will move in the same direction as the commercial paper rate, since both debt instruments are influenced by domestic financial conditions. However, the movement of

TABLE 19.1

Discount rate cyclical low	Stock market cyclical peak	Lead time in months
August 1924	September 1929	61
February 1934	March 1937	37
August 1937	September 1939	26
October 1942	May 1946	44
April 1954	April 1956	25
April 1958	December 1959	20
August 1960	February 1966	65
April 1967	December 1968	20
December 1971	January 1973	13

Treasury bills occasionally diverges for short periods, since they are also bought by foreign investors and foreign central banks. Trends in Treasury-bill yields are analyzed by means of essentially the same techniques as the other money market rates discussed above.

THE IMPORTANCE OF CHANGES IN THE DISCOUNT RATE

The relative importance of a change in the discount rate, as compared with a change in any other interest rate, is that it is an indication of official central bank policy. Since the central bank is in a position to influence other interest rates, such a change reflects the desire of the central bank to raise or lower the general level of interest rates. It is therefore a good indication of the future direction of these market-oriented rates and has a strong psychological influence on both debt and equity markets. In addition, since the Federal Reserve does not reverse policy decisions on a week-to-week basis, a change in the discount rate implies that the trend in market interest rates is unlikely to be reversed for at least a few months. Just as a corporation does not like to cut dividends shortly after they have been raised, so does the central bank wish to create a feeling of continuity and consistency. A change in the discount rate is therefore helpful in confirming trends in other rates which, when taken by themselves, can sometimes give misleading signals because of temporary technical or psychological factors.

Since the incorporation of the Federal Reserve System, with the exception of the depression and war years of 1937 and 1939 and more recently 1976, every single bull market peak in equities has been preceded by a rise in the discount rate. The leads have varied. In 1973 the discount rate was raised on

CHART 19.5 The discount rate and the stock market.

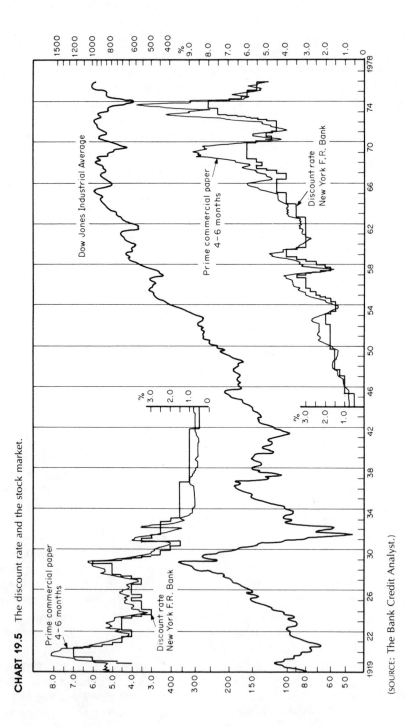

Dow Jones Industrial Average

Prime commercial paper
4–6 months

Discount rate
New York F.R. Bank

Prime commercial paper
4–6 months

Discount rate
New York F.R. Bank

(SOURCE: The Bank Credit Analyst.)

254

January 12, 3 days before the bull market high, whereas the 1956 peak was preceded by no less than five consecutive hikes. It is worth considering the number of months separating the point where the discount rate reached its cyclical low from the point marking a cyclical high in the equity market. For example, in the 1970–1973 bull cycle, the discount rate was cut to its lowest point (4½ percent) in December 1971, 13 months before the bull market top in January 1973. Other bull market cycles since 1919 are as shown in Table 19.1. As the table shows, historically the lead time can vary from 5½ years, as in 1960–1966, to as little as 13 months in 1971–1973.

As can be seen in Chart 19.5, cuts in the discount rate usually precede stock market bottoms, although the relationship is far less precise than that observed at market tops. Note, for example, that the rate was lowered no fewer than seven times during the 1929–1932 debacle, whereas it was not changed at all during the 1946–1949 bear market.

20

Long-Term Interest Rates

As discussed in Chapter 18, the long-term bond market comprises the U.S. government sector, the corporate sector, and the tax-exempt sector. The yields of a series representative of each are shown in Chart 20.1. During the period under consideration it can be seen that all sectors basically move in the same direction most of the time, as might be expected. At specific points, the supply/demand relationship peculiar to one or another of the sectors sets it apart from the rest. For example, the long-term corporate market reached its low point, i.e., highest yield as shown on Chart 20.1, in October 1974 (along with most bonds of shorter maturity), while the municipal and government indexes did not reach their low point until October 1975. Moreover, the government yield index troughed in January 1977, whereas its municipal counterpart reached its low many months later. Chart 20.2 shows a composite bond market index constructed from the average of all three sectors. This index is useful because it places movements of all three areas in perspective and serves as a base from which relative-strength analysis can be undertaken.

Technical analysis of bonds is very similar to that of stocks in that trend reversals in yield indexes or price indexes of bonds can be identified by price pattern formations, trendlines, momentum and moving averages, etc. In a sense, it is possible to extend a crude form of breadth analysis, for an

CHART 20.1   Key interest rates, 1955–1978: AAA, Government Long-Term, and Bond Buyers 20 Bond yields.

(SOURCE: *National Bureau of Economic Research.*)

advance or decline by one sector, if unconfirmed by the other two, is likely to prove spurious since it will result in a change in the competitive spread between the various sectors. One major difference between bonds and stocks is that high-quality bonds generally lead the debt market in both directions, whereas it is generally the poorer-quality stocks which lead the equity market down; both classes appear to bottom out simultaneously.

CHART 20.2 Composite long-term bond yield index, 1974–1978. This chart of the *Pring Market Review*'s composite long-term term bond yield index has been plotted inversely to correspond with bond prices. The dashed lines at +5 and −5 percent are used as a rough benchmark for "overbought" and "oversold" areas. Note the positive divergence between the 13-week momentum index and the index itself between late 1974 and late 1975.

*Includes: Moody's Corporate Aaa bonds
Bond Buyer's 20 municipal bonds
St. Louis Federal Reserve long–term gov'ts.

(SOURCE: Pring Market Review.)

RELATIONSHIP BETWEEN BOND AND STOCK YIELDS

Chart 20.3 shows the ratio of Moody's Aaa corporate yields divided by the indicated yield on the Standard & Poor's 500 stock index. A fall in the index shows that the return on stocks based on the indicated dividend is becoming more attractive in relation to bonds. When the line rises, stocks (on a yield basis) are becoming more expensive. When the line has been rising for some time, it is usually indicating a bull market in equities, whereas a declining line is normally associated with a bear market. Quite often the bond/stock index peaks out ahead of the stock market, giving advance warning of a reversal in the primary trend. Usually this lead time is relatively short, as in

CHART 20.3 Moody's Aaa/Standard & Poor's 500 Yield, 1926–1977.

1959 and 1972, but in 1936–1937 the line peaked out well ahead of the stock market, indicating that as stocks rose in price they were becoming cheaper and cheaper in relation to bonds, since dividends were growing at a faster rate than stock prices.

Chart 20.4 helps to show the degree of overvaluation of stocks in an even longer historical context. The index is similar to the one just described, but is derived by subtracting one yield from another, rather than dividing. The resulting index is called a *yield gap,* since it measures the difference in yield between bonds and stocks. Normally, stock yields are higher than bond yields in view of the greater risk associated with stocks, but sometimes, as in the 10 to 15 years represented on the chart, bond yields have been higher. During such periods the yield gap becomes negative and is known as the "reverse" yield gap. This negative gap is a direct result of growing investor confidence and expectations arising from the virtually uninterrupted period of postwar prosperity. Under such conditions stocks are obviously less risky than in the more volatile economic conditions of the past.

Chart 20.4 shows that even at the bottom of the 1973–1974 bear market, the most severe in postwar history, stocks were still overvalued on a yield basis in relation to bonds in a long-term historical context. This was true even though they appeared to be inexpensive in relation to the previous 10 years. In this connection, Chart 20.5 shows the postwar period in greater detail.

TREND DETERMINATION OF LONG-TERM BONDS

Analysis of the trend in bond prices (or yields) is approached in the same way as analysis of the various equity market indicators. Because the move-

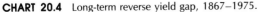

CHART 20.4   Long-term reverse yield gap, 1867–1975.

(SOURCE: *White, Weld & Co., Inc.*)

ment of bonds tends to be much smoother than those of stocks, whipsaws resulting from the use of moving averages are usually far less troublesome.

SHORT-TERM MOVEMENTS

One good method for determining short-term (4- to 12-week) movements in bonds is to plot a price arithmetically (or inverted yield) above a 30-day rate-of-change (momentum) index, as in Chart 20.6. The bond used in the chart

CHART 20.5 Reverse yield gap, 1949–1978. Recent bond/stock yield spread between average quarterly yield on Moody's Composite (average long-term Corporate Bond Series—Aaa, Aa, A, and Baa) and the indicated quarterly (seasonally adjusted) dividend yield on Standard & Poor's 425 Industrial Stock Price Index.

(SOURCE: *White, Weld & Co., Inc.*)

CHART 20.6 Government National Mortgage Association Certificates versus 30-day momentum.

(SOURCE: Pring Market Review.)

is an 8 percent Government National Mortgage Certificate (GNMA), a widely traded U.S. government agency debt instrument which is a good bellwether for the medium-term U.S. government market. The technique is a very simple one of drawing trendlines for both the GNMA and its 30-day rate of change. A trendline break that is confirmed for both the index and its momentum index gives a reliable indication of a reversal in the trend of the GNMA itself. The level of the 30-day rate-of-change index is also useful for judging when the price of the GNMA is likely to run into support or resistance. Such "overbought" or "oversold" indications are shown by the two dashed lines.

PART 4

Other Aspects of
Market Behavior

Sentiment Indicators

I find more and more that it is well to be on the right side of the minority since it is always the more intelligent.

GOETHE

During primary bull and bear markets the psychology of all investors moves from pessimism and fear to hope, overconfidence, and greed. For the majority the feeling of confidence is built up over a period of rising prices, so that optimism reaches its peak around the same point that the market is also reaching its high. Conversely, the majority is most pessimistic at market bottoms, at precisely the point when the acquisition of stocks should be taking place.

The better-informed market participants, such as insiders and stock exchange members, act in a contrary manner to the majority by selling at market tops and buying at market bottoms. Both groups go through a complete cycle of emotions, but in completely opposite phases. This is not to suggest that members of the public are always wrong at major market turns and that professionals are always correct, but that in aggregate the opinions of these groups are usually in direct conflict.

Data are available on many of these market participants, so that over a period of years it has been possible to derive parameters that indicate when a particular group has moved to an extreme historically associated with a major market turning point.

Unfortunately, there is a possibility that many of the indexes that have proved useful historically may now be partially distorted because of the advent of listed options trading in 1973 and the introduction of stock index futures in 1982. This possibility arises because the purchase and sale of options and index futures are a substitute for short selling and other speculative activity formerly carried out on the Stock Exchange.

Generally speaking, the data relating to market participants that have not been unduly affected by options trading before the mid-1960s are unavailable. Some degree of caution should therefore be exercised in the interpretation of these data in view of their relatively short history. For these reasons, some of the more popular indicators measuring investor expectations which almost certainly have been distorted by options trading and other technical factors, such as the odd-lot statistics, are not discussed here; but since a description of technical analysis would not be complete without some reference to investor sentiment, some of the more reliable indicators are considered below. Incorporation of three or four indexes measuring sentiment is useful from the point of view of assessing the majority view, from which a contrary opinion can be taken.

MEMBERS' SHORT INDEX

Each week data are published by the NYSE which break down the total round-lot short sales into two categories, namely, those made by stock exchange members and those made by nonmembers. A ratio of members' short sales to the total short sales is calculated each week and then smoothed by a 10-week moving average (see Charts 21.1 and 21.2a). Over the years, stock exchange members in aggregate have proved to be consistently on the right side of the market. Consequently, when the 10-week Members' Short Index reaches the 85 percent level, it indicates that over the previous 10-week period only 15 percent of total NYSE short sales have been made by the public. A 65 percent reading in the ratio, on the other hand, shows that a somewhat higher 35 percent of all short sales have been made by the public. A high level of shorting by the public (30 to 35 percent) is considered bullish, and a low level (15 to 20 percent) bearish. Readings between 70 and 80 percent are considered normal and have little forecasting value. Sometimes the ratio is smoothed by a 2-month moving average, which is shown on Chart 21.2b along with a similar index for the American Stock Exchange. The dashed lines on the chart are representative of the extreme levels of the index, although it can be seen, for example, that in the mid-sixties high readings did not necessarily immediately result in a falling stock market.

A high reading in the index indicates a reluctance on the part of the

CHART 21.1 DJIA versus Members' 10-Week Short Ratio.

(SOURCE: Pring Market Review.)

public to go short, since this group is anticipating a further market advance. But chances are that these expectations have already been translated into stock purchases, leaving these participants with little or no cash reserves with which to push stock prices higher. On the other hand, if the ratio is at a low 65 percent reading, the oppressive nature of public short selling indicates that an extremely pessimistic attitude toward the market has developed. Chances are that most of the discouraging news has already been built into the price level and that the market is likely to advance.

In this respect it is worth noting that the index has a habit of achieving a series of declining peaks as the market works its way higher (for example, 1965 and 1966). These divergences should be viewed as growing technical weakness, just as the two descending troughs in 1962 indicated technical strength in November of that year, since the public was shorting proportionally more stock even though stock prices held above their earlier lows.

The Members' Short Index can also be interpreted in other ways. For example, it can be seen from Chart 21.1 that during the period under scrutiny whenever the index moved above the 85 percent level and then fell below it, an important decline resulted. Such periods are marked with downward sloping arrows. Occasionally, as in the 1959, 1961, and 1962 signals, the market rallies before the decline sets in. In the 1972 situation the DJIA rallied for about 9 months after the warning from the Members' Short Index. However, during that period the broad market sold off quite sharply so that the signal actually corresponded with the bull market high for indexes such as the Value Line Composite which reflect the performance of secondary issues. Chart 21.2a shows that in the 5-year period between 1978

CHART 21.2a   DJIA and three measures of market sentiment.

(SOURCE: Pring Market Review.)

and 1983 the Members' Short Index rose above the 85 percent level five times and that each such rise was followed by an important decline.

At the other end of the spectrum, a decline below the 65 percent level followed by a move above it offered a very good buy signal in 1962, 1966, 1970, and 1974.

Although it is possible that the Members' Short Index may have been distorted by options trading, it is also apparent that the option alternative is open to both members and nonmembers alike, since the ratio relates two categories of short selling to each other. This is not the case for many other indexes constructed from short-sale data, since most of these compare short sales to some other figure, e.g., odd-lot shorts to odd-lot sales or total NYSE short position to total NYSE volume.

CHART 21.2b   DJIA versus Members 4-Week Short Ratio.

Dow Jones Industrials (monthly high-low-close)

NYSE members short ratio (2-month average)

AMEX members short ratio (2-month average)

J A J O J A J O J A J O J A J O J A J O J A J O J A J O J A J O J A J O J A J O J A J O J A J O J A J O J A J O J A J O J A J O J A J O J A J O J
1957 58   59   60   61   62   63   64   65   66   67   68   69   70   71   72   73   74   1975

(SOURCE: *J. C. Bradford, Nashville, Tenn.*)

PUBLIC SPECIALISTS' RATIO

Chart 21.3a shows a 10-week moving average of what might be regarded as the weekly ratio which pits the smart money against one of the least informed categories. It measures the round-lot short selling done by the public against the NYSE specialists on the floor of the Exchange. This indicator, which has been plotted inversely to correspond with peaks and troughs in the market, seems to be most useful when used in conjunction with the 60 and 30 percent levels. For instance, whenever it rises above or toward the 30 percent level and then falls below it or reverses direction (vice versa for the 60 percent level), it triggers reliable sell and buy signals, respectively.

SHORT INTEREST RATIO

The short interest is a figure published around the end of the month which reports the number of shares that have been sold short on the NYSE. Similar

CHART 21.3a DJIA and three indicators.

(SOURCE: Pring Market Review.)

data are also published by the other exchanges. The short interest is both a flow-of-funds statistic, since every share sold short has to be repurchased (covered), and a measure of sentiment. This is true because a large number of shares sold short indicates a predominantly bearish attitude, and vice versa. Over the years technicians have discovered that the ratio of the short interest to the average daily volume of the preceding month offers more reliable signals than the short interest taken by itself. The short interest ratio is shown on Chart 21.3a. The ratio is most bullish when it is at a reading of 1.8 or higher. In Chart 21.3a it has been plotted inversely so that readings in excess of 1.8 are shown below the lower dashed line. Typically, readings in excess of 2.0 are even more bullish. A short interest ratio of less than 1 has normally reflected a very bullish consensus. The short interest ratio appears to work best as a bullish indicator after a lengthy decline rather than after a sustained upmove. Thus, in 1967 and 1968, buy signals were generated but were followed only by weak rallies. On the other hand, the signal given in late 1962 occurred around the time of the second part of a double bottom,

CHART 21.3b   Dow Jones Industrial Average versus mutual fund liquidity and 12-month moving average, 1966–1977.

when the short interest was rising and the total volume was shrinking, thereby offering a classic warning of the dynamic bull market which was to follow.

INSIDER TRADING

Stockholders who hold in excess of 5 percent of the total voting stock of a company and corporate officers or other employees who have access to important corporate information are required to file with the Securities and Exchange Commission (SEC) any purchases or sales within 10 days. As a group, these "insiders" are generally correct in their decisions, having a tendency to sell proportionately more stock as the market rises, and vice versa. An 8-week moving average of the weekly insider sell/buy ratio is shown at the bottom of Chart 21.2a. The chart shows that as prices work their way higher, insiders step up their sales as a percentage of purchases. Market peaks are signaled when, after a period of a few months or more of a rising ratio, the trend is reversed. A rise above the 2:1 level and a reversal in direction of the index is normally sufficient therefore to offer a bearish signal. Unfortunately, the lag in the data and the lag caused by the MA calculations can result in a late signal. In 1973 and 1977, for example, the ratio turned down well after the peak in prices.

When the 8-week MA moves above the 3.5 level it is usually better to wait not only for a reversal in trend but also for the indicator to decline below this important benchmark before coming to a bearish conclusion. Typically, when such a signal is given the market sooner or later embarks on a major shakeout.

At market lows the 1:1 level appears to offer the best warning of an impending advance. If the index either falls below the 1 level and then rises above it, or even just declines to briefly touch it, as in early 1978 or March 1980, a rally usually results.

ADVISORY SERVICES

Since 1963 Investors' Intelligence[1] has been compiling data on the opinions of publishers of market letters. It might be expected that this group would be well informed and offer advice of a contrary nature by recommending acquisition of equities at market bottoms and offering selling advice at market tops. The evidence suggests that the advisory services in aggregate act in a completely opposite manner and therefore represent a good proxy for "majority" opinion.

Chart 21.2a shows the percentage of bullish market letter writers in relation to the total of all those expressing an opinion. The data have been smoothed by a 10-week moving average to iron out misleading fluctuations. The resulting index shows that the advisory services follow the trend of equity prices by becoming most bullish near market tops and predominantly pessimistic around market bottoms. Investors would clearly find it more profitable to take a position contrary to that of the advisory service industry.

This index also gives a good indication of how market psychology can swing from outright pessimism to extreme overconfidence. In early 1968, for example, virtually all services were putting out bearish forecasts right at a major low. Then, as prices began to rise, their prognostications became more optimistic and turned to outright bullishness by the time prices reached their highest level. This indicator would have proved very useful during the 1973–1974 bear market, for although the averages experienced two substantial declines in 1973, the index showed that while confidence among the advisory services was low, it was not sufficiently weak to indicate that a major bottom had been reached.

Both Charts 21.2a and 21.4 show that whenever the Advisory Services Sentiment Indicator has moved below the 35 percent level and then risen above it, important buy signals have resulted. The two weakest signals occurred during the 1969–1970 bear market in 1969, and both were fol-

[1]Larchmont, N.Y.

CHART 21.4 Advisory service sentiment.

* Bulls as a percentage of bulls and bears

(SOURCE: *Investors' Intelligence, Inc., Larchmont, N.Y.*)

lowed by a bear market rally. At market tops a decline from the eighties or high seventies below the 75 level appears to offer a fairly consistent warning of impending trouble.

The principles of nonconfirmation and divergence can also be applied to the interpretation of this index. For example, the Dow peak in 1973 was not confirmed by a new high in the Advisory Services Sentiment Indicator. During the 1969–1970 bear market, prices worked their way lower, but confidence was markedly higher in May 1970 than in July 1969, thereby setting up a positive divergence.

MUTUAL FUNDS

Data on mutual funds are published monthly by the Investment Company Institute. The statistics are useful because they monitor the actions of both the public and the institutions. In recent years money-market and tax-exempt mutual funds have become widespread, so the data used here have been modified to include only equity funds. There are two useful measurements of mutual fund activity. The first relates to mutual fund cash as a percentage of assets, and the second to mutual fund cash and annual redemptions. Both should be treated in a strict sense as flow-of-funds indicators but are discussed here as indicators of sentiment.

Mutual Fund Cash/Assets Ratio

At all times mutual funds hold a certain amount of liquid assets, so that investors wishing to cash in or redeem their investment can be accommodated. When the cash position is expressed as a percentage of the total value of mutual funds' portfolios (a figure known as total asset value), a useful indicator is derived (see Chart 21.3). The index moves in the opposite direction to the stock market, since the proportion of cash held by mutual funds rises as prices fall, and vice versa. There are three reasons for this characteristic. First, as the value of a fund's portfolio falls in a declining market, the proportion of cash held will automatically rise even though no new cash is raised. Second, as prices decline, the funds become more cautious in their buying policy, since they see fewer opportunities for capital gains. Third, the decision is made to hold more cash reserves as insurance against a rush of redemptions by the public. In a rising market the opposite effect is felt, as advancing prices automatically reduce the proportion of cash, sales increase, and fund managers are under tremendous pressure to capitalize on the bull market by being fully invested.

The cash/assets ratio can be interpreted in two ways. First, as illustrated in Chart 21.3, two parameters are used as benchmarks for buying and selling. In most instances such signals result in an unduly long lead time before peaks and troughs, and an alternative approach is to wait for a reversal in the trend of the index. A useful method of accomplishing this is to construct a 12-month moving average of the ratio, using crossover points as buy and sell indicators. Most of the time this technique is very useful, but occasionally, when the action of the index is indecisive (e.g., the 1971–1972 period), whipsaws can develop. In such instances it is as well to examine the action of other expectational and technical indicators, with the objective of forming an overall opinion rather than trying to fathom the course of one particular indicator.

Mutual Fund Cash/Redemptions

Another way of looking at the pressure on mutual funds is to compare their cash position with the previous 3 months of redemptions. In this instance the cash reserves are used as a proxy for institutional buying power, and the redemptions as an indication of selling pressure on the market by the public. This ratio is shown in Chart 21.5. When cash on hand is considerably higher than redemptions, i.e., when the ratio is in excess of 18, selling by the public does not appear to place undue pressure on the institutions. Con-

CHART 21.5 DJIA versus Mutual Fund Cash/3-Month Redemption Ratio.

(SOURCE: Pring Market Review.)

versely, when the ratio falls to 8 or below, this combination of low cash reserves (buying power) and strong selling pressure results in declining prices. Quite often a change in the direction of the trend can be as important as the actual level of the index. Consequently, a moving average can prove useful in assessing important juncture points in the index.

MARGIN DEBT

Trends in margin debt are probably better classified as flow-of-funds indicators, but since the trend and level of margin debt is also a good indication of investor confidence (or lack of confidence), it is discussed in this section.

Margin debt is money borrowed from brokers and bankers using securities as collateral. The credit is normally used for the purchasing of equities. At the beginning of a typical stock market cycle, margin debt is relatively low; it begins to rise very shortly after the final bottom in equity prices. As prices rise, the margin trader becomes more confident, wishes to take maximum advantage of an advancing market, and purchases more stock by taking on additional margin debt.

During a primary uptrend, margin debt is a valuable source of new funds for the stock market. The importance of this factor can be appreciated when it is noted that margin debt increased by $6.3 billion between 1974 and 1977. The essential difference between stock purchased for cash and that bought on margin is that the latter at some point must be sold in order to pay off the debt, whereas stock purchased outright can theoretically be held indefinitely. Consequently, during stock market declines margin debt reverses its positive role and becomes an important source of stock supply.

This occurs for four reasons. First, margin requirements are fairly closely regulated, so the financial position and sophistication of margin-oriented investors is relatively superior to that of other market participants. When this group realizes that the potential for capital gains has greatly diminished, a trend toward liquidation begins. Thus, margin debt has flattened or declined within 3 months of all but one of the 14 stock market peaks since 1932.

Second, primary stock market peaks are invariably preceded by rising interest rates, which in turn increase the carrying cost of margin debt, therefore making it less attractive to maintain.

Third, since 1934 the Federal Reserve Board (the "Fed") has been empowered to set and vary margin requirements, which specify the amount that can be lent by a broker or bank to customers for the purpose of holding securities. This measure was considered necessary in view of the substantial expansion of margin debt in the late 1920s, the liquidation of which greatly contributed to the severity of the 1929–1932 bear market. When stock prices have been rising strongly for a period of time, speculation develops, often resulting in a sharp rise in margin debt. Sensing that things could get out of control at this stage, the Fed raises the margin requirement, which has the effect of reducing the buying power of the general public from what it might otherwise have been. Normally, it takes several margin-requirement changes to significantly reduce the buying power of margin speculators, since the substantial advance in the price of stocks—which was responsible for the requirements' being raised in the first place—normally creates additional collateral at a rate which is sufficient to offset the rise in reserve requirements.

Fourth, once stock prices have begun their decline, the collateral value of the securities used as a basis for the margin debt falls, and the margin speculator is faced with the option of putting up more money or selling stock in order to pay off the debt. At first, the margin call process is reasonably orderly, as most traders have a sufficient cushion of collateral to protect them from the initial drop in prices. Alternatively, those who are undermargined often choose to put up additional collateral or cash. Toward the end of a bear market, prices fall more rapidly, and this unnerving process, combined with the unwillingness or inability of margin customers to come up with additional collateral, triggers a rush of margin calls, which substantially adds to the supply of stock which must be sold regardless of price. This self-feeding downward spiral of forced liquidation continues until margin debt has contracted to a more manageable level.

As a potential influence on stock prices, margin debt can be examined with regard to both its trend and its level. Chart 21.6 shows the New York Stock Exchange Composite and the amount of margin debt outstanding with brokers. (The margin debt index has been revised from time to time, which accounts for the broken nature of this series.) It can be seen that each bear

CHART 21.6   New York Stock Exchange Composite versus margin debt level.

(SOURCE: The Bank Credit Analyst.)

market since 1949 has been accompanied by some form of liquidation in margin debt. Also important is the amount of margin debt in relation to the value of all securities; this measure gives an indication of the presence of the speculative content. This ratio, shown at the bottom of Chart 21.7, uses the market value of stocks listed on the New York Stock Exchange as a proxy for the value of all securities. The scale incorporating the margin debt ratio has been compressed before 1947, for easier presentation of data. The ratio is affected by three factors: the absolute level of margin debt (both at brokers and banks), the number of shares listed on the New York Stock Exchange, and the price of those shares. Over a period of 12 to 24 months the number of shares outstanding does not fluctuate significantly, and thus within a particular cycle it is the level of margin debt and stock prices that determines the course of the ratio.

Generally speaking, when the ratio approaches 1.5 percent and then begins to fall, the bull market in stocks is approaching maturity. Moreover, in the postwar period a reading close to 1.5 percent has normally been associated with a hike in the margin requirement.

Since stock index futures were introduced in 1982, it is quite possible that

CHART 21.7 Margin debt as a percentage of total NYSE capitalization.

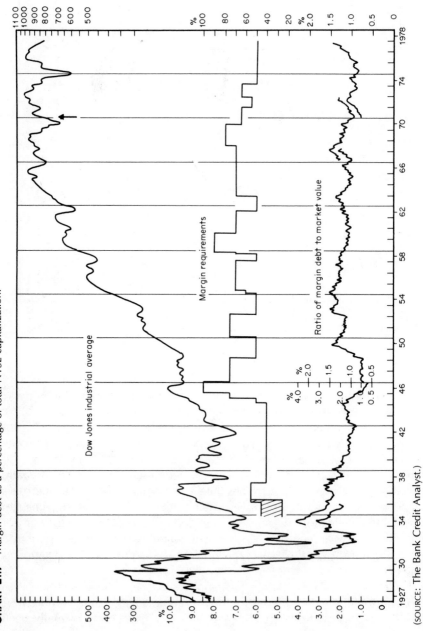

Dow Jones industrial average

Margin requirements

Ratio of margin debt to market value

(SOURCE: The Bank Credit Analyst.)

280

CHART 21.8   NYSE and two measures of sentiment.

(SOURCE: Deliberations, *Toronto, Ontario, Canada.*)

margin statistics will no longer prove to be so reliable. This factor should be borne in mind in future interpretations of these statistics.

Stock Index Futures as Measures of Sentiment

Stock index futures have had a very brief trading history in comparison with other market instruments, and any results obtained in this period of 2 to 4 years should be treated with great caution. One indicator which seems to have worked reasonably well, but only from a trading point of view, is the amount of premium or discount of a theoretical 3-month forward contract over the cash or spot index. Chart 21.8 shows this relationship smoothed by a 10-day moving average for the S&P Composite.

Typically, the peak in the Premium Discount Index occurs at around the same time as the short-term peak in prices. A move to a discount by the futures generally represents a buying opportunity. As more data over several cycles become available, this indicator may well offer some useful longer-term benchmarks. It is shown here merely to point up that as new market vehicles are introduced, technicians should review them with the ultimate goal of creating new tools for the technical arsenal.

Contrary Opinion as a Sentiment Indicator

Since, as already mentioned, the crowd is typically wrong at major market turning points, and since the news media normally reflect majority opinion, a sentiment indicator based solely on reports, cover stories, network news items, and other public sources would probably be extremely useful. In practice, it is of course not possible to construct a precise indicator. However, a careful study of popular magazine publications (such as *Time, Newsweek, U.S. News & World Report, Fortune,* or *Business Week*), the network evening news, financial books on the best-seller list, and other such sources can offer a very useful supplement to the indicator approach.

Typically, at the top or bottom of an established move the story of a market crashing, the gold price soaring, or some other extreme event is in itself newsworthy and the story will appear as either a prominent article or a cover story. I do not mean to imply that the media are incompetent because they emphasize financial stories at the wrong time—quite the reverse in fact, because their function is to publish newsworthy stories. From a market aspect, of course, nothing is more newsworthy than a panic-stricken or euphoric market. Unfortunately, by the time the facts have been widely disseminated, they have usually been well discounted by the markets; it is thus highly likely that the media are publicizing the end rather than the beginning of a move. Occasionally a cover story or article will prove timely for investment purposes, as happened with the famous "Birth of the Bull" *Time* cover at the beginning of the 1982–1983 advance. In this case some interpretation would have been necessary since the stock market had grabbed the news on record volume and a very sharp price rise, both of which are characteristic of the beginning of a major move. It is very important, therefore, to make sure that such stories are consistent with the other technical indicators.

Typically, the news story will not be an isolated example but will appear in many publications in one form or another. It is therefore possible to identify a basic theme. After a sustained run-up in stock prices, for example, one article may be quoting experts who are forecasting significantly higher prices, and another may feature analysts touting their favorite stocks or the tremendous incomes being earned by America's leading stockbrokers. Such a trend will almost invariably indicate that the pendulum has swung too far in the bullish direction. At major market lows the opposite type of story will emerge, highlighting a panic decline, some financial problem seemingly impossible to resolve, or a major bankruptcy. A major feature during the early evening network news right from the floor of the Exchange usually proves to be a classic tip-off that the decline is either over or in its very late stages.

At other times an isolated article or story on an obscure topic will offer a vital clue that a trend has gone too far. For example, in late 1981, just before a major debt market sell-off, an article pointing out the profit potential for Treasury-bill/Treasury-bond spreads was printed in one of the major magazines. In the summer of 1983, just before a major sell-off, another magazine ran a long article on stock index futures. Although experienced investors are familiar with such concepts and trading vehicles, this type of article is very unusual for a general-purpose magazine. Another classic was a CBS evening news feature on the price of sugar in 1980 which occurred within 1 or 2 days of the bull market peak. It is doubtful whether the sugar price has been discussed on that program either before or since.

The art of forming a correct contrary opinion based on an observation of the media is not easy, since such articles and features usually are published or aired at a time when no one in his or her right mind would expect a market reversal, and since there are no obvious overbought or oversold parameters on which to base a judgment of historical behavior. Putting this approach into practice is therefore not a simple matter, and this discussion is intended only to illustrate the possibilities which exist for augmenting a more orthodox technical approach.

SUMMARY

1. Sentiment indicators are a useful adjunct to the trend-determining techniques discussed earlier. They should be used for the purpose of assessing a majority of consensus opinion from which a contrary position can be taken.

2. Since it is difficult to derive actual levels from which definitive investment action can be taken, none of these measures of investor psychology should be used in isolation; each should therefore be analyzed from the point of view of confirming the rest. Only in this way can an accurate overall assessment of market sentiment be made.

22

Speculative Activity in the Stock Market

Speculation has been defined as the undertaking of substantial risk in the hope of gain. Some degree of speculation is always present in market activity, in the sense that there are always individuals willing to bear a risk. However, since virtually all bull markets in their late stages have clearly defined characteristics of speculation, an examination of some indicators that measure this phenomenon of excessive confidence is well worthwhile.

Over the course of the stock market cycle, investors move from outright pessimism and sometimes panic at market bottoms to an outlook of overconfidence and avarice at market tops. On the assumption that, once set in motion, a trend in market psychology perpetuates itself, it is important to determine the level of emotion at any point compared with previous periods and also to detect any reversal in its trend at a relatively early stage.

MEASURING SPECULATION

As discussed in previous chapters, there are four main aspects or dimensions of psychology in the stock market: price, volume, time, and breadth. Price reflects the level of enthusiasm; volume, the intensity of enthusiasm; breadth, the extent of participation; and time, the extent of the period. The farther these four factors work in any one direction, the greater the significance of the counterreaction. Thus, by late 1929, stock prices had been rising almost uninterruptedly for 8 years. Prices had increased fivefold, and volume at the time of the peak was exceptionally heavy. The counterreaction was naturally extreme, with an almost total collapse in equity prices. Since speculation is one of the most emotional aspects of the stock market, examination from all four dimensions—price, volume, time, and breadth—is relevant.

Price

One method of evaluating speculation is to compare the prices of low- and high-quality issues. The rationale is that low-quality stocks are more volatile and, in a bull market, will rise proportionately faster than better-quality stocks. The high potential for profit in these equities makes them very popular with speculators. In addition, members of the public who like to buy in 100-share "round" lots but do not have the capital to purchase higher-priced stocks in these quantities find low-priced equities a natural vehicle.

The upper portion of Chart 22.1 shows the Standard & Poor's Low-Priced and High-Grade stock indexes. The relatively high volatility of the low-priced stocks is self-evident and is a good reflection of the exaggerated emotions of investors during a market cycle. At market bottoms the Low-Priced Index either lags or coincides with the Dow Jones Industrial Average and is therefore a confirming indicator. At market peaks the index usually leads by anywhere from 0 to 15 months. Considered in isolation, the index itself is not too helpful in determining levels of speculation, though obviously a sustained but controlled uptrend points to a good underlying improvement in confidence, while a more exponential trend after a slow but lengthy rise is a good tip-off to a speculative peak.

The lower portion of Chart 22.1 shows what amounts to a relative-strength line comparing the Low-Priced Index to the Standard & Poor's High-Grade Stock Index. It is calculated by dividing the Low-Priced by the High-Grade Index. Whenever this ratio is below 100, the value of the higher-grade index is greater than that of the low-priced. Such a condition reflects a relatively defensive posture by speculators and is normally associated with major bottom areas. With the exception of 1961, the ratio has always been above 100 at major tops.

There is no absolute level that indicates a peak in speculation. However, the high readings in the late 1920s, 1937, 1946, and 1968 (all of which followed lengthy periods of rising stock prices) were clearly pointing out that activity was reaching an extreme from which a major counterreaction could

CHART 22.1 Low-priced versus high-priced stocks.

(SOURCE: Pring Market Review.)

be expected. It is important to distinguish between the high levels which occur in this index after a long and substantial rise in equities and, for example, those that occurred in 1933–1934 and 1951, which were strong upward reactions in low-priced stocks following a long and sharp decline. In retrospect it can be seen that the 1971–1972 rally was really a temporary interruption of what proved to be a long corrective period.

Volume

Chart 22.2 shows the average monthly volume of the American Stock Exchange expressed as a percentage of that on the New York Stock Exchange. The rationale for using this index is basically the same as the high-grade/ low-price comparison. Generally speaking, because of less stringent listing

CHART 22.2 American Stock Exchange volume as a percentage of New York Stock Exchange volume (monthly).

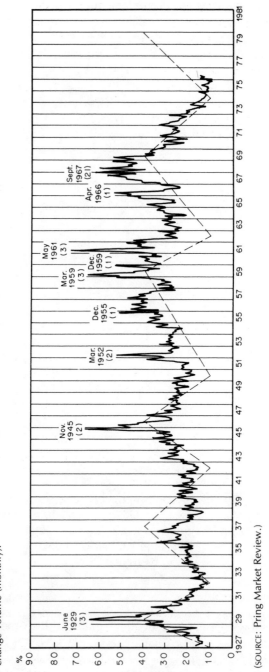

(SOURCE: Pring Market Review.)

requirements, stocks trading on the ASE are of lower quality than those on the NYSE. Since speculators normally deal in low-quality issues, rises and falls in the index therefore reflect volume trends toward more or less speculation. Historically, levels of 50 percent or more have occurred in the area of tops. Normally these high readings lead ultimate peaks in the Dow by several months or more. Conversely, levels of 20 percent or less (when speculation in terms of volume has been low) have often been good buying points, although purchases would have been more profitably made if this somewhat erratic indicator had been used in conjunction with the others.

Breadth

One prerequisite for a strong surge in speculation is that equities should have been rising on a broad front for a relatively long period of time. For the general level of confidence to mature into a speculative orgy, it is first necessary for the broad spectrum of stocks to advance rather than for the price rise to be confined to a relatively select group.

If only a few investors are making money, overconfidence is unlikely to develop, but if virtually everyone is profiting, the ingredients are in place for a self-feeding spiral resulting in an excess of optimism.

Breadth is portrayed in Chart 17.2 (see page 224) by an advance/decline line constructed on the basis of the $\sqrt{A/u} - D/u$ formula discussed in Chapter 17. Until 1969 every cyclical peak in the Dow since 1931 was confirmed by the A/D line. In 1968 the line made a new cyclical high unaccompanied by the DJIA, while in 1973 the opposite occurred. These examples illustrate the necessity for strong breadth rather than a strong average to presage a speculative flurry. The 1968–1969 rise in the A/D line was a cumulation of the rise in speculation begun in 1962, but it was not reflected in the Dow. On the other hand, a notable high for the Industrial Average was achieved in January 1973 against an overall declining trend in breadth.

Previous speculative peaks were preceded not only by strong rises in breadth but also by a rise that had extended for a number of years. Only after a long advance was confidence able to develop into excessive optimism.

Time

For a strong speculative wave to get under way, it is necessary not only to correct the excesses of the previous speculative peak but also to establish a fairly lengthy period of rising stock prices, so that a feeling of gradually improving confidence can erase the fears and caution of the corrective processes. Since many investors suffer staggering losses during the declining period, time is also needed either to restore their financial viability or to develop a new generation of participants who have not undergone the sobering experience of a speculative cleansing. Once confidence resumes, it can become a self-feeding spiral as investors undertake risks as a group which they would never contemplate as independent and clear-thinking individuals.

In observing the patterns of the speculative indicators discussed above, it becomes clear that this repetitive emotional transition from greed to fear and back to greed forms an approximate cycle. Since the 1920s, for example, there have been three outstanding speculative peaks (1928–1929, 1946, and 1967–1968) occurring about 20 years apart. In turn, these major peaks were separated by two other peaks at roughly 10-year intervals, namely 1937 and 1959, so that there were really five peaks of speculation in all, each falling in the latter part of their respective decade. Between these periods of excesses, troughs also occurred at 10-year intervals when risk-bearing was at a minimum. These points happened around the years 1932, 1942, 1950, 1962, and 1974. Following these low points there was a period either of bounce-back or of speculative recovery, such as 1934 or 1951–1952, or the beginning of a slow but sustained rise in speculation, as in 1942–1946 or 1962–1968. This idealized cycle has been superimposed on the volume and price indicators discussed above. There are some obvious drawbacks in utilizing this approach, since volume, price, and breadth do not always coincide. For example, in 1936–1937 the high-grade/low-priced ratio was quite high, and breadth had risen sharply for a fairly lengthy 5 years. On the other hand, ASE/NYSE volume was high (34 percent) compared with 1932 (10 percent), but it was still well below other speculative peaks. Conversely, the ASE/NYSE volume reached its highest recorded level in 1961, at around 74 percent, against a relatively short 6-month advance in breadth and a price ratio that showed low-priced stocks only marginally above high-grade issues.

YIELD

As another approach to the 10-year-cycle concept of speculation, stock yields are worth examining, since yields reflect one form of equity valuation. Consequently, if stocks are overvalued, i.e., possess low yields, some degree of speculation is implied, and vice versa. Chart 22.3 shows the yield of the Barron's 50-Stock Average on which the idealized 10-year cycle has been superimposed. With the obvious exception of 1936–1937, when yields rose as speculation and stock prices advanced, the cycle fits very well.

CHART 22.3 Dividend yields (Barron's 50-Stock Average) and the 10-year cycle in speculation.

(SOURCE: Pring Market Review.)

The Influence of Options and Stock Index Futures

To some extent, traditional methods of speculation may be distorted by the advent of listed options and trading in stock index futures. Unfortunately, data on these new vehicles do not go back far enough to be of any predictive value; indeed, it is not clear what proportion of such trading is due to arbitrage and hedging and what to speculation. Although their development may dilute some of the activity associated with lower-quality issues, the concept of a wasting asset or ultra-high gearing is not palatable to all speculators. Consequently, it should be fair to assume that though some of the indicators discussed above may not reach the fervent levels witnessed on previous occasions, they should continue to give some indication of the general trend and level of speculative activity.

SUMMARY

1. From the point of view of the long-term investor, the establishment of a major cyclical peak in speculation is an important factor, since speculation is normally the last but most dynamic stage of any bull market.

2. Since the 1920s, there have been five such peaks (1928–1929, 1936–1937, 1946, 1959, and 1967–1969), separated by about 10 years. A major decline followed these excesses of optimism from which the market, as measured by the A/D line, did not recover to a new high for at least 4 years. In most cases this retracement took much longer.

3. In addition to these speculative peaks, there is also an approximate 10-year cycle of troughs characterized by a dearth of speculative activity and a general disgust with equities. Following these major cyclical lows,

there is normally an initial rebound or recovery in speculation. These recovery periods were not followed by severe and lengthy declines since insufficient time had elapsed for formation of major distributions. For example, while the 1951–1952 period showed breadth advancing sharply, accompanied by high readings in the ASE/NYSE volume and high-grade/low-price ratios, the A/D line had merely returned to its 1946 level over a comparatively short period.

4. These indicators of confidence or speculation are not precise tools like those discussed earlier; rather, they offer a longer-term perspective on how far the trend of optimism or pessimism has developed. Consequently, they are useful background indicators that can lead to a more enlightened interpretation of the mechanical techniques.

Putting the Indicators Together

It is now appropriate to examine an actual market cycle by putting all the indicators together and observing how they work in practice. The 1970–1974 period has been chosen because that particular cycle offers a substantial variety of technical conditions that are worth studying.

Using the Dow Jones Industrial Average, Chart 23.1 illustrates the market action of this period in a simplified wave form, showing the three upward phases of the 1970–1973 bull market and the three downward phases of the 1973–1974 bear market. The description will focus upon these two primary moves and the intervening secondary corrections.

The cycle begins in the dark days of late May 1970. The market had been declining dramatically for 6 weeks on gradually expanding volume, the trend of virtually all the technical indicators was down, and there seemed no end in sight to falling prices. Nevertheless, there were some tentative indications that prices would soon bottom out, since short-term interest rates and long-term government bonds had already reversed their cyclical trends in late 1969.[1]

By the end of May it was obvious that a selling climax had taken place. While this did not necessarily mean that the ultimate low had been reached, it did imply that the May bottom would hold at least temporarily and that

[1] See Charts 19.1 and 20.1.

293

CHART 23.1 Dow Jones Industrial Average and major movements, 1970–1974.

prices were unlikely to decline for a while. At the same time, many of the oscillators were recording extreme "oversold" conditions. The annual rate of change of the Dow, for instance (see Chart 12.6) was at a postwar low, while the 10-week moving average of the A/D ratio (Chart 17.1) was at a very negative level. In addition, many of the sentiment indicators were pointing up an extreme degree of pessimism. This can be observed from Charts 21.1, 21.2a, and 21.3b which represent the Members' Short Ratio, the Advisory Service Index, and the Mutual Funds Cash/Asset Ratio respectively.

At this juncture many of the indicators were pointing out that a new bull market was in the process of being born, but as yet no long-term trends had been broken, no long-term moving averages had been crossed, no bases had been built, and certainly no positive divergences had been observed among the major averages. It was not until the summer months of 1970 that more tangible signs of a cyclical reversal appeared. First, a base was formed by most averages as the early June rally petered out and a successful test of the May lows was achieved. Then as prices rose in July and August, a clearly defined bear market trendline was penetrated on the upside (see Chart 23.1). During this period, the 18-month weighted moving average of the 4- to 6-month commercial paper rate turned down (see Chart 19.4), confirming that a cyclical reversal in short-term rates had taken place. Finally, longer-term indicators of price and volume momentum turned up (see Chart 16.2). These indicators offered fairly conclusive proof that a new bull market had begun in May, especially as they were accompanied by a Dow theory buy signal in December. Finally, encouragement was given by the World Stock Index, which had crossed above its 40-week moving average (Chart 24.2), accompanied by a rising trend in the smoothed momentum index (Chart 24.1).

Prices generally rose until March 1971, following which an 8-month correction took place. Advance warning of this intermediate decline was given by several interest-sensitive indexes. The Federal Funds rate, for example, had already given a sell signal in February as it moved above its 10-week moving average, and its momentum index had crossed above its zero reference line (see Chart 19.1). This signal was validating the action of the Utility index, which had topped out in January and had refused to confirm the March high in the DJIA. The A/D line had also peaked ahead of the industrial average. Many of the oscillators had also reached extremely overbought conditions earlier in the year, but this was quite a normal and healthy phenomenon for the early stages of a bull market. Only a decline in momentum accompanied by a break in the trend of the index being monitored really flashes a red light.

The position at the March peak in the Dow was therefore one in which the interest-sensitive and breadth indexes had begun to diverge, and the oscillators were declining from an overbought condition. In addition, many of the sentiment indicators were also at bearish extremes. Certainly no distribution had formed, the strong uptrend since May 1970 was still intact, and the longer-term momentum indicators were still positive, like the primary trend of the commercial paper rate, as evidenced by the strongly rising 18-month weighted moving average. The situation appeared to be one of cyclical strength but potential intermediate weakness.

Not surprisingly, prices broke and continued falling until August. During this period, the strong July 1970–April 1971 uptrend of many averages was decisively violated on the downside. But since these trends were unsustainably steep, this development merely indicated that the market was adjusting to a more subdued rate of advance. By August the technical picture suggested that the market was oversold and a rally was called for. The 13-week rate of change of the DJIA, for example (see Chart 12.5), reached a low reading of −10 percent, and the percentage of Dow stocks in bullish trends fell to below 30 percent (see Chart 17.5). The rally did take place, and at the same time debt markets began to recover from their decline, which had started earlier than the stock market.

This was a very difficult period, since most long-term factors pointed to a continuation of the bull cycle, and the intermediate trends of interest-sensitive securities (normally a good lead indicator for the stock market) had also turned positive. Given the oversold nature of the market in August and the fact that the April–August downtrend had been violated on the upside, it would have been easy to come to the conclusion that the reaction was over, especially as volume expanded very sharply during late August. But this proved to be one of those times when patience would have paid off, since not all the indicators were in a positive position.

The 30-Day Most Active Indicator was the most notable, since it was unable to cross over its bullish area (+3) despite the surge in volume. In addition, while some of the major averages such as the DJIA were able to better their July highs, others (such as the weekly A/D line) failed to surpass theirs. The Members' Short Index had also crept back toward a very bearish 85 percent reading. Finally, despite the positive trend in the bond and money markets, the Utility Index continued to remain in its intermediate downtrend, while the World Index showed absolutely no indication of a reversal in its intermediate downtrend.

It was not until early December, when the market was much lower, that the Most Active Indicator became positive and the Utility Index was able to reverse its downtrend. By this time there were many more positive signs that the bull market was about to resume. First, the debt markets failed to make new lows in November and had therefore set up some positive divergences with the stock market. Second, the 10-week oscillator of the weekly A/D line had failed to significantly penetrate its August low, thereby creating a further positive divergence between it and the A/D line itself. Third, the indicators of long-term momentum measuring price and volume (Chart 16.2), while falling slightly, had not confirmed a bear market by falling below their zero reference lines. Finally, the Dow Jones Transportation Index had refused to confirm the November low in the Dow, thereby indicating that the Dow theory bull market was still intact.

The rally continued until April 1972, when the DJIA returned to the 950 resistance level, which again served to halt the advance as it had done one year earlier. The Dow did not sell off as it had in 1971, but began a period of consolidation in the 900–950 area that was to last for most of the balance of the year. The action over the ensuing months provided the first indication that the bull market was reaching maturity. First, the up phase of the 4-year cycle was rapidly running out of time, since it was 2 years old by May 1972. This did not necessarily mean that the rise could not continue longer (as shown by the 1962–1966 experience); but in view of renewed weakness of (1) the debt markets during this period, (2) the Utility Average, (3) the A/D line, and (4) the Most Active Index, some ominous rumblings were developing. Indeed, not only was the A/D line falling while the DJIA was marking time, but it had also failed to surpass its old 1971 high (see Chart 17.1). Moreover, even though long-term interest rates held steady until January 1973, the Federal Funds Indicator (Chart 19.1) went negative in the late spring of 1972, suggesting that the intermediate trend of short-term interest rates was up. Later on, the 18-month weighted moving average of 4- to 6-month commercial paper (Chart 19.4) started to rise, thereby confirming that the cyclical trend in short-term rates had also been reversed. To make matters worse, the Transportation Average, which had previously outperformed the Dow during the 1971 decline, began to fall off rather badly. Finally, all the sentiment indexes were portraying a picture of widespread confidence and optimism, which, from a contrary-opinion standpoint, suggested that a top was being made.

By October 1972 many of the oscillators measuring intermediate movements began to reach oversold conditions or, in the case of the 10-week A/D ratio, had created a positive divergence. The indications therefore were that a short-term rally would then take place. In the DJIA this proved to be somewhat more of an intermediate rise, as it rallied 15 percent from 900 to 1065, a new all-time high. Because of the rally, even greater divergences were set up, as this strong performance was not confirmed by many of the other indicators. As if things were not bad enough, short-term interest rates during this period began to rise even more sharply, accompanied by a discount rate hike and a rise in margin requirements in December. By late January, the long end of the bond market (Chart 20.1) also began to fall sharply. The situation in January 1973 was one in which the DJIA had broken out of what appeared to be a 9-year consolidation pattern, but the accompanying technical structure was so weak that the move proved to be spurious. The bear market, which had begun for most issues in mid-1972, had finally reached the blue-chip sector. During the early months of 1973 it also became apparent that the World Stock Index had turned down, although it was not until late spring that the index fell below its 40-week moving average (Chart 24.2). The first leg down of the new bear market was temporarily halted in July. The DJIA, the A/D line, and several other indicators made a new low in August, after a brief rally. But this secondary bottom was unconfirmed by the S&P 500 (Chart 12.1) and the upside-downside volume line (Chart 14.4). Moreover, two important oscillators—the 10-week A/D line ratio (see Chart 17.1) and the Trendline Over-200-Day Indicator (Chart 17.7)—were both well up from their July bottoms at the time of the new Dow low in August. These many divergences and oversold readings suggested that the market was in a position to mount a substantial rally, for the first time since the fall of 1972. However, that some of the longer-term indicators were still in the early stages of deterioration suggested that this rally was likely to be a bear market correction rather than the first leg of a new bull market. For example, both the 18-month weighted moving average of the commercial paper rate and the Federal Funds Indicator were indicating that the trend of short-term interest rates was still adverse for stock prices. In addition, the sentiment indicators were reflecting a fair degree of pessimism, but not enough to be commensurate with a bear market low. This can be observed from the Members' Short Index (Chart 21.1) and the Advisory Services Sentiment Indicator (Chart 21.2a).

In 7 weeks the Dow rose 12 percent, from 880 right back to the 1000 level on rapidly expanding volume. The speed and strength of the rally confused many into believing that the bear market was over. This deceptive characteristic is most common during the first rally of a bear market, since business conditions are usually still good and negative arguments seem less persuasive under a background of rising stock prices.

However, most of the indicators measuring long-term movements remained in a bearish trend throughout this period. Despite the softening in short-term interest rates, the 18-month weighted moving average of the commercial paper rate was still in a rising trend, and there had been no meaningful rally in long-term bonds. The Dow theory, which had signaled a bear market in April, was still negative, while most of the long-term momentum indicators were below their zero reference lines and falling. Still, some of these more sensitive longer-term indicators began to turn up, and for the first time in many years they gave a misleading signal; generally speaking, however, the proof of a new bull market was far from conclusive. In addition to the negative tone of many of the longer-term indicators, the rally had taken place during a period of rising interest rates, whereas falling interest rates normally lead or coincide with bear market bottoms. In any event, by October the market became overbought and was losing momentum in the face of a very major level of resistance around the Dow 1000 level. When the market runs into significant resistance under such conditions, it is always wiser to await the reaction which invariably takes place and then reassess the state of the indicators.

In this case the correction extended for 200 Dow points and left no doubt that the bear market was still very much alive.

The second bear market rally was not difficult to predict. The DJIA had fallen to an extremely significant support area at 800, while the various oscillators had again reached oversold territory. In the case of the 10-week A/D ratio, this was to be its lowest reading of the bear market. Although no major positive divergences were apparent, the Federal Funds Indicator, which had turned positive in November, was still signaling that lower interest rates lay ahead.

The ensuing rally was almost as deceptive as the previous one, but for different reasons. To start with, the oversold condition in December 1973 had been much greater than that of the previous July or August, leading many observers to believe that the December selling climax marked the end of the bear market. Moreover, the A/D line and many of the lower-priced stocks were initially acting much stronger than the Dow itself, as can be seen from a comparison of the two indexes in Chart 17.1.

This strength was short-lived, since the A/D line fell away very sharply following the late March peak in the Dow. Moreover, the 18-month weighted moving average of the commercial paper rate had remained in a negative trend throughout this period and was now joined by the Federal Funds Indicator, which also deteriorated in late March. While the Federal Reserve was obviously easing monetary policy during the December–March period, it did not at any time lower the discount rate. As the rally progressed, the Members' 10-Week Short Index and the Advisory Services Sentiment Indicator both turned over and began to deteriorate.

The ensuing reaction proved to be the third and final leg of the worst bear market since the 1930s. The 1974 bottom was initially signaled by a positive reading in the Federal Funds Indicator in October as well as a major set of divergences between the DJIA, the S&P 500, and the Transportation and Utility averages during October and December, when most indexes formed classic double bottoms. Several positive divergences were also observed in many of the oscillators. For example, the December reaction in the percentage of stocks above their 200-day moving average was far above the October low, thereby indicating a position of growing technical strength. By October most of the sentiment indexes had reached extreme levels of pessimism, adding further confirmation that a major bottom was being formed. By the end of January all the indicators had formed and broken out of large bases, Dow theory was signaling a new bull market, and most of the long-term momentum indexes had turned up accompanied by an expanding level of volume. These positive technical developments were also confirmed by the debt markets, most of which had made their cyclical bottoms in the fall. Finally, the World Stock Index, confirmed by virtually all the foreign stock indexes, had made a sharp reversal, and in January 1975 it rose explosively. There was little doubt that the 1974–1976 bull market had begun.

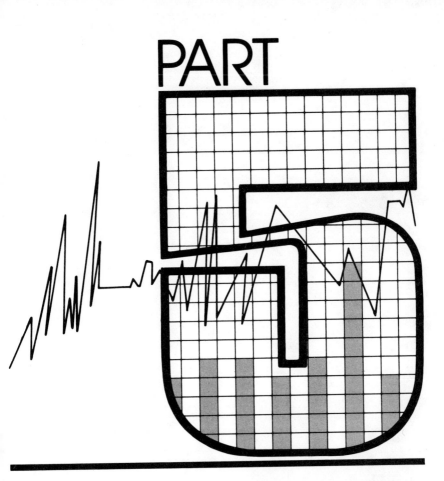

PART

Specific
Financial Markets

Technical Analysis of International Stock Markets

Since equities are bought and sold throughout the world for essentially the same reasons, the principles of technical analysis can be applied to any stock market. Unfortunately the degree of sophistication in statistical reporting of many countries does not permit the kind of detailed analysis that is available in the United States.

Nevertheless, it is possible to obtain data on price, breadth, and volume for nearly all countries. Information on industry groups and interest rates is also widely available.

Chart 24.1 shows the *Pring Market Review* World Stock Index, which is constructed from the market averages of 12 individual countries, each in turn weighted by that country's share of the sum total of all their gross national products. The World Stock Index is a good starting point from which to analyze the cyclical trends of the various stock markets, just as a composite index or the Dow Jones Industrial Average would be used as a focal point in assessing the U.S. market. This is true because the stock

CHART 24.1   World Stock Index versus 12-month momentum.

(SOURCE: Pring Market Review.)

markets of the individual countries tend to move in the same direction, just as the majority of U.S. stocks gravitate in the general direction of the DJIA most of the time. The individual stock markets do not all reach their peaks or troughs concurrently. The United Kingdom market, for example, has a tendency to lead, while the Japanese and Canadian markets are usually late turning down. If the world is treated as one unit comprising many parts (i.e., the various stock markets), it is possible to construct several indicators measuring world breadth, momentum, volume, etc.

In Chart 24.1, the presence of the international 4-year cycle is indicated by the arrows. It can be seen that the peaks in 1961, 1965, 1969, 1973, 1977, and 1981 are separated by approximately 4 years, and the troughs in 1962, 1966, 1970, 1974, 1978, and 1982 by the same period. The trend in the World Stock Index is therefore the starting point for analyzing the primary trends for individual markets, including that of the United States.

Shown beneath the World Stock Index is its 12-month rate-of-change index and a 14-month exponential moving average. This moving average, when used in combination with the moving average of the World Stock Index itself, has offered a useful confirmation of primary trend reversals in world equities.

Another way to analyze the global technical position is to calculate the percentage of individual-country indexes that are above their 40-week mov-

CHART 24.2   World Stock Index versus percentage of markets in positive trend.

(SOURCE: Pring Market Review.)

ing averages (see Chart 24.2). The chart shows that this measure of momentum is continually moving from the 0 (bullish) to the 100 percent (bearish) extremes. By the time the index has reached these outer parameters, the probabilities are that the larger portion of a price move has already taken place, although confirmation of an actual reversal should be obtained from a bearish signal in the World Stock Index itself in the form of a moving-average crossover or other trend reversal technique.

Extreme readings in the index are usually associated with primary reversals, but occasionally they mark the termination of an intermediate move. The action of the index following a decline, especially to a zero reading, can be very useful from the point of view of assessing the overall technical structure of the world equity markets. For example, the 60-point advance in this momentum index from 0 to 60 in early 1974 was accompanied by a relatively small price advance of about 10 points, while a similar rise of 50 percentage points in the index in late 1975 resulted in a proportionately larger price rise of 20 points in the World Index. The first example of strong momentum accompanied by a weak price rise was indicative of technical weakness and was followed by a substantial decline. The second, where

CHART 24.3 World Stock Index versus world industrial production.

(SOURCE: Pring Market Review.)

strong momentum was accompanied by a healthy price rise, was followed by a more sustainable advance, although prices eventually fell again due to the rapidly maturing position of the cycle.

Once the cyclical trend in the World Stock Index has been established, it is possible to determine more accurately the course of each individual stock market within the global equity cycle. Not all countries will rise or decline with the World Stock Index, because the principle of variation (see Chapter 15) applies just as much to countries as to individual stocks or groups. In addition, the long-term economic financial and political situations of coun-

CHART 24.4 World Stock Index versus world advance/decline line.

*Weighted by GNP. U.S., Japan, Germany, France, U.K., Italy,
Canada, Australia, Netherlands, Spain, Sweden.

(SOURCE: Pring Market Review.)

tries will vary, so that a good world bull market in equities may be brief or
almost nonexistent for a country undergoing severe financial distortions; this
was the Italian and French experience in the 1974–1977 global bull market.
Generally speaking, as time progresses and improvements in technology
and communications break down geographical and trading patterns, countries will become more interdependent, so that their stock market and business cycles are likely to become more closely related. The three stages of the
1974–1977 bull market shown in Charts 24.5 through 24.7 point up this
principle of commonality (see Chapter 15) quite well. The arrows above and
below the various stock indexes correspond with intermediate buy and sell
signals on the DJIA, as derived from a momentum indicator.[1] The charts

---

[1] This momentum indicator was developed by I. S. Notley of the Trend and Cycle Department, Dominion
Securities, Toronto, Canada.

CHART 24.5 Commonality applied to world stock indexes, phase 1.

show that the termination of each upleg was followed sooner or later by a fall in each individual stock index. As the global cycle developed into the third phase, several stock markets (such as the French and Italian) failed to make a new bull market high, resulting in a third upleg magnitude failure.

A further aid in assessing the technical position of an individual country can be obtained through the construction of a relative-strength index be-

CHART 24.6   Commonality applied to world stock indexes, phase 2.

tween the stock index of that country and the World Stock Index itself. The relative-strength line itself will not indicate whether a market will rise or fall in an absolute sense, but only whether it will outperform or underperform the rest of the world. If it has been established that the World Stock Index is in a rising trend, it will be as well to invest in a country with a strong trend of relative strength. A relative-strength index for Japan and the United States in the period from 1959 to 1978 is shown in Charts 24.8 and 24.9. During this period there were isolated points such as 1970–1972 and 1974–1977 when investment in the United States would have given relatively good results, but overall its performance against the rest of the world since 1959 was inferior.

CHART 24.7 Commonality applied to world stock indexes, phase 3.

In complete contrast, Japan's relative-strength line rose strongly during the same period and experienced only minor declines. It is worth noting that the Japanese relative strength in each cycle has a tendency to peak out around the time that the United States stock market is reaching its bear market low. These points are indicated on the chart by arrows.

An analysis of the global technical position should incorporate an assessment of the technical structure of the stock markets in the various countries concerned, as well as the composite measures of momentum, breadth, etc., discussed above. The trend-determining techniques outlined in Part 1 should be used as a basis, but it will be found through experimentation that different markets respond to different techniques because of the variations in their structures and cycles.

CHART 24.8 United States relative strength versus World Index.

(SOURCE: Pring Market Review.)

CHART 24.9 Japanese relative strength versus World Index.

(SOURCE: Pring Market Review.)

This global technical approach should therefore form an integral part of an assessment of the technical health of any individual stock market, including that of the United States. As time progresses, the economies and financial structures of the countries that make up the world economy are becoming increasingly interwoven, making it extremely difficult for any stock market to move in an opposite direction to the prevailing trend of world markets in general.

Technical Analysis of Individual Stocks

INTRODUCTION

It is important to form a view on the likely trend of the overall market, and it is also helpful to have some idea of how to go about selecting individual stocks. Naturally, all investors would like their investments to appreciate rapidly in price, but stocks which may satisfy this wish tend to be accompanied by a substantially greater amount of risk than many investors are normally willing to accept. Stocks which move up rapidly in price usually have a high beta (i.e., are very sensitive to market movements), a very thin float (i.e., are illiquid and very price-sensitive to a small increase in volume), or a very strong earnings momentum resulting in constant upward revisions in the price/earnings multiple. Others may be in a turnaround situation in which the price has fallen to unrealistically low levels, so that even the slightest good news will have an explosive effect on the price.

These are all fundamental factors and really fall outside the scope of this book. However, it is important to understand that investors can be very fashion-conscious when it comes to stock ownership. When the price is bid up to unrealistically high levels and the popular press is airing all the good news in the form of cover stories, major articles, etc., the chances are that the bullish arguments are understood by virtually all the market participants. At this point everyone who wants to buy has already bought, and the stock is said to be "overowned." This happened to the pollution-control stocks in the late 1960s, the so-called glamour growth stocks in 1973, the oils in 1980, and certain "hi-tech" stocks in the early 1980s. When the news is so bad that it appears that profits will never recover or that the company might even go into bankruptcy, the opposite condition sets in and the stock is said to be "underowned." Real Estate Investment Trusts in 1974 and tire stocks in 1980 present examples of underownership. Not all companies go through such extreme overownership and underownership cycles, but it is still important to recognize that these cycles exist.

A position of overownership does not usually take place during one cyclical advance but has the tendency to develop over several advances, creating what is called a "secular rise." Similarly, a position of underownership, in which a stock becomes totally out of fashion, can take many years to develop.

STOCK SELECTION FROM A SECULAR POINT OF VIEW

General

The selection process should begin by trying to identify whether a stock is in a secular advance or decline in order to try to establish its position within its ownership cycle. Chart 25.1, example a, shows Allis Chalmers (ALL), a company which went through several such cycles between 1948 and 1983. Stocks in basic industries, such as ALL, are called "cyclical stocks" since they offer great profit opportunities over one or even two business cycles but are rarely profitable using the buy-hold approach.

Because of the long-term growth characteristics of the global economy, most stocks exhibit characteristics of a long-term secular advance interrupted by mild secular corrections. Chart 25.1b shows the long-term trend of Bristol Myers (BMY). Between 1948 and 1953, and later between 1967 and 1974, the stock was in a small secular decline, since successive bear market lows were lower than their predecessors. During the remainder of the period shown on the chart Bristol Myers was in a secular uptrend. The dominant period of rapid price advance occurred between 1953 and 1967. By 1968 the breaking of the 10-year uptrend line in the stock and the 12-year uptrend in relative strength suggested that the stock was in an overowned state and might need a lengthy corrective period. By 1974 Bristol Myers had experienced a "double" bear market in which it lost almost two-thirds of its value. Having corrected the excesses of the previous secular advance, BMY was then in a technical position to begin a new advance.

Republic Steel, shown on Chart 25.1c, provides an opposite example to Bristol Myers; this stock spent most of its time between 1959 and 1982 in a secular bear market. From the point of view of investing and using a 5- to 7-year time horizon, it would have been relatively difficult to make money in Republic compared to Bristol Myers.

These three examples point up the differing life cycles and trend characteristics of individual stocks. Investors who are able to identify secular trends in price and relative strength are in a position to profit from extremes in the ownership cycle. Consequently, a very long term price chart of stocks can provide a very useful starting point for stock selection.

Major Price Patterns (Long Bases)

As the Chapter 4 discussion of price patterns pointed out, generally the larger the pattern, the greater the ensuing move is likely to be, in terms of both magnitude and time. One of the best approaches to stock selection is to search through the chart books for issues which are emerging from or pulling back to long-term bases. Since there are almost always some stocks in this position, it should be noted that whenever the chart books are full of emerging long-term bases, as happened in the early 1940s and late 1970s, the odds of a long-term, broad-based general market advance are greatly enhanced.

Some examples of these large formations in action are shown in Charts 25.1 and 25.2. Following its mid-1970s secular correction, Bristol Myers (Chart 25.1b) broke out of a 14-year inverse head-and-shoulders consolidation pattern in 1980; this break was accompanied by a similar move in the company's RS line.

Smithkline Beckman (SKB), shown in Chart 25.2a, formed a broadening formation with a flat top during the 1967–1975 period, ending the long interval of consolidation which began in 1959. The RS line had broken above its 13-year downtrend in 1974 almost a year before the price of the stock achieved the same distinction. A second opportunity to purchase SKB occurred in mid-1977 as the price pulled back to the upper portion of the base. The dramatic rise above the flat top, once this correction was completed, is typical of the type of move to be expected from the completion of such patterns. It should be noted that this is not a classically symmetrical formation since the flat top declined slightly; moreover, there were clearly some false breakouts, both upward in 1961 and 1965 and downward in 1960. The 1961 breakout was accompanied by relatively low volume, whereas the 1965 move developed within a trend of declining RS. In sharp

CHART 25.1*a* Allis-Chalmers Corp.

(SOURCE: *Securities Research Co., a Division of United Business Service Co.*)

Price Scale

Allis Chalmers Mfg.
prior to 5/12/71

Standard Steel
acquired 1/69

Amer. Air Filter
merged 10/31/78

Simplicty Mfg.
sold 3/16/83

PRICE
Monthly
Ranges

EARNINGS
12 Mos. Ended

Dividend
omitted
11/16/68

Dividend
omitted
12/20/81

THOUSANDS OF SHARES

1966 1967 1968 1969 1970 1971 1972 1973 1974 1975 1976 1977 1978 1979 1980 1981 1982 1983

CHART 25.1*b*   Bristol Myers Co.

Clairol, Inc.
acquired 4/59

Drackett Co.
acquired 8/2/65

PRICE
Monthly
Ranges

RATIO-CATOR
Monthly

Extra
1.3¢

Extra
1.9¢

Extra
1.9¢

Extra
1.9¢

Extra
1.3¢

Extra
1.3¢

Extra
1.3¢

Extra
1.3¢

Extra
.3¢

Extra
.2¢

Extra
.4¢

Extra
.6¢

Extra
.7¢

Adj. for
3 for 1
7/28/59

Adj. for
2 for 1
10/28/63

Adj. for
2 for 1
10/31/66

1948 | 1949 | 1950 | 1951 | 1952 | 1953 | 1954 | 1955 | 1956 | 1957 | 1958 | 1959 | 1960 | 1961 | 1962 | 1963 | 1964 | 1965 | 1966

(SOURCE: *Securities Research.*)

318

Price Scale

Jobst Institute Inc.
acquired 3/31/83

Mead Johnson
merged
11/14/67

Foster Milburn
merged 7/1/69

Renuzit Home Products
acquired 8/26/69

Zimmer Mfg.
acquired 1/72

Unitek Corp.
merged 4/78

EARNINGS
12 Mos. Ended

S¹

H

S

DIVIDENDS
Annual Rate

Extra
1. 3¢

Adj. for
2 for 1
5/31/77

Adj. for
2 for 1
5/27/83

1967 1968 1969 1970 1971 1972 1973 1974 1975 1976 1977 1978 1979 1980 1981 1982 1983

CHART 25.1c Republic Steel Corp.

(SOURCE: *Securities Research.*)

Price Scale

EARNINGS
12 Mos. Ended

DIVIDENDS
Annual Rate

RATIO-CATOR
Monthly

Special
$1.00

Special
$1.40

Special
55¢

Special
35¢

Special
25¢

Earns. 12 mos.
3/31/83 D15.92

Earns. 12 mos.
6/30/82 D 3.63
9/30/82 D10.70
12/31/82 D15.47

THOUSANDS OF SHARES

1966 1967 1968 1969 1970 1971 1972 1973 1974 1975 1976 1977 1978 1979 1980 1981 1982 1983

CHART 25.2a Smithkline Beckman Corp.

(SOURCE: *Securities Research.*)

Price Scale>

Smith Kline & French
Labs. prior to
7/1/73

New earns. line
reflects Beckman
merger

Beckman Instruments
merged 3/4/82

SmithKline Corp.
prior to 3/4/82

Allergan Pharmaceuticals
merged 4/1/80

Humphrey Instruments
acquired 2/80

DIVIDENDS
Annual Rate

Extra
5¢

Extra
3¼¢

RATIO-CATOR
Monthly

RS
breakout

Adj. for
2 for 1
6/1/77

Adj. for
2 for 1
6/1/79

1967 1968 1969 1970 1971 1972 1973 1974 1975 1976 1977 1978 1979 1980 1981 1982 1983

CHART 25.2*b* Whirlpool Corp.

Nineteen Hundred Corp.
prior to 6/15/50

Whirlpool Corp.
prior to 9/15/55

Whirlpool-Seeger
prior to 4/1/57

Clyde Porcelain Steel
merged 3/31/52

Seeger Refrigerator
merged 9/15/55

Birtman Electric
merged 4/1/57

Servel, Inc.
acquired 1/3/58

Listed
NYSE 1/3/55
ASE prior

New earns. line
includes cos.
merged in 1957

RATIO-CATOR
Monthly

Extra
1.8¢

Extra
1¢

Extra
2.9¢

Extra
1.6¢

Extra
.18¢

Extra
1¢

Adj. for
2 for 1
12/22/48

Adj. for
2 for 1
3/31/52

Adj. for
2 for 1
1/3/55

Adj. for
2 for 1
6/10/65

1948 1949 1950 1951 1952 1953 1954 1955 1956 1957 1958 1959 1960 1961 1962 1963 1964 1965 19

(SOURCE: *Securities Research.*)

CHART 25.2c Fedders Corp.

(SOURCE: *Securities Research.*)

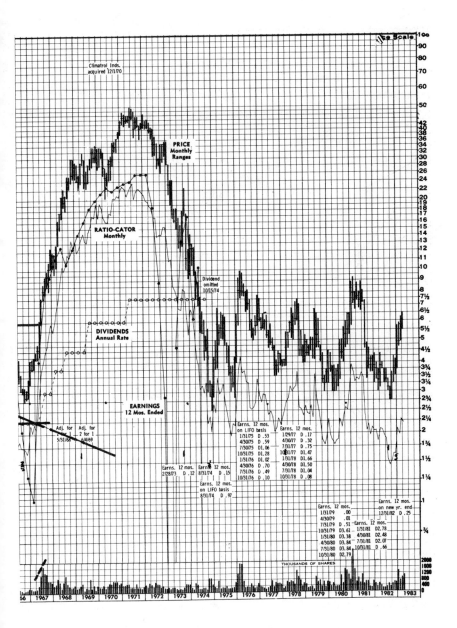

Climatrol Inds.
acquired 12/1/70

PRICE
Monthly
Ranges

RATIO-CATOR
Monthly

Dividend
omitted
10/15/74

DIVIDENDS
Annual Rate

EARNINGS
12 Mos. Ended

Adj. for   Adj. for
      2 for 1
5/31/68   6/4/69

Earns. 12 mos.   Earns. 12 mos.
2/28/73   D .12   8/31/74   D .15

Earns. 12 mos.
on LIFO basis
8/31/74   D .97

Earns. 12 mos.
on LIFO basis
1/31/75   D .53
4/30/75   D .59
7/31/75   D1.06
10/31/75 D1.28
1/31/76   D1.02
4/30/76   D .70
7/31/76   D .49
10/31/76 D .10

Earns. 12 mos.
1/29/77   D .17
4/30/77   D .32
7/31/77   D .75
10/31/77 D1.47
1/31/78   D1.66
4/30/78   D1.50
7/31/78   D1.04
10/31/78 D .08

Earns. 12 mos.
1/31/79   .00
4/30/79   .01
7/31/79   D .61
10/31/79 D3.61
1/31/80   D3.38
4/30/80   D3.84
7/31/80   D3.84
10/31/80 D2.79

Earns. 12 mos.
1/31/81   D2.78
4/30/81   D2.48
7/31/81   D2.07
10/31/81 D .66

Earns. 12 mos.
on new yr. end
12/31/82 D .25

THOUSANDS OF SHARES

66 1967 1968 1969 1970 1971 1972 1973 1974 1975 1976 1977 1978 1979 1980 1981 1982 1983

contrast, during the 1976 breakout, volume expanded sharply and relative strength was also improving.

Whirlpool (Chart 25.2b) offers a fine example of an ascending triangle that took 8 years to complete. Occurring similarly to the SKB breakout, the Whirlpool breakout was accompanied by good volume and preceded by a long-term reversal in relative strength. Following the rise that took place between the mid-1960s and the early 1970s, the stock consolidated its gains in the form of what might be loosely described as a 10-year inverse head-and-shoulders pattern. Whether the 1977 sell-off qualifies as a left shoulder is open to debate. The important point is that the 1982 breakout above the significant area of resistance marked by the neckline was accompanied by improving relative strength and expanding volume.

Finally Fedders Corporation (Chart 25.2c) formed a huge rectangle base between 1948 and 1957. This example has been chosen for two reasons: first, to illustrate that when a valid breakout occurs the surprises are usually on the upside, and second, to point out that whereas a large base normally implies a long and steady rise following the breakout, once a dynamic rise of the type experienced by Fedders has occurred, investors should be on the lookout for some price vulnerability and should not greedily assume that such a dynamic move can extend indefinitely.

SOME BASIC PRINCIPLES OF STOCK SELECTION DURING A PRIMARY BULL MARKET

General

A bull market has been defined as a period in which most stocks are moving up most of the time. A bear market, in contrast, is a period in which most stocks are declining the vast majority of the time. When investing or speculating in the market, it is clearly important to be committing money during the bull phase; although some stocks can rise during a bear market, the odds of success are obviously diminished under such conditions. For this reason, most books and analyses of the technical approach concentrate on the major trend of the market. Investors and speculators, however, should not be totally concerned with "where the Dow is"; rather, they should also be aware of what the stocks in their portfolios are worth. Individual investors must ask not only whether it is generally a good time to buy stocks but also which stocks should be bought.

The performance of specific issues can differ widely, not only over the course of the total bull move but also during its various stages. This phenomenon was discussed in Chapter 13, which described the group rotation process. Once it has been established that now is a good time to purchase stocks in relation to the primary trend or intermediate trend or both, two questions need to be answered:

1. Which industry groups look technically sound not only in their own right but also in relation to the market?

2. Which stock or stocks within the group look strong technically in their own right, in relation to the market as a whole, and in relation to the group or industry index?

Although it is clearly important to examine the price action of the various groups and stocks with the help of moving averages, rates of change, trendlines, etc., the above questions are best answered through an analysis of relative-strength trends.

Stock Selection at a Major Market Bottom

Once it is established that the market is in a low-risk buying area, a review of the technical position of the various industry groups should be undertaken. Because certain groups have a *tendency* to lead, these areas represent a good starting point.

Even though relative-strength lines often trace out accumulation and distribution patterns, the best results seem to come from the breaking of important uptrend and downtrend lines. This is not meant to imply that price patterns in RS lines should be ignored, for indeed they should be considered. However, the violation of a well-established trendline tends to give better signals than price pattern breakouts in terms of both timeliness and reliability. For this reason many analysts like to use longer-term moving-average crossovers as a confirmatory signal that an important change in the trend of RS has taken place.

Chart 25.3 shows two Standard & Poor's retail stores indexes between 1972 and 1983. Since retail stores are considered a leading group, it would be reasonable to expect these indexes to show an improving trend in RS at the beginning of the cycle. However, this was certainly not the case at the 1974 bear market low. The indexes themselves were able to rally along with the market in late 1974–early 1975, but the RS line continued on its downward path. That a leading group cannot put on an impressive performance at the beginning of the cycle when typically it should be at its strongest is normally a powerful indication of underlying technical weakness. In the case of the retail stores indexes the implication was that even if the index itself could put on a rally and result in a profitable trade, there were likely to be far better opportunities in other stock groups where relative strength was actually improving. The chart shows that the indexes did manage to rally into January 1976 but subsequently declined in price for another 4 years.

CHART 25.3   Standard & Poor's retail stores—food chains and general merchandise chains.

(SOURCE: *Securities Research.*)

By the time the market bottomed in 1982, the retail stores indexes were much lower, but the technical action had improved dramatically. The secular low was touched in December 1980. However, an improvement in RS did not become apparent until late 1981 when the down trendline, which had begun in 1974, 7 years before, was broken on the upside. By the summer of 1982 it became apparent that this group had begun an important bull market, for not only did the retail stores indexes fail to confirm the 1981 low in the DJIA, but they had already broken above the down trendline (*CD*) in May of 1982, 3 months before the bull market had begun. Since this declining trendline could be drawn back to 1973 and was therefore 9 years in length, it should have been clear that something very significant had occurred in the long-term technical position of the indexes.

By late August 1982, 3 weeks after the start of the bull market, the index broke out from a massive 4-year, complex inverse head-and-shoulders accumulation pattern, thereby leaving little technical doubt that this group had embarked on a major bull move.

Although the situation in 1974 did not look particularly exciting, especially in view of the deteriorating RS line, the technical position of the retail stores indexes looked extremely attractive in August 1982. Not only was a bull market emerging, but the group itself was clearly in a position to outperform the averages, given both the reversal in its long-term RS and the actual price performance of the group itself.

Once this fact was established, the question that would then arise was which retail merchandise stock or stocks would constitute the most

CHART 25.4a   K Mart Corp.

(SOURCE: *Securities Research.*)

profitable investment. Possible candidates incorporated in the construction of the index were K Mart, Wal-Mart, Woolworth, J. C. Penney, and Sears. These five stocks are shown in Chart 25.4a to e. Clearly, the outstanding stock throughout the 8-year period between 1975 and 1983 was Wal-Mart, which rose from just over $1 to over $40.

By August 1982, at the beginning of the bull market, Wal-Mart and its RS line had been in an uptrend for 7 years. Since there was no sign of a reversal in either of these trends, there was no technical justification for selling the stock. On the other hand, since Wal-Mart had been rising sharply for a very extended period, it could quite easily have become vulnerable to profit taking if some bad news had come out. Should it therefore have been bought? Because buying the leading stock or group at the beginning of a bull market normally pays off, it would have made sense to allocate some funds to Wal-Mart even though the stock looked overextended. As it happened, the stock doubled over the next year. However, from an investment management point of view it would nevertheless have made sense to spread the risk.

In this respect one stock, Sears, stands out—for whereas other stocks had violated major downtrends on the upside, Sears had actually completed and broken out from a major inverse head-and-shoulders pattern. In the ensuing 12 months the performance of Sears closely matched that of Wal-Mart,

CHART 25.4b J. C. Penney Co., Inc.

(SOURCE: *Securities Research.*)

proving that the diversification strategy would have worked quite well. The performance of the remaining stocks in the group, though less exciting than that of Wal-Mart and Sears, still outranked the market as measured by the DJIA.

Trend Changes in Relative Strength within a Primary Trend

The example used above concerned a group of stocks whose relative-strength trend had been improving over a long period of time, i.e., between two stock market cycles. Since moves of an intermediate nature often prove to be highly profitable, it makes sense to consider changes in an RS trend within a primary move, for there is a *tendency* for different groups to outperform the averages at various stages of a bull or bear market.

Such changes in relative strength can often first be noticed around important intermediate turning points of the market itself. This can be seen from Chart 25.5, which illustrates the performance of the S&P Electronics—

CHART 25.4c Sears, Roebuck & Co.

(SOURCE: *Securities Research.*)

Semiconductor/Components Index. In 1976 this group made a new bull market high, but this was not confirmed by the RS line, which had peaked earlier in 1975. When the bull market trendline (*AB*) of the index itself was violated on the downside, the negative action of the RS line was confirmed. Even more bearish was that the index had just completed a 9-month head-and-shoulders distribution pattern (more obvious from a monthly high, low, close chart). By early 1978[1] the technical position of this group had completely reversed itself. The index itself reached a 2-year low in March 1978, but the RS line bottomed out early in 1977 and had been in an uptrend for almost a year. By April 1978 both the index itself and the RS line had broken above their downtrend lines, thereby offering a strong buy signal for semiconductor stocks in general. Again the question of which stocks to buy would arise. What is interesting is that all the stocks used in the construction of the index outperformed the market during the following months. The choices, which are shown in Chart 25.6a to e, were AMP, Intel, Motorola, National Semiconductor, and Texas Instruments.

[1] It is debatable whether 1978 marked a bear market or an intermediate low. In a strict Dow theory sense it represented a bear market low. For broader-based indexes such as the Value Line Composite for March 1978, however, it was an intermediate low; it has therefore been treated as such in this example.

CHART 25.4d   Wal-Mart Stores, Inc.

(SOURCE: *Securities Research*.)

CHART 25.4e   F. W. Woolworth Co.

(SOURCE: *Securities Research.*)

National Semiconductor had an improving RS line and had broken out from a double bottom formation by April 1978, but there had been no discernible reversal in trend in terms of either the price itself or its RS line. Moreover, by that time the stock, at about $16, was 60 percent above its low. Motorola was also relatively unattractive since the choppy nature of the stock suggested that any technical signals could not wholeheartedly be relied upon. This is a point very well worth noting since certain stocks possess characteristics that result in constant whipsaws, yet other stocks almost consistently give reliable technical signals. Given the choice, reliability is to be preferred, even though the volatile alternative might offer

CHART 25.5   Standard & Poor's Electronics—Semiconductors/Components

(SOURCE: *Securities Research.*)

greater profit potential if it is not a whipsaw signal. Even though an important break of a 5-year downtrend in Motorola's relative strength had taken
place, the general technical unreliability of the stock suggested that there
might be better possibilities elsewhere.

Texas Instruments, on the other hand, looked to be a better prospect;
both the stock and its RS line had pushed above very important trendlines
accompanied by a modest expansion in volume. Here at last was a possible
candidate.

AMP also looked promising. This stock had just broken above a
downtrend which had been in force for nearly 5 years. On the whole it had
been a more reliable stock than Motorola, and its recent action had been
superior to that of Texas Instruments. This could be seen because AMP made
a marginal new low in 1978 compared to TI's low, which was almost 20
percent lower than that set in 1977. Finally, the RS line of AMP not only
broke above a 4½-year down trendline but also completed and broke out
from an inverse head-and-shoulders pattern. On balance, therefore, AMP
looked to be a better bet than TI.

Then too, some consideration had to be given to Intel. This issue was the
only one that did not make a post-1976 low in 1978. It also broke above a
very important downtrendline in April. Although this line was not as long as
that of AMP or TI, it had been touched many times during its descent and

CHART 25.6a AMP, Inc.

(SOURCE: *Securities Research.*)

CHART 25.6*b*   Intel Corp.

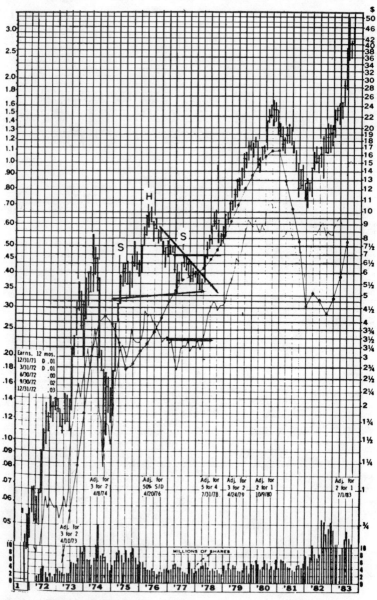

(SOURCE: *Securities Research.*)

CHART 25.6c Motorola, Inc.

(SOURCE: *Securities Research.*)

therefore represented a significant resistance area. The line was relatively shorter than the other candidates because the stock had made a new all-time high in 1976, which was really a point in its favor. This also accounts for the failure of the RS line to form a discernible downtrend during this period, although a small head-and-shoulders pattern had been completed. Finally, what made Intel such an intriguing prospect was that the April 1978 breakout above the $7 area strongly suggested that the head-and-shoulders distribution pattern that seemed to be forming between mid-1975 and early 1978

CHART 25.6d National Semiconductor Corp.

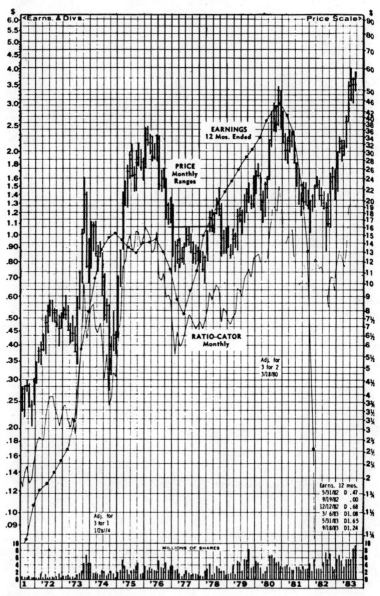

(SOURCE: *Securities Research.*)

CHART 25.6e Texas Instruments, Inc.

(SOURCE: *Securities Research.*)

was not in fact going to "work." As the chart shows, this conclusion would have proved to be correct, and the failure proved to be a signal for a very worthwhile move.

SUMMARY

1. Most stocks go through ownership cycles which normally take a long period to complete. It is important to identify whether a stock is in a secular uptrend or downtrend, in order to better understand its position within its ownership cycle.

2. Substantial profit potential is available to the long-term investor who can identify stocks breaking out from extended bases when accompanied by expanding volume and an improving long-term trend in relative strength.

3. Though a bull market generally carries most stocks with it, the performance of individual issues can vary considerably both over the course of the primary upmove and within it.

4. The best method of stock selection is first to analyze trends in relative strength for the appropriate stock group and then to isolate those stocks which are outperforming the others within the group. Purchases should only be made when price trends and volume support the improving relative strength.

Technical Analysis of Gold

INTRODUCTION

Prices in financial markets are essentially determined by psychology or the attitude of investors and speculators to the fundamentals. Gold perhaps arouses greater emotion than any other commodity or market. Some investors call it the "barbaric metal," but others believe that only a return to the gold standard will restore the world's financial structure to stability.

Gold has a tendency to respond emotionally to global political events, though this sensitivity in my opinion is greatly overexaggerated. Since emotion moves in trends, gold prices also move in trends—and trends in gold are no more difficult to detect than those in other financial markets. In fact, the price of gold is relatively easier to analyze from a technical viewpoint than that of virtually any other commodity because of the depth of the analytical tools available: trend analysis of the gold price itself, the relationship between gold and gold shares, the relationship between gold and other precious metals, and the relationship between gold and its advance/decline line.

At any given time there are three forces working on the price of gold: (1) gold as money, i.e., as both a currency and a store of value, (2) gold as an industrial metal, and (3) gold as an emotional thermometer. Since the supply of any currency, unlike the supply of gold, can be expanded at will, the major influence on the gold price is investors' hopes or fears about the future course of inflation. Gold is also purchased as an alternative reserve asset if the U.S. dollar, the world's principal reserve currency, is weak.

At the beginning of the business cycle the inflation rate is generally falling. The price of gold is also usually falling, since investors at this time have no need to purchase gold as an inflation hedge. As the business cycle progresses, the price of gold moves up (in a cyclical, but not necessarily a secular, sense) and worries about inflation grow. The industrial demand for gold follows a similar path since it too reaches a peak at the end of the cycle. The emotional demand for gold is a result of political scares. It is not related to the business cycle but has the effect of exacerbating rallies in a bull market and cushioning declines during bear markets. For example, the invasion of Afghanistan took place during a bull market and had a very powerful effect on the gold price, whereas the Sadat assassination and the Iran-Iraq war, which occurred during a bear market, had only small but temporary upward effects.

ANALYSIS OF THE GOLD PRICE ITSELF

The gold price, which is expressed here in U.S. dollars, responds to trend-determining techniques such as price pattern behavior, moving averages, and rates of change. For longer-term movements, decisive crossovers of the 40-week moving average have proved to be very helpful (see Chart 26.1). However, it should be noted that the gold price, unlike the stock market or other commodities, has been trading only since 1968—a relatively short period, especially in terms of categorizing cyclical characteristics. Readers may wish to refer to the chapters on trend-determining techniques in Part I and relate these discussions to the gold price charts included in this chapter.

GOLD AND GOLD SHARES

General Principles

In most cases the prices of gold shares lead the price of gold. In instances where a gold share or, more important, a gold share index breaks out from a price pattern, some form of advance warning for the future price action of gold bullion is given. Even where no advance notice appears, it is still important to make sure that a specific move in the gold price is confirmed by similar action in the gold share indexes, and vice versa. When no such confirmation exists, the move should be considered suspect.

There are several reasons why this relationship between the prices of gold and gold shares works so well.

CHART 26.1 Gold and two measures of momentum.

(SOURCE: Pring Market Review.)

First, investors in gold shares are concerned with the flow of profits from those shares, which is predominantly determined by the average price of gold bullion over a particular period. If investors in the shares feel that the average price is likely to fall, they discount this fact by selling well in advance, and vice versa.

Second, gold shares are more leveraged than bullion. Not only do gold mines borrow money to go into production, but as the gold price rises or falls, so marginal ore deposits become commercially profitable or un-profitable, thereby adding to or subtracting proportionately more from the value of the mine than the change in the actual price of the metal.

CHART 26.2 Gold and gold shares weekly, 1970–1983.

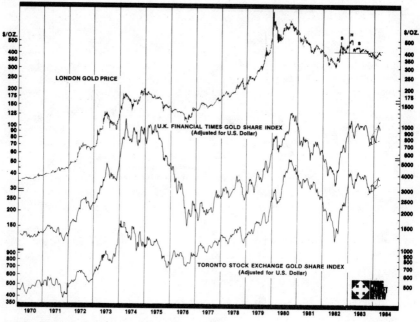

(SOURCE: Pring Market Review.)

Third, the profits of gold mines are a function not only of the gold price but of the cost of production. These costs are basically subject to the same influences as other corporations, with the result that trends in profits are also influenced by the business cycle. Since profits are a leading indicator and inflation (which is discounted in the trend of bullion prices) is a lagging indicator, the net effect (other things being equal) is for gold shares to lead the price of bullion.

Some Examples

The top of Chart 26.2 shows the price of the London P.M. fix from 1970 to 1983. Underneath are two important gold share indexes, the Toronto Gold Share Index (TSE), and *The Financial Times* (of London) Gold Share Index (FT). The latter essentially comprises South African stocks which are traded in London. Both share indexes have been converted from local currencies to U.S. dollars for the sake of consistency. The chart shows that the TSE Index reached a cyclical high in March 1974, whereas the bullion price topped out 9 months later, in December 1974. The South African Index also gave a warning signal by peaking out in March 1974, again failing to confirm the late 1974 high in the bullion price.

Up to March 1974 all three indexes had been moving together, as each confirmed a new high made by the other two. It is also worth noting that the two share indexes were actually making distributional tops in 1974 from which they later broke down. At the beginning of 1975 it was fairly clear that the technical structure of the gold asset markets was breaking down; not only had the shares failed by a wide margin to confirm the bullion, but also they had actually given important indications that they were going to lead the bullion price lower.

At the bottom of the bear market in mid-1976 this technical position had partly reversed itself. Whereas the bullion price made its low in August 1976, the TSE Index refused to make a new low, thereby setting up a positive divergence. Although this was clearly a positive sign, a really bullish signal did not come until later that year when the bear market trendlines of both the bullion price and the TSE Index were penetrated on the upside.

The equity/bullion relationship is useful for assessing shorter-term as well as longer-term movements in the gold price, as Chart 26.3 shows. For much of the time, little can be gleaned from the relationship between the three series, but there are points at which the shares give a clear-cut lead for the bullion either in terms of an actual divergence or in terms of relative-strength superiority. For example, in November 1979 all three indicators were consolidating their October losses, but by the middle of the month the shares had begun to move up sharply, especially the FT Index which had broken out of an inverse H&S pattern. Although this lead given by the shares was a very bullish sign, no action should have been taken until the bullion price itself had also broken out of its trading band. It is important to make sure that both the shares and the bullion are going to be in gear.

The cyclical peak in gold bullion in January 1980 was one of those few occasions when the shares *lagged* behind the bullion price. During the December 1979–February 1980 period, the gold bullion price formed a small H&S pattern in the face of rising share prices. Given the leading characteristic of the gold share prices, it might have been expected that the distribution pattern being traced out by the bullion would "fail." Since it did not fail, and since investors and speculators in commodity markets take positions in the physical metal and not the shares, it would have been wise to conclude that the gold price was likely to head lower when the trend in the bullion price broke. Although the shares tend to lead the bullion price, there are times when they lag. A price move in bullion which remains unconfirmed by the shares and vice versa is almost always a sign that the prevailing trend is likely to reverse. Such a development is signaling that the gold asset markets are out of gear.

CHART 26.3 Gold and gold shares weekly. [SOURCE: *Martin J. Pring (ed.), The McGraw-Hill Handbook of Commodities and Futures, McGraw-Hill, New York, 1985, p. 46-4.*]

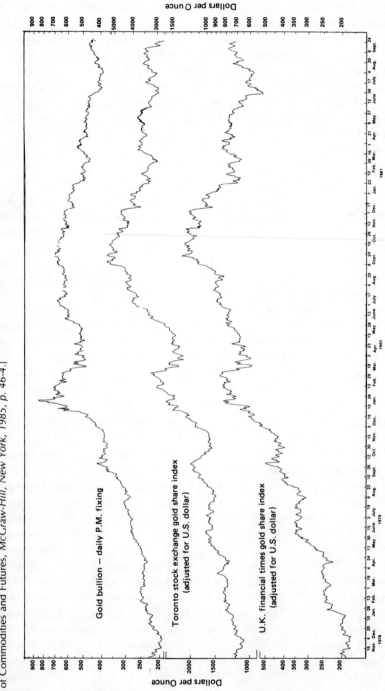

Another point worth noting is that the asset which takes the lead, whether bullion or gold shares, generally has the largest ensuing price swing. Thus gold bullion peaked at 850 in January 1980 and led the shares on a decline. Bullion lost almost half its value (that is, it fell from 850 to 450), whereas gold shares lost only about 30 to 40 percent of theirs.

By May 1980 the decline for all three series had run its course. That both share indexes had formed and completed important bottoms ahead of bullion was highly significant. First, this occurrence gave advance warning that an imminent upside breakout in the metal was likely to take place, and second, it added tremendous validity to the breakout when it did in fact occur.

The September 1980 peak in the gold price was also instructive, since it found the gold asset markets once again in a major disagreement. Gold shares reached a new cyclical peak, yet the bullion price was well below its January high. The ensuing decline was extremely bloody for both shares and bullion.

GOLD AND THE GOLD ADVANCE/DECLINE LINE

As described in Chapter 17, a weekly A/D line for the NYSE is constructed by taking a cumulative plurality of the number of issues advancing over those declining. The gold A/D line which is shown in Chart 26.4 is constructed by taking a cumulative weekly plurality of the price of gold expressed in 12 different currencies. If the cumulative total is currently at 155 (the cumulative line can be started from any arbitrary number) and the price of gold when expressed in 12 currencies advances in terms of dollars and eight other currencies, and declines against three currencies, then the plurality is $+6$, that is, $9 - 3$. This plurality is then added to the cumulative line, and the next total becomes 161. There is no reason why the gold A/D line should not be constructed from any number of currencies, although the larger the universe, the greater the task of data collection and manipulation.

The idea behind the construction of the A/D line is to try to estimate whether the price rise (or decline) of gold bullion is broad, where many currencies are participating, or narrow, where gold is moving up merely on U.S. dollar weakness.

The gold A/D line is interpreted in the same way as the gold/gold share relationship. Generally the A/D line leads the price of gold both up and down. If the lead of either the U.S. dollar price of gold bullion or the gold A/D line remains unconfirmed, the continuation of the prevailing trend is doubtful, because of the disagreement. Chart 26.4 shows that the A/D line did not confirm the December 1974 high, the August 1976 low, or the June 1982 low; important trend reversals followed. Also there was a major dis-

CHART 26.4 The gold bullion advance/decline line.

(SOURCE: Pring Market Review.)

agreement in September 1980 when the A/D line made a new secular high but the gold price did not.

Advance/decline data can also be used in oscillator form. For instance, the indicator shown at the foot of Chart 26.4 is a 6-week moving average of a 13-week moving average of the weekly A/D ratio.

GOLD AND OTHER PRECIOUS METALS

Over the course of the business cycle, the four precious metals traded on futures markets—gold, silver, platinum, and palladium—proceed in the same direction. Indeed, at almost every trading session they move in tandem, and only their magnitude varies.

The three critical markets to monitor are gold, silver, and platinum. If all three are confirming new highs or lows in a prevailing trend, all may be

CHART 26.5 Gold in relation to silver and platinum.

(SOURCE: Pring Market Review.)

considered well. When one begins to falter, a warning flag, but not a signal, of a trend reversal is given. A more important area to monitor is the relative-strength action between the various metals, for often a change in a relative-strength trend will also signal a reversal in the trend of the price of gold, as seen in Chart 26.5, which shows the price of gold with the gold/silver ratio and the 26-week rate of change of the ratio. The RS line has been plotted inversely; thus, when it is rising, silver is the superior performer, and when it is falling, gold is outperforming silver. In Chart 26.5, the gold price was being outperformed by silver in 1975 and during the first part of 1976. However, when gold made its bear market low, this relationship reversed its trend. At this time the ratio also fell back to the 45 level—which appears to mark an important extreme, for rarely does it exceed this limit. Similarly, the 25 level appears to mark the opposite extreme. In the chart, these extremes are marked by a dashed line, as are the oversold and overbought levels of the 26-week rate of change.

Chart 26.5 shows that when both indexes reach an extreme reading at the same time and then reverse direction, a reversal in the prevailing gold price usually results. For example, in mid-1973 a move in the gold/silver ratio to 45, accompanied by a decline in the rate-of-change indicator to 40, signaled a decline in the gold price. Sometimes only one indicator offers a warning signal. For example, in February 1983 the rate-of-change index rallied above − 30, which resulted in a sharp slide in the gold price.

It should be noted that which extreme the ratio or ROC index reaches does not matter; that they reach an extreme and reverse their trend is what is important in forecasting the gold price. Clearly, this approach only rarely warns of a trend change, but when such a warning occurs, it is usually worth paying attention to.

SUMMARY

1. Changes in the trend of the gold price can be determined with the help of price patterns, moving averages, volume patterns on the futures, rates of change, etc.

2. Gold shares and the gold A/D line usually lead the price of gold. If their lead remains unconfirmed by the gold price or vice versa, this represents a disagreement which will in all probability result in a reversal in the prevailing trend.

3. Changes in the trend of the gold price are usually accompanied by a change in the trend of gold/silver ratio, or gold/platinum ratio, or both. It is of little concern whether or not gold is outperforming the other two metals; what is important is that the trend in the relationship has changed.

27

Technical Analysis of Currencies

INTRODUCTION

The principles of analyzing currencies from a technical aspect are basically the same as those of any other financial market or stock. The one major difference is that the price of a currency is always relative to the prices of all other currencies. Hence a long position in the Swiss franc vis-à-vis the U.S. dollar may prove unprofitable even if the Swiss franc is generally strong against most other currencies. This is true because the U.S. dollar may be even stronger.

There are therefore two questions which must be asked by the trader who invests or speculates in currencies: First, which currency should be bought (or sold)? Second, which cross rate should be bought (or sold)? In other words, having established in principle that the Swiss franc is basically a good currency to buy, the next decision is which currency the Swiss franc is likely to be strongest against.

From a speculative point of view, there are really only five currencies which are actively traded: the Canadian dollar, British pound, Swiss franc, German mark, and Japanese yen. All five are listed on the International Monetary Market (IMM) in Chicago, and the last four are also listed on the London International Financial Futures Exchange (LIFFE) in the United Kingdom. IMM contracts can also be traded in London before the U.S. markets open on an exchange-for-physicals (EFP) basis.

These and other currencies can also be bought or sold in the forward market through the currency trading departments of major international banks. However, liquidity problems and transactions costs make the IMM a more attractive vehicle for trading by speculators. From a practical point of view, therefore, possible strategies are limited to these five currencies and their respective cross rates.

ISOLATING A STRONG OR WEAK CURRENCY

The first and most important task is to analyze the overall technical position of a currency. The price of a currency is a cross relationship, i.e., the pound sterling expressed in D-marks or the pound expressed in Canadian dollars. It is therefore important to begin with some overall measure which acts as a proxy for the general fortunes of a particular currency similarly to the way that a stock market index such as the S&P 500 is used as a proxy measure for the stock market as a whole. For a currency the starting point is usually a trade-weighted (TW) index. Trade-weighted indexes are constructed from a basket of currencies measured against the base currency, the performances of which are weighted according to the volume of trade transacted with the country issuing the base currency. The trade-weighted index for the U.S. dollar is heavily weighted in favor of the Canadian dollar since Canada is the main trading partner of the United States. The Swiss franc, on the other hand, would play a very small role in a trade-weighted index for the U.S. dollar because relatively little trade goes on between the United States and Switzerland. Trade-weighted indexes are constructed by the Morgan Guarantee Bank and the Bank of England. Chart 27.1 shows a TW index of the U.S. dollar as calculated by Morgan Guarantee, with a 12-month ROC. A 9-month moving average of the index and a 9-month moving average of the ROC index are represented by dashed lines.

Techniques discussed in Chapters 7 (moving averages) and 8 (momentum) can usefully be applied to the interpretation of this chart. It is also possible to devise a fairly helpful mechanical system. Buy signals are given whenever the trade-weighted index crosses above its 9-month moving average and this is confirmed by a crossover of the 12-month ROC index above its 9-month moving average. Such signals remain in force until *both* crossovers occur in a negative way. A sell signal is not triggered if the trade-weighted index alone crosses below its moving average, since a valid signal requires a confirmation from the rate-of-change index. Periods when the U.S. dollar was a "sell" under these rules are indicated by the shaded areas. The chart shows that on balance the signals have been relatively long-lasting and have offered few whipsaws.

Another technique which has proved useful in analyzing the overall tech-

CHART 27.1 U.S. trade-weighted index and the 12-month rate of change.

(SOURCE: Pring Market Review.)

nical structure of a currency is to compare its trade-weighted index (this time calculated by the Bank of England) with an advance/decline line, as shown on Chart 27.2. The advance/decline line for the U.S. dollar, shown in the middle of the chart, is constructed by taking a simple cumulative weekly plurality of the U.S. dollar in relation to a basket of currencies using a Friday close as a basis. If the dollar rises against 8 currencies and falls against 4, the plurality (+4) is added to the cumulated total of the previous week. In this example, 12 currencies and gold have been used in the construction, but there is no reason why a larger basket of currencies could not have been used in the analysis. The comparison between the trade-weighted index and the advance/decline line is useful because the two series do not always move together. When they are moving in concert, the prevailing trend is reaffirmed, but when they move in opposite directions or one does not confirm the other, a warning of a probable reversal in trend is given.

Some of these instances are shown by the dashed lines on Chart 27.2. For example, the two high peaks in the trade-weighted index in 1979 were not confirmed by a similar action in the A/D line. Although the trade-weighted index did not sell off dramatically, a new high was seen only after about 10 months. In turn, this new high was not confirmed by the A/D line in 1980 which was unable to surpass its 1979 high. A dramatic sell-off followed.

CHART 27.2   U.S. dollar and the advance/decline line.

(SOURCE: Pring Market Review.)

Similarly, the September low in the A/D line was not confirmed by the TW index, and this was followed by a major trend reversal, this time to the upside. One other point worth noting is that between 1978 and early 1980 the A/D line formed and broke out from a broadening formation with a flat top. Throughout the ensuing bull market each index confirmed the other as new highs were being achieved. The use of this relationship was therefore limited to pointing up that technically everything was in gear during this period.

Two other useful indicators are shown at the foot of Chart 27.2. These are a simple average of five currencies and gold calculated on a 13-week and a 26-week rate-of-change basis. The construction of the 13-week rate-of-change index starts by adding the individual 13-week ROC indexes of the five currencies and gold (expressed against the U.S. dollar) and dividing the average by 6. The incorporation of five currencies and gold into the rate-of-change analysis offers a further dimension of breadth to be compared against the trade-weighted index itself. Their interpretation vis-à-vis the TW index is the same as any other momentum study, as discussed in Chapter 8.

The discussion has so far been limited to the U.S. dollar, but there is nothing to preclude the construction of similar indicators for the other currencies. Indeed, as an important starting point, it is useful to chart the TW indexes of the major currencies. For example, Chart 27.1 shows that the U.S. trade-weighted index was forming a top in 1976, whereas the trade-weighted index for the Japanese yen shown on Chart 27.3 reveals the formation of a very large inverse H&S between 1974 and 1976. It can be seen from this simple comparison that the U.S. dollar was likely to decline and that the yen was probably embarking on a major bull market. It was relatively simple at the time therefore to conclude that the yen should be bought against the U.S. dollar.

ANALYSIS OF INDIVIDUAL CURRENCY RELATIONSHIPS

Charts 26.4 through 26.8 represent the major currencies against the U.S. dollar from 1978 to 1983. The format is quite helpful because it includes the currency, two moving averages, and two rates of change. Since a rate-of-change index measures momentum over a given cycle, the use of two indexes helps to show whether the two cycles are in gear. For instance, if they are both moving in the same general direction, this is a normal occurrence; their *relationship* is not offering any forecasting value. On the other hand, if they have been moving in opposite directions for some time or if they are widely apart, a warning is given that the cycles are not in gear and that *perhaps* an important change in the prevailing trend is going to take place. A classic example of this phenomenon can be seen in winter 1980 on Chart 27.5, which shows the British pound. At the time of the bull market peak, the 26-week ROC reached a 16-month high, yet the 13-week ROC had been trending in the opposite direction since the summer of that year and was able to rally only anemically at that time. A similar type of divergence can be seen for the other currencies during that same period.

In Chart 27.4 the Canadian dollar shows many of these divergences. At the beginning of 1979, for example, a bullish divergence developed, since the 26-week ROC index was in a sideways-to-declining trend during late 1978 and early 1979, while its 13-week counterpart was basically in a rising phase. The result of this divergence, which was completely opposite in nature to that of the British pound discussed above, was to signal a reversal of the previous downward trend. Chart 27.4 also reveals that while it is normal for such divergences to result in a sharp sell-off (for a negative

CHART 27.3 Trade-weighted Japanese yen and 12-month rate of change.

(SOURCE: Pring Market Review.)

CHART 27.4 Canadian dollar.

CHART 27.5 British pound.

CHART 27.6 Deutsche mark.

(SOURCE: Pring Market Review.)

CHART 27.7 Swiss franc.

(SOURCE: Pring Market Review.)

CHART 27.8 Japanese yen.

(SOURCE: Pring Market Review.)

divergence) or rally (for a positive divergence), these do not always occur and instead a fairly lengthy period of consolidation can develop. The negative divergence of mid-1979 between the Canadian dollar 26- and 13-week rate-of-change indexes (Chart 27.4) gives a good example.

As with so many tools of technical analysis, the ones discussed here do not make possible the quantification of the limits of a major divergence. This has to be a matter of subjective judgment. However, in many cases such as the mid-1980 divergence in the 13- and 26-week ROC indexes for the D-mark, the discrepancy becomes quite obvious, even to the most casual observer, and on that basis can be treated with a relatively high degree of confidence.

MECHANICAL TECHNIQUES

Through observation of the historical price action of charts it is often possible to develop mechanical "fail-safe" systems. Such systems always represent a compromise between timely and conservative signals. It is easy to design a system that gives buy and sell signals very close to tops and bottoms, but the problem is that the more sensitive the signal, the more likely it is to be vulnerable to whipsaws. Similarly, the use of a 200-day or other long-term moving average eliminates most of the whipsaws; however, by the time the signals are triggered, the market, stock, commodity, or currency being tracked has usually moved a long way.

One method which has proved extremely profitable, but which I nevertheless introduce with some hesitancy, is to combine a moving-average crossover with a signal from a rate-of-change index. Usually it is better to

CHART 27.9 British pound.

(SOURCE: Pring Market Review.)

choose different time periods for the MA and ROC indicators, so that the signals have a better chance of taking into account two different market cycles. Chart 27.9 shows the pound sterling with a 10-week MA, a 13-week ROC, and a 6-week ROC between 1972 and 1979. Buy signals are triggered when the currency crosses above its 10-week MA and both ROC indexes cross above the zero reference line. A sell signal can be given only when *all* three indicators cross below their respective benchmarks. Between

1971 and 1983, 15 (or 75 percent) of the 20 buy and sell signals represented gains, for a total gain of $2.75. If an investor had adopted this system, using 10 percent on a futures contract and assuming that the movement in the nearby contract months did not differ appreciably on a net basis from the spot, and had invested the profits from each signal, an initial investment of $10,000 in 1971 would have grown to over *$4 million* by 1983. These hypothetical transactions ignore commission costs and capital gains taxes, but even when these are taken into account, the results would still be staggering. I should point out that this system is not necessarily going to offer such large rewards in the future. Experimentation with other currencies has also proved profitable, but the results have always been inferior to the hypothetical example discussed above. This example of the British pound *must* be treated as the exception rather than the rule, but it is introduced to give readers an incentive to experiment along these lines.

SUMMARY

Technical analysis of individual currency cross rates is very similar to that of other financial markets. However, since the value of a currency is a *relative* relationship, it is possible to analyze both sides of that relationship on an overall basis to discover whether the particular currencies in question are generally technically strong or weak.

1. Technical analysis of individual currencies should begin from an analysis of an overall measurement known as a trade-weighted index.

2. Advance/decline lines and weighted rate-of-change indexes are also useful in the analysis of currencies.

3. Once a strong currency has been isolated, it is important to find a weak currency to sell against the strong one.

28

Technical Analysis of Commodity Markets

INTRODUCTION

Since commodity markets are so highly leveraged and volatile, it is probably true to say that technical analysis is used more widely by market participants in this area than any other. Most commodity transactions are consummated within a very short time, quite often within the course of a single day. For this reason, commodity traders have tended to concentrate on charts and systems geared to the very short term. The basic principles outlined in Chapters 3 to 10 can be applied to individual commodities. This chapter will describe how to identify important trend reversals in the overall commodity price structure and how to capitalize on these situations with the help of relative-strength analysis. This chapter is oriented toward commodity traders who wish to obtain a longer-term and macro background for these challenging markets. A brief discussion of seasonal aspects is also included.

ESTABLISHING A REFERENCE POINT

Technical analysis of commodity markets should not begin with a particular commodity but rather with a larger reference point. For commodities, there is no widely followed index such as the DJIA, which is constantly quoted in the popular press. This is probably because no convenient method of weighting commodities has been found to be widely acceptable. Because of specific fundamental factors totally unrelated to the business cycle, individual commodities more commonly move counter to the general commodity trend than do individual stocks. This is another reason for the slowness of any overall measure of commodity movements to gain popularity.

In the United States the most widely followed index is the Commodity Research Bureau (CRB) Futures Price Index, which is constructed from 27 different commodities. This organization also publishes a spot commodity index based on the cash price of 22 commodities. The Futures Price Index is shown in Chart 28.1.

Commodities are also traded actively in the United Kingdom, and several indexes are also published out of London. *The Economist* publishes a composite index weighted by the amount of world trade in each commodity, which in a sense could be regarded as the ultimate global commodity index. *The Economist* also publishes the same data in terms of pounds sterling. *The Economist* dollar index is shown in Chart 28.2.

The relative performances of the various composite indexes can and do vary considerably. Chart 28.3, for example, compares the performance of the CRB Composite Index with that of the Dow Jones Futures Index, another U.S.-based commodity measure, and Chart 28.2 compares the Reuters Index, an alternative U.K.-based index, with the *Economist* index. The two charts show that, whereas the indexes move in concert a substantial portion of the time, there are some glaring instances in which they do not.

For example, the performance of both the Reuters and the Dow Jones indexes differed greatly from their CRB and *Economist* counterparts during the 1982–1983 period. The Reuters Index made a new all-time high in 1983, whereas the *Economist* index merely retraced part of the 1981–1982 bear market. The Dow Jones Futures Index rallied in an almost uninterrupted uptrend between 1975 and 1977, unlike the CRB index, which moved marginally higher in a series of violent rallies and reactions. Clearly, these different performances reflect alternative weightings by various commodities, suggesting that there really is no "perfect" indicator for overall commodity price movements.

Since it is important to be able to use an indicator from which relative strength may be monitored, a selection must be made. The CRB index has been chosen for the following reasons: First, the formula for spot commodity prices developed by the Commodity Research Bureau has been adopted by the U.S. government for reporting purposes (the spot and futures index formulas are relatively similar). Second, this organization also publishes subindexes which, along with the spot index, can be used for comparative analytical purposes. Finally, the CRB index and its subindexes can be easily

CHART 28.1 CRB Composite Index, 1960–1983.

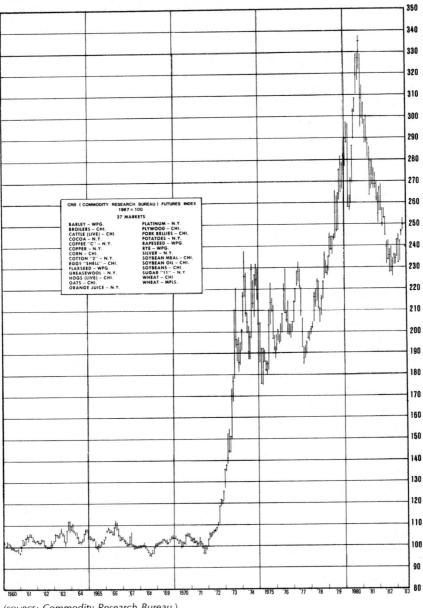

CRB (COMMODITY RESEARCH BUREAU) FUTURES INDEX
1967 = 100
27 MARKETS

BARLEY – WPG.	PLATINUM – N.Y.
BROILERS – CHI.	PLYWOOD – CHI.
CATTLE (LIVE) – CHI.	PORK BELLIES – CHI.
COCOA – N.Y.	POTATOES – N.Y.
COFFEE "C" – N.Y.	RAPESEED – WPG.
COPPER – N.Y.	RYE – WPG.
CORN – CHI.	SILVER – N.Y.
COTTON "2" – N.Y.	SOYBEAN MEAL – CHI.
EGGS "SHELL" – CHI.	SOYBEAN OIL – CHI.
FLAXSEED – WPG.	SOYBEANS – CHI
GREASEWOOL – N.Y.	SUGAR "11" – N.Y
HOGS (LIVE) – CHI.	WHEAT – CHI
OATS – CHI.	WHEAT – MPLS.
ORANGE JUICE – N.Y.	

(SOURCE: *Commodity Research Bureau.*)

367

CHART 28.2 *Economist* All Commodity Index versus Reuter's Commodity Index.

(SOURCE: *Dominion Securities Pitfield Graphics.*)

CHART 28.3 CRB Composite Index versus Dow Jones futures.

(SOURCE: *Dominion Securities Pitfield Graphics.*)

CHART 28.4   CRB Composite Index and a momentum indicator.

(SOURCE: *Dominion Securities Pitfield Graphics.*)

obtained in either data or chart form from the Commodity Research Bureau. The data are also relatively easy to obtain from the financial press or popular data bases.

ANALYZING MAJOR AND INTERMEDIATE TRENDS

Success from the long side is usually much easier to achieve during a bull market as measured by the CRB index than in the stock market during a bull market. The techniques for determining trends with these indicators are basically the same as in other financial markets. In this respect, price patterns, trendlines, moving averages, and rate-of-change indicators have all proved to be useful in identifying basic trend reversals. Chart 28.4, for example, shows the CRB Futures Index with a deviation from a 12-month moving average. This indicator was very useful in helping to identify the 1982 bottom. In late 1982 the CRB index reached its ultimate low, but the oscillator had made its low many months before and had in fact been tracing out a series of higher lows as the index itself declined. These positive divergences pointed up a distinct shrinkage in downside momentum. In addition, the bear market trendline had been touched five times during its descent and therefore represented a major area of resistance in its own right. Consequently, when it was broken on the upside in November 1982 a major buy signal was registered. In Chart 28.5 the CRB index is again portrayed, this

CHART 28.5 CRB Composite Index and two measures of breadth.

(SOURCE: ContiCommodity Services, Inc.)

time with a weekly advance/decline line. The indicator shown is not the actual line but a ratio derived from advance/decline data on the 27 commodities included in the CRB index. It is important to note that this oscillator also refused to confirm the high set in the CRB index in September 1983. The third indicator shown on this chart represents the number of contracts making net new lows. This also failed by a wide margin to confirm the September high. The maximum number of contracts making new lows was reached in August, a month before the high in the index itself.

Finally, the percentage of markets above their 50-week MA is shown at the bottom of Chart 28.5. It can be seen that whenever the index rises to the 75 percent level and then starts to fall there is little potential for a commodity price rise. The opposite situation arises when it falls below the 25 percent level and then begins to rise. The very low level in October 1982 corresponded with an excellent buying opportunity as it marked the cyclical low.

However, it should not be assumed that, because the CRB index was able to rally from the 220 level in late 1982 to over 270 by mid-1983, it was easy to make money in the commodity markets from the long side—for it was not. Even though most commodity markets were fairly choppy, on balance it would still have been more profitable to have played the markets from the long rather than from the short side.

RELATIVE STRENGTH ANALYSIS USING COMMODITY SUBINDEXES

General

Since the trend of individual commodity markets can be diverse, it is worthwhile to analyze the various subindexes. Unlike stocks, which usually show some recognizable form of group rotation, commodities in general are lagging indicators. Consequently, there is no conceptual group rotation pattern which can act as a framework. Each group therefore has to be assessed on its own technical merits. The analysis of subindexes is really most useful, first, in identifying a prospective area in which to trade and, second, as a basis for relative strength analysis. The approach used is very similar to that described in Chapter 25 for individual stocks.

Isolating a Strong Subgroup

First the relative-strength position of the group in question has to be established.

Chart 28.6 shows the CRB Composite Index with the metals subcomponent. It can be seen that the composite made an important low in August 1977. This was not confirmed by the metals index, which had made its low in January 1976. This positive action by the metals index would have signaled to alert technicians that it was likely to outperform the composite index in the ensuing period. More substantial evidence that this was a growing possibility emerged when both the metals index and its RS line (against the CRB composite) broke above intermediate down trendlines AB. The chart shows that while the CRB Composite rallied over the following year, the performance of the metals index was far superior. A similar situation arose in mid-1982, when both the RS line and the index itself successfully assaulted major down trendlines. Chart 28.7 gives the mid-1982 period in more detail.

These three series show that, following its initial bounce, the metals index fell back to successfully test its low, unlike the composite index. As the previous high was bettered in September, the index and its RS line moved back above their down trendlines (CD), and the index crossed above its 30-week moving average, setting the scene for a dynamic rally. Again it

CHART 28.6 CRB Composite Index versus CRB Metals Index, 1976–1983.

(SOURCE: *Dominion Securities Pitfield Graphics.*)

was possible to make money on the long side if the composite index had been bought between September 1982 and February 1983; but a better result by far would have derived from participating in the metals markets.

Selecting a Specific Commodity

Although an investment or speculation in the metals markets would have done well in general terms, it should not be blindly assumed that a long position in all metals would have been profitable during this period. This can be seen from Chart 28.8, which shows the performance of London spot lead and N.Y. spot silver, both expressed in relative-strength terms against the CRB Metals Index. In the late summer of 1982, silver broke above its steep bear market downtrend, the last few weeks of which are shown on the chart. As silver began to break above its declining RS line, lead's relative strength began to break down. As Chart 28.8 shows, a long position in silver would have produced substantial profits, compared to a long position in lead, which declined in price during late 1982.

CHART 28.7 CRB Composite Index versus CRB Metals Index, 1981–1983.

(SOURCE: *Dominion Securities Pitfield Graphics.*)

Identifying Changes in Relative Strength

Relative strength analysis is also helpful in pointing up deteriorating as well as improving technical situations. For example, Chart 28.7 shows that the relationship between the metals index and the CRB Composite was changing dramatically in the early part of 1983, since the sharp February commodity price decline broke both the uptrend of the metals index itself and the uptrend of its RS line. Even though the composite picked up steam and rallied sharply into the summer, the deteriorating technical structure of the metals markets would not have enabled participants from the long side to have made any money. When the metals began to break down, investors or speculators who were bullish on the overall trend of commodity prices should have been considering other alternatives. In this respect, analysis of relative-strength trends would have proved useful. Chart 28.9 shows the CRB Grain Index with its relative strength against the metals index. In the late spring several technical observations could be made. First, the Grain Index itself had been making a series of bullish ascending peaks and

CHART 28.8 New York spot silver versus London spot lead.

Relative Strength

14
12
10
8
6

New York Silver

··· 30 Week Moving Average

Relative Strength

0.30
0.28
0.26
0.24
0.22
0.20
0.18

London Lead

··· 30 Week Moving Average

| MAR | MAY | JUL | OCT | DEC | FEB | APR | JUL | SEP |
| 82 | 82 | 82 | 82 | 82 | 83 | 83 | 83 | 83 |

(SOURCE: *Dominion Securities Pitfield Graphics.*)

troughs. When it crossed its 30-week moving average in June, it also broke above a small intermediate down trendline. Both these developments suggested that the test of the February low had been successful. Since the CRB Composite Index had previously broken out of a major inverse head-and-shoulders pattern and found support around the neckline, the chances were that the overall commodity bull market was still intact. This being the case, it was quite clear from an examination of the relative-strength line of the grains against the metals that the former were likely to put in the best performance. This was because the RS index had, first, broken above an important down trendline *EF* and, second, completed a downward-sloping inverse head-and-shoulders pattern. The ensuing price action in summer 1983 proved this analysis to have been correct.

CHART 28.9   CRB Grain Index versus CRB Composite, 1981–1983.

(SOURCE: *Dominion Securities Pitfield Graphics.*)

SEASONAL ASPECTS

Seasonality in commodity prices is influenced by temporary changes in the supply-demand relationship caused by factors which occur about the same time each year. Agricultural commodities appear to have the strongest seasonal tendencies. On the supply side, such factors as harvest, planting, weather patterns, and navigation on the great lakes are very important. Demand is affected by seasonal consumption, feed demand, export patterns, soybean crushings, etc. Seasonal tendencies do not always work, since longer-term fundamental factors often outweigh them.

Table 28.1 is therefore offered as a rough guide for seasonal tendencies. Readers wishing to study this subject in greater detail are referred to *Seasonality in Agricultural Futures Markets.*[1]

[1]Written and published by ContiCommodity Services, Inc., Board of Trade Building, Chicago.

TABLE 28.1 Seasonal Tendencies

Commodity	Strong months	Weak months
Wheat	December and May	July
Corn	May and July	December
Beans	May and July	November and January
Meal	January and July	March
Oil	May and July	December
Hogs	February and June to July	April and October
Cattle	February and June	April and October
Pork bellies	February and July	March and August
Copper	May	December
Cocoa	July	December
Sugar	May	October
Cotton	May to July	October to December
Lumber	May to July	September to November
Plywood	May to July	September to November

Metals prices also appear to be affected by seasonality. Typically the best seasonal buying opportunity occurs sometime between late October and early January. Important peaks in prices develop in the February–May period and again following a summer rally, and seasonal highs develop in the late summer and early fall.

SUMMARY

1. Whereas the overall trends of commodity prices are subject to primary bull and bear markets, individual commodity prices are generally more independent of the general price movement than are individual stock prices.

2. Overall commodity price movements are best monitored through a commodity price index. The Commodity Research Bureau Composite Index is recommended for this purpose.

3. Major buying and selling points for commodities can be identified from price trend, momentum, and breadth analyses.

4. Relative strength analysis of the various commodity subindexes and the commodities making up the subindexes should be used as a starting point for investment decisions about individual commodities.

Epilog

At the outset the suggestion was made that the keys to success in the stock market were knowledge and action. The "knowledge" part of the equation has been discussed as comprehensively as possible, but the final word has been reserved for investor "action," since the way in which knowledge is used is just as important as the understanding process itself.

It remains to point out some common errors which all of us commit more often than we would like to. The most obvious of these can be avoided by applying the following principles.

1. *Perspective.* The interpretation of any indicator should not be based on short-term trading patterns; it should always consider the longer-term implications.

2. *Objectivity.* A conclusion should not be drawn on the basis of one or two "reliable" or "favorite" indicators. The possibility that these indicators could give misleading signals demonstrates the need to form a balanced view derived from *all* available information.

3. *Humility.* One of the hardest lessons in life is learning to admit a mistake. The knowledge of all market participants in the aggregate is, and always will be, greater than that of any one individual or group of individuals. This knowledge is expressed in the action of the market itself as represented by the various indicators. Anyone who "fights the tape" or the verdict of the market will swiftly suffer the consequences. Under such circumstances, it is as well to become humble and let the market give its own verdict; a review of the indicators will frequently suggest its future direction. Occasionally the analysis proves to be wrong, and the market fails to act as anticipated. If this unexpected action changes the basis on which the original conclusion was drawn, it is wise to admit the mistake and alter the conclusion.

4. *Tenacity.* If the circumstances outlined above develop but it is considered that the technical position has *not* changed, the original opinion should not be changed either.

5. *Independent thought.* Should a review of the indicators suggest a position that is not attuned to the majority view, that conclusion is probably well founded. On the other hand, a conclusion should never be drawn simply because it is opposed to that of the majority. In other words, contrariness for its own sake is not valid. Usually the majority conclusion is based on a false assumption, so it is prudent to examine such assumptions to determine their accuracy.

6. *Simplicity.* Most things done well are also done simply. Because the market operates on common sense, the best approaches to it are basically very simple. If one must resort to complex computer programming and model building, the chances are that the basic techniques have not been mastered and therefore an analytical crutch is required.

7. *Discretion.* There is a persistent temptation to call every possible market turn, along with the duration of every move the stock market is likely to make. This deluded belief in one's power to pull off the impossible inevitably results in failure, a loss of confidence, and damage to one's reputation. For this reason, analysis should concentrate on identifying major turning points rather than predicting the duration of a move—because there is no known formula on which consistent and accurate forecasts of this type can be based.

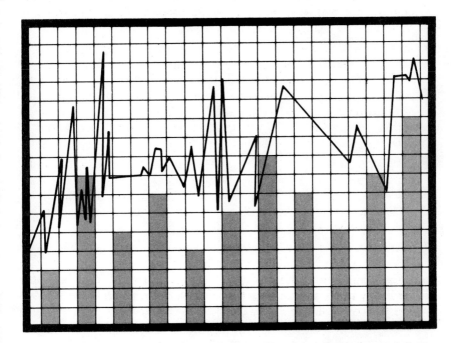

Appendixes

A

The Elliott Wave Principle

The Elliott Wave Principle was established by R. N. Elliott and first published in a series of articles in *Financial World* in 1939. The basis of Elliott Wave theory developed from the observation that rhythmic regularity has been the law of creation since the beginning of time. Elliott noted that all cycles in nature, whether of the tide, the heavenly bodies, the planets, day and night, or even life and death, had the capability for repeating themselves indefinitely. Those cyclical movements were characterized by two forces—one building up, the other tearing down.

This concept of natural law also embraces an extraordinary numerical series discovered by a thirteenth-century mathematician named Fibonacci. The series which carries his name is derived by taking the number 2 and adding to it the previous number in the series. Thus $2 + 1 = 3$, then $3 + 2 = 5$, $5 + 3 = 8$, $8 + 5 = 13$, $13 + 8 = 21$, $21 + 13 = 34$, etc. The series becomes 1, 2, 3, 5, 8, 13, 21, 34, 55, 89, 144, 233, etc. It has a number of fascinating properties, among which are:

1. The sum of any two consecutive numbers forms the number following them. Thus $3 + 5 = 8$ and $5 + 8 = 13$, etc.

2. The ratio of any number to its next higher is 61.8 to 100, and any number to its next lower is 161.8 to 100.

3. The ratio 1.68 multiplied by the ratio 0.618 equals 1.

FIGURE A.1

FIGURE A.2

FIGURE A.3

The connection between Elliott's observation of repeating cycles of nature and the Fibonacci summation series is that the Fibonacci numbers and proportions are found in many manifestations of nature. For example, a sunflower has 89 curves, of which 55 wind in one direction and 34 in the opposite direction. In music, an octave comprises 13 keys on a piano, with 5 black notes and 8 white. Trees always branch from the base in Fibonacci series, and so on.

Combining his observation of natural cycles with his knowledge of the Fibonacci series, Elliott noted in an 80-year period that the market moved forward in a series of five waves, and then declined in a series of three waves. He concluded that a single cycle comprised eight waves, as shown in Figure A.1 (3, 5, and 8 are of course Fibonacci numbers).

The longest cycle in the Elliott concept is called the Grand Supercycle. In turn each Grand Supercycle can be subdivided into eight supercycle waves, each of which is then divided into eight cycle waves. The process continues to embrace Primary, Intermediate, Minute, Minuette, and Sub-Minuette waves. The various details are highly intricate, but the general picture is represented in Figures A.1 and A.2.

Figures A.2 and A.3 show Elliott in historical perspective. Figure A.2 illustrates the first five waves of the Grand Supercycle, which Elliott deemed to have begun in 1800. As the wave principle is one of form, there is nothing to determine when the three corrective waves are likely to appear. However, the frequent recurrence of Fibonacci numbers representing time spans

TABLE A.1   Time Spans between Stock Market Peaks and Troughs

Year started	Position	Year ended	Position	Length of cycle (years)
1916	Top	1921	Bottom	5
1919	Top	1924	Bottom	5
1924	Bottom	1929	Top	5
1932	Bottom	1937	Top	5
1937	Top	1942	Bottom	5
1956	Top	1961	Top	5
1961	Top	1966	Top	5
1916	Top	1924	Bottom	8
1921	Bottom	1929	Top	8
1924	Bottom	1932	Botom	8
1929	Top	1937	Top	8
1938	Bottom	1946	Top	8
1949	Bottom	1957	Bottom	8
1960	Bottom	1968	Top	8
1962	Bottom	1970	Bottom	8
1916	Top	1929	Top	13
1919	Top	1932	Bottom	13
1924	Bottom	1937	Top	13
1929	Top	1942	Bottom	13
1949	Bottom	1962	Bottom	13
1953	Bottom	1966	Bottom	13
1957	Bottom	1970	Bottom	13
1916	Top	1937	Top	21
1921	Bottom	1942	Bottom	21
1932	Bottom	1953	Bottom	21
1949	Bottom	1970	Bottom	21
1953	Bottom	1974	Bottom	21
1919	Top	1953	Bottom	34
1932	Bottom	1966	Top	34
1942	Bottom	1976	Top	34
1919	Top	1974	Bottom	55
1921	Bottom	1976	Top	55

between peaks and troughs are probably beyond coincidence. These time spans are shown in Table A.1.

More recently, 8 years occurred between the 1966 and 1974 bottoms and the 1968 and 1976 tops, and 5 years between the 1968 and 1973 tops, for example.

It can readily be seen that the real problem with Elliott is interpretation. Indeed, every wave theorist (including Elliott himself) has at some time or another become entangled with the question of where one wave finished and another started. As far as the Fibonacci time spans are concerned, although these periods recur frequently, it is extremely difficult to use this principle as a basis for forecasting; there are no indications whether time spans based on these numbers will produce tops to tops, or bottoms to tops, or something else, and the permutations are infinite.

The Elliott Wave is clearly a very subjective tool. Its subjectivity in itself can be dangerous because the market is very subject to emotional influences. For this reason, the weight given to Elliott interpretations should probably be downplayed. The old maxim "A little knowledge is a dangerous thing" applies probably more to Elliott than to any other market theory. The sources listed in the Bibliography will give a fuller understanding of the principles involved, since the theory has been described here only in its barest outline.

Selected
Charts

CHART B.1 Stock prices, bond prices, and money market rates, 1831–1938. Due to its construction the stock price series used here does not reflect the long-term uptrend in stock prices that took place between 1832 and 1929. The comparison between stock prices, bond prices, and commercial paper rates should therefore only be used for the purpose of cyclical reversals and not secular trends.

(SOURCE: *Leonard Ayres*, Stock Prices and Turning Points in Business Cycles.)

CHART B.2 Dow Jones Industrial Average versus Constant-Dollar Dow Jones Industrial Average, 1897–1976.

(SOURCE: *Media General Financial Services.*)

CHART B.3 Dow Jones Industrial Average, 1930–1944.

(SOURCE: Pring Market Review.)

CHART B.4   Dow Jones Industrial Average, 1944–1959.

(SOURCE: Pring Market Review.)

CHART B.5   *Financial Times* Industrial Ordinary Index (Chart 7-1*b* reproduced with 13-week momentum).

(SOURCE: Pring Market Review.)

CHART B.6 Dow Jones Transportation Average, 1929–1977.

Monthly index
9 - month moving average

(SOURCE: Pring Market Review.)

CHART B.7   Dow Jones Transportation Average, 1930–1944.

(SOURCE: Pring Market Review.)

CHART B.8   Dow Jones Transportation Average, 1944–1959.

(SOURCE: Pring Market Review.)

CHART B.9 Dow Jones Transportation Average, 1959–1978.

Dow Jones Transportation Averages
—— Monthly average
– – – 14–month exponential moving average

12 Month rate of change
—— Monthly average
– – – 14–month exponential moving average

(SOURCE: Pring Market Review.)

CHART B.10 Dow Jones Transportation Average, relative strength, 1929–1977.

(SOURCE: Pring Market Review.)

CHART B.11 Dow Jones Utility Average, 1930–1944.

(SOURCE: Pring Market Review.)

CHART B.12 Dow Jones Utility Average, 1944–1959.

(SOURCE: Pring Market Review.)

CHART B.13 Dow Jones Utility Average, relative strength, 1929–1977.

Monthly index
9 – month moving average

(SOURCE: Pring Market Review.)

CHART B.14 Industry advance/decline line, 1965–1977.

1965 1966 1967 1968 1969 1970 1971 1972 1973 1974 1975 1976 1977

(SOURCE: Pring Market Review.)

CHART B.15 Secondary stock offerings versus the Dow Jones Industrial Average, 1958–1976.

(SOURCE: Pring Market Review.)

CHART B.16   Dow Jones Industrial Average versus Odd Lot Short-Sale Index.

(SOURCE: *Courtesy of J. C. Bradford.*)

CHART B.17   Annual rate of change of stock prices versus short-interest ratio.

(SOURCE: *Dow Jones Industrials.*)

CHART B.18 Composite long-term bond index.

COMPOSITE LONG-TERM BOND YIELD INDEX
(Plotted Inversely)

* Includes: Moody's Corporate Aaa Bonds
Bond Buyer's Municipal Bonds
Long-term U.S. Government Bonds

● BANK CREDIT ANALYST

(SOURCE: Pring Market Review.)

398

Glossary

Advisory Services Privately circulated publications which comment upon the future course of financial markets, and for which a subscription is usually required.

Bear Trap A signal which suggests that the rising trend of an index or stock has reversed but which proves to be false.

(Market) Breadth Breadth relates to the number of issues participating in a move. A rally is considered suspect if the number of advancing issues is diminishing as the rally develops. Conversely, a decline which is associated with fewer and fewer stocks falling is considered to be a bullish sign.

Bull Trap A signal which suggests that the declining trend of an index or stock has reversed but which proves to be false.

Customer Free Balances The total amount of unused money on deposit in brokerage accounts. These are "free" funds representing cash which may be employed in the purchase of securities.

Cyclical Investing The process of buying and selling stocks based on a longer-term or primary market move. The cycle approximates to the 4-year business cycle, to which such primary movements in stock prices are normally related.

Insider Any person who directly or indirectly owns more than 10 percent of any class of stock listed on a national exchange, or who is an officer or director of the company in question.

Margin Occurs when an investor pays part of the purchase price of a security and borrows the balance, usually from a broker; the "margin" is the difference between the market value of the stock and the loan which is made against it.

Margin Call The demand upon a customer to put up money or securities with a broker. The call is made if a customer's equity in a margin account declines below a minimum standard set by the exchange or brokerage firm. This happens when there is a drop in price of the securities being held as collateral.

Members Members of a stock exchange who are empowered to buy and sell securities on the floor of the exchange either for a client or for their own account.

399

Odd Lots Units of stock of less than 100 shares; these do not customarily appear on the tape.

Odd-Lot Shorts Odd lots that are sold short. Since odd lots are usually the vehicle of uninformed traders, a high level of odd-lot shorts in relation to total odd-lot sales often characterizes a major market bottom. A low level of odd-lot shorts compared with total odd-lot sales is a sign of a market top.

Option The right to buy or sell specific securities at a specified price within a specified time. A "put" gives the holder the right to sell the stock, a "call" the right to buy the stock. In recent years options on specific stocks have been listed on several exchanges, so that it is now possible to trade these instruments in the same way that the underlying stocks can be bought and sold.

Overbought An opinion about the level of prices. It may refer to a specific indicator or to the market as a whole after a period of vigorous buying, following which it may be argued that prices are overextended for the time being and are in need of a period of downward or horizontal adjustment.

Oversold An opinion about the level of prices. It is the opposite of overbought, i.e., a price move that has overextended itself on the downside.

Over-the-Counter (OTC) Market An informal collection of brokers and dealers. Securities traded include almost all federal, state, municipal, and corporate bonds and all widely owned equity issues not listed on the stock exchanges.

Price/Earnings Ratio The ratio of the price of a stock to the earnings per share, i.e., the total annual profit of a company divided by the number of shares outstanding.

Rally A brisk rise following a decline or consolidation of the general price level of the market.

Reaction A temporary price weakness following an upswing.

Secondary Distribution or Offering The redistribution of a block of stock some time after it has been sold by the issuing company. The sale is handled off the exchanges by a securities firm or group of firms, and the shares are usually offered at a fixed price which is related to the current market price of the stock.

Short Covering The process of buying back stock that has already been sold short.

Short-Interest Ratio The ratio of the short position to the average daily trading volume of the month in question. A high short-interest ratio (above 1.8) is considered bullish, and a low one (below 1.15) is considered bearish.

Short Position (Interest) The total amount of short sales outstanding on a specific exchange at a particular time. The short position is published monthly.

Short Selling Short selling is normally a speculative operation undertaken in the belief that the price of the shares will fall. It is accomplished by borrowing stock from a broker in order to sell shares one does not own. Most stock exchanges prohibit the short sale of a security below the price at which the last board lot was traded.

Specialist   A member of a stock exchange who acts as a specialist in a listed issue and who is registered with the exchange for that purpose. The member agrees to efficiently execute all orders and, insofar as is reasonably practical, to maintain a fair and orderly market in the issue or issues for which he or she is a specialist.

Yield Curve   The structure of the level of interest rates through various maturities. Usually the shorter the maturity, the lower the interest rate. Thus, 3-month Treasury bills usually yield less than 20-year government bonds. The slope of the yield curve relates to the speed with which rates rise as the maturity increases. In periods of tight money, short-term rates usually yield more than longer-term rates, and the curve is then called an inverse yield curve.

Bibliography

Appel, G.: *Winning Stock Market Systems,* Signalert Corp., Great Neck, N.Y., 1974.

Ayres, L. P.: *Turning Points in Business Cycles,* August M. Kelly, New York, 1967.

Benner, S.: *Benner's Prophecies of Future Ups and Downs in Prices,* Chase and Hall, Cincinnati, 1875. Reprinted in *Journal of Cycle Research,* vol. 8, no. 1, January 1959.

Bernstein, J.: *The Handbook of Commodity Cycles: A Window on Time,* John Wiley and Sons, Inc., New York, 1982.

Bretz, W. G.: *Juncture Recognition in the Stock Market,* Vantage Press, New York, 1972.

Coppock, E. S. C.: *Practical Relative Strength Charting,* Trendex Corp., San Antonio, Tex., 1960.

Dewey, E. R.: *Cycles: The Mysterious Forces that Trigger Events,* Hawthorne Books, New York, 1971.

—— and E. F. Dakin: *Cycles: The Science of Prediction,* Henry Holt, New York, 1947.

Drew, G.: *New Methods for Profit in the Stock Market,* Metcalfe Press, Boston, 1968.

Edwards, R. D., and John Magee: *Technical Analysis of Stock Trends,* John Magee, Springfield, Mass., 1957.

Eiteman, W. J., C. A. Dice, and D. K. Eiteman: *The Stock Market,* McGraw-Hill Book Company, New York, 1966.

Fosback, N. G.: *Stock Market Logic: A Sophisticated Approach to Profits on Wall Street,* The Institute for Econometric Research, Fort Lauderdale, Fla., 1976.

Frost, A. J., and Robert R. Prechter: *The Elliott Wave Principle—Key to Stock Market Profits,* New Classics Library, Chappaqua, N.Y., 1978.

Gann, W. D.: *Truth of the Stock Tape,* Financial Guardian, New York, 1932.

Gartley, H. M.: *Profits in the Stock Market,* Lambert Gann Publishing, Pomeroy, Wash.

Gordon, W.: *The Stock Market Indicators,* Investors Press, Palisades Park, N.J., 1968.

Granville, J.: *Strategy of Daily Stock Market Timing,* Prentice-Hall, Englewood Cliffs, N.J., 1960.

Greiner, P., and H. C. Whitcomb: *Dow Theory,* Investors' Intelligence, New York, 1969.

Hamilton, W. D.: *The Stock Market Barometer,* Harper & Bros., New York, 1922.

Hurst, J. M.: *The Profit Magic of Stock Transaction Timing,* Prentice-Hall, Englewood Cliffs, N.J., 1970.

Jiler, W.: *How Charts Can Help You in the Stock Market,* Commodity Research Publishing Corp., N.Y., 1961.

Krow, H.: *Stock Market Behaviour,* Random House, New York, 1969.

Merrill, A. A.: *Filtered Waves: Basic Theory,* Analysis Press, Chappaqua, N.Y., 1977.

Nelson, S.: *ABC of Stock Market Speculation,* Taylor, New York, 1934.

Pring, M. J.: *How to Forecast Interest Rates,* McGraw-Hill Book Company, New York, 1981.

———: *International Investing Made Easy,* McGraw-Hill Book Company, New York, 1981.

Rhea, Robert: *Dow Theory,* Barrons, New York, 1932.

Shuman, J. B., and D. Rosenau: *The Kondratieff Wave,* World Publishing, New York, 1972.

Smith, E. L.: *Common Stocks and Business Cycles,* William Frederick Press, New York, 1959.

Index

ABOUT THE AUTHOR

Martin J. Pring, one of the most respected names in the field of forecasting financial markets, is editor of *The Pring Market Review*, a technically oriented forecasting publication covering the U.S. stock and bond markets, commodities, and currencies. He is also president of The International Institute for Economic Research. He is the author of three highly acclaimed McGraw-Hill publications: *The McGraw-Hill Handbook of Commodities and Futures, International Investing Made Easy*, and *How to Forecast Interest Rates*. He has lectured in Europe and North America on global financial markets.